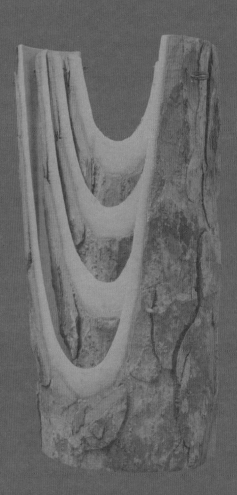

# ROOTED REVIVED REINVENTED

## BASKETRY IN AMERICA

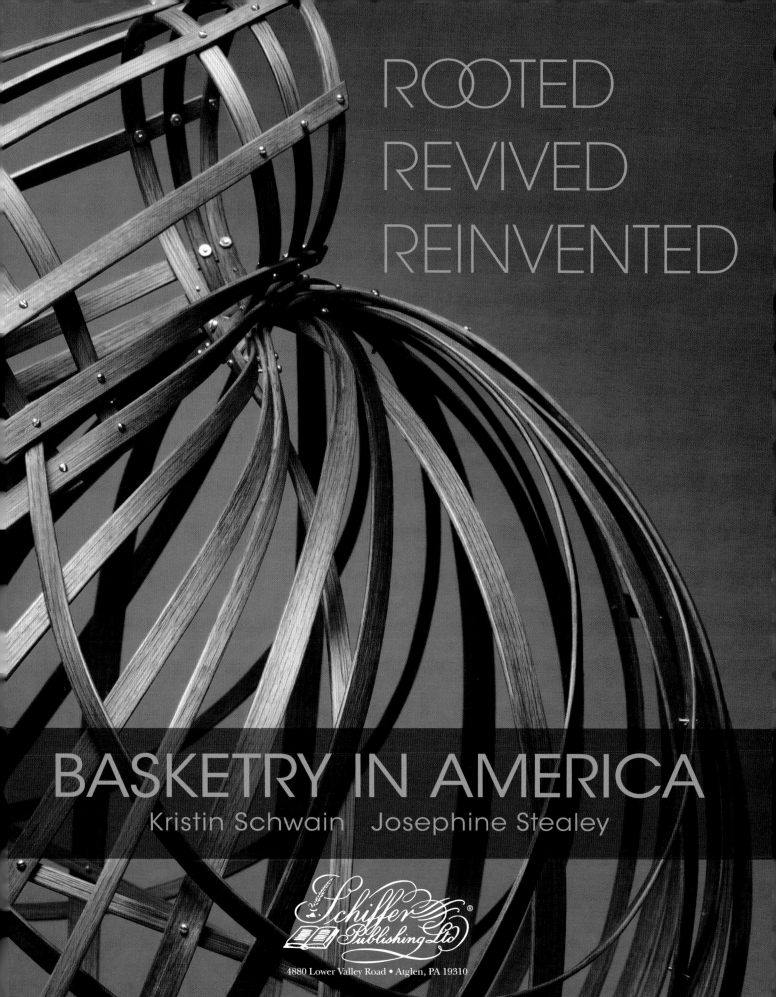

# ROOTED
# REVIVED
# REINVENTED

# BASKETRY IN AMERICA

## Kristin Schwain   Josephine Stealey

Schiffer Publishing Ltd

4880 Lower Valley Road • Atglen, PA 19310

Designed by RoS
Type set in ITC Avant Garde Gothic/Chaparral Pro
Front cover image: Leon Niehues, *Bentwood Sphere*, 2015. Loaned by the artist.
Back cover image: John Mc Queen, *Out of True,* 2014. Courtesy of the Duane
Reed Gallery

ISBN: 978-0-7643-5373-4
Printed in China

Partially funded by:

Published by Schiffer Publishing, Ltd.
4880 Lower Valley Road
Atglen, PA 19310
Phone: (610) 593-1777; Fax: (610) 593-2002
E-mail: Info@schifferbooks.com
Web: www.schifferbooks.com

For our complete selection of fine books on this and related subjects, please visit
our website at www.schifferbooks.com. You may also write for a free catalog.

Schiffer Publishing's titles are available at special discounts for bulk purchases
for sales promotions or premiums. Special editions, including personalized
covers, corporate imprints, and excerpts, can be created in large quantities for
special needs. For more information, contact the publisher.

We are always looking for people to write books on new and related subjects. If
you have an idea for a book, please contact us at proposals@schifferbooks.com.

# Contents

CHAPTER 1

Introduction: The Story of
Contemporary American Basketry

*Kristin Schwain & Josephine Stealey*

7

CHAPTER 2

Native American Basketry from the
Multicultural South: Craft, Labor,
and Heritage

*Jason Baird Jackson*

31

CHAPTER 3

Coiled Baskets of the South Carolina
Lowcountry: Who Knew the Art World
Would Embrace Baskets
as Works of Art?

*Sybil E. Gohari*

39

CHAPTER 4

The Oak-Rod Baskets of Brown County,
Indiana

*Jon Kay*

47

CHAPTER 5

Fashioning Nantucket Mink: From
Nantucket Lightship Basket to
Friendship Purse

*Margaret Fairgrieve Milanick*

57

CHAPTER 6

Beyond Summer Camp and Merit
Badges: The Studio Craft Movement,
Education, and the American Basket

*Perry Allen Price*

65

CHAPTER 7

New Basketry Beginnings: 1970–1990

*Patricia Malarcher*

75

CHAPTER 8

Diverse Structures,
Dissolving Boundaries

*Carol Eckert*

87

CHAPTER 9

The Space Between

*Jeannine Falino*

97

Rooted, Revived, Reinvented: Basketry in America

107

Part I: Cultural Origins           108
Part II: The New Basketry          115
Part III: Living Traditions        124
Part IV: Baskets as Vessels        132
Part V: Beyond the Basket          143

Acknowledgments                    163
Notes                              167
Bibliography                       189
Index                              202
About the Contributors             206

CHAPTER 1

INTRODUCTION:
The Story of Contemporary
American Basketry

by Kristin Schwain & Josephine Stealey

## American Basketry and the Industrial Revolution

Baskets are an integral part of American history and identity. Long before Europeans arrived in the New World, Native Americans were producing baskets for domestic and ceremonial uses. European settlers and enslaved Africans brought their own traditions that took root in the American context. Each tradition evolved in response to the availability of materials, cultural encounters, economic pressures, technological developments, and the aesthetic sensibilities of individual makers.

The story of contemporary American basketry begins in the second half of the nineteenth century, when the expansion of the Industrial Revolution and the rise of mass production fundamentally altered the production, distribution, and use of baskets. Imported materials and new craft supplies democratized basket making and opened its practice to a wider audience. At the same time, the endowment of handwork with pedagogical and therapeutic potential led middle- and upper-class European Americans to put their faith in art appreciation and production as antidotes to civilization's ills. Baskets became more than ethnographic artifacts, souvenirs, and household decorations: They became works of art.

Fig. 1. Lewis Hine (1874-1940), *A Basket Factory, Evansville, Ind. Girls Making Melon Baskets,* 1908. Photograph. *Courtesy of Library of Congress, Prints & Photographs Division, National Child Labor Committee Collection, LC-DIG-nclc-04484.*

With the expansion of the Industrial Revolution, factories manufactured utility baskets that were once made by hand, particularly for use in agriculture. In 1911, photographer Lewis Hine visited a factory in Evansville, Indiana, that produced melon baskets with child labor (figure 1).[1] In the photograph, an assortment of materials, situated in barrels, are ready to be compiled. A young girl stands in an assembly line alongside others, performing her specialized role in the process. Mass-produced baskets like this were inexpensive, standardized, and quick to produce, and as a result, swiftly adopted across the country. By the 1930s and 1940s, Americans' familiarity with them facilitated their use as visual shorthand in Works Progress Administration (WPA) photography. Photographer Russell Lee captures a young man from Oklahoma leaning against a large stack of baskets filled with peaches ready for purchase (figure 2). The large number suggests both a substantial yield and a strong customer base, and consequently, the success of the government's economic policies. Another photograph presents at least sixteen rows of empty baskets in La Pryor, Texas, ready to be filled with harvested spinach (figure 3). The lines of baskets continue beyond the frame, underscoring the great potential of American agriculture. It shows, too, the role baskets continued to play in the era of mass production.[2]

Fig. 2. Russell Lee (1903-1986), *Grocery Boy Leaning on Basket of Peaches* (Muskogee, Oklahoma), 1939. Photograph. *Courtesy of Library of Congress, Prints & Photographs Division, FSA/OWI Collection, LC-DIG-fsa-8a26777.*

Fig. 3. Russell Lee (1903-1986), *Pile of Spinach Baskets* (La Pryor, Texas), 1939. Photograph. *Courtesy of Library of Congress, Prints & Photographs Division, FSA/OWI Collection, LC-DIG-fsa-8a25437.*

Fig. 4. H. Davis Company, *Colorful Basket Making for Girls and Boys* (kit), circa 1930s and 1940s. *Courtesy of Kristin Schwain*.

Mass production and the global commodity culture it generated expanded the number of people making baskets by supplying enthusiasts everywhere with the materials they needed. For example, in a classic book from the era, *Raffia Basketry as a Fine Art* (1915), Gertrude and Mildred Ashley advised their readers to purchase specific items: "blunt-pointed carpet-needles, size No. 20"; imported raffia palm, "which grows in the island of Madagascar"; and reeds from "China and the Philippine Islands," particularly "split reed No. 3 and round reeds Nos. 4 and 6."[3] New technologies streamlined the collection and preparation of materials and simplified basketry construction. Beginning in the mid-nineteenth century, perforated cardboard became a multipurpose craft supply that was quickly adopted for use in craft kits for children and adults (figure 4).[4] Samuel Gabriel and Sons sold a basket-weaving kit in the 1930s that included pieces of perforated cardboard that formed the top and bottom of the baskets, wooden dowels that connected the two pieces, and strips of paper that were woven in and out of stays. The H. Davis Company distributed *Colorful Basket Making for Girls and Boys*. In this set, perforated cardboard was replaced by wood. Makers placed the dowel sticks into precut holes in the base, soaked the enclosed reeds in water for fifteen minutes, and wove the reeds in and out of these sticks. According to the directions, the resulting baskets were "beautiful and useful things."

The American Arts and Crafts movement established the framework for the revaluation of handwork in modern life and elevated basket making into an art form. A national reform effort with regional variations, it posited a critique of the manufacturing process as well as the poorly constructed products that resulted from it.[5] Influenced by the art criticism of John Ruskin and the reform ideals of William Morris, the movement's proponents sought to improve the quality of life by reuniting workers with the products of their labor and by making beautiful handmade objects. A leader of the Deerfield, Massachusetts, Arts and Crafts movement, basket maker Madeline Yale Wynn lamented the status of commercial baskets in an article published in *Good Housekeeping* in 1901: "We find them decked out with extraneous ribbons and paper flowers, colored with pitiful, shallow pink colors, with crude, shameless greens; fluted, ruffled, pinched in, gathered, warped out of all normal shape."[6] In their place, Wynn sought "a basket of fine, honest intent and beautiful make" and rallied her readers to create baskets themselves. Describing her efforts with the Deerfield Basket Industry, she continued, "We do not threaten commercial upheavals, but we sit in our Valley of Delight and make baskets; good, honest baskets for use, with such beauty as we can evolve." Wynn's despair over commercial baskets did not include a renunciation of the economic system that produced them, but rather a reconciliation of handcraft and consumption: "Our hands are daily growing in skill, enthusiasm reigns, and we joy in the doing. Behold! We have made baskets; yes, and sold them, and orders have come to us. For every basket there has been a buyer."[7]

Wynn and many of her Arts and Crafts enthusiasts also sought to counteract what they perceived as the banality, over-civilization, and "weightlessness" of modern life by embracing peoples they deemed "primitive" as well as the more authentic, embodied, and spiritual lives they led.[8] According to anthropologist Molly Lee, the "Indian basket became a key symbol of this burgeoning anti-modernism."[9] Leading figures in the study and promotion of Native arts at the turn of the century called attention to the craze. In 1904, Smithsonian curator Otis Mason coined the term "canastromania" (from the Latin word *canistra*, meaning basket) to describe the "basket fever" that had gripped the nation.[10] Indeed, Indian baskets were omnipresent. People could view collections of Native baskets in museums, clubs, galleries, and world's fairs across the country. For example, the Peabody Museum of Archaeology and Ethnology opened to the public in 1877 with a focus on "the early inhabitants of America, and their relation to those of other parts of the world."[11] Those who could not visit the Peabody or the United States National Museum could read George Wharton James's two popular books, *Indian Basketry* (1901) and *How to Make Indian and Other Baskets* (1903). In the latter publication, James acknowledged "the making of Indian and other baskets is a fad" and cautioned that the "true worker desirous of emulating Indian work" must "approach it in the Indian spirit":

> The basket to the uncontaminated Indian meant a work of art, in which hope, aspiration, desire, love, religion, poetry, national pride, mythology, were all more or less interwoven. Hence, the work was approached in a spirit as far removed from that of mere commercialism, passing whim or fancy, as it was from that of levity, carelessness, or indifference.[12]

Middle- and upper-class European Americans sought to escape the crassness of modern life by looking at and making baskets with the presumed natural purity and religious sincerity of the Native American artist.

One of the underlying assumptions of the Arts and Crafts movement—that the cultivation of taste was pivotal to the development of character—resulted in the introduction of basketry as part of art and manual training programs in the public schools. Concerned with the influx of immigrants and the growing threat of urban and working-class unrest, middle- and upper-class tastemakers believed that the appreciation and production of art would promote social stability and inculcate the public into middle-class values and standards of deportment. American studies scholar Eileen Boris contends that art and manual training programs "promised to develop both the complete child and competent workman; they would also train both the consumers and producers necessary for an expanding corporate order."[13] One of many books written for educators and enthusiasts, William S. Marten's *Inexpensive Basketry* (1912) proposed a course of study for elementary classrooms predicated on the production of coil baskets, which he argued served three essential functions (figure 5).[14] The first was "the correlative value of the materials used." By gathering local materials, students became invested in their environment and teachers could capitalize on their engagement to introduce the study of botany and other subjects. Second, basket making helped develop motor

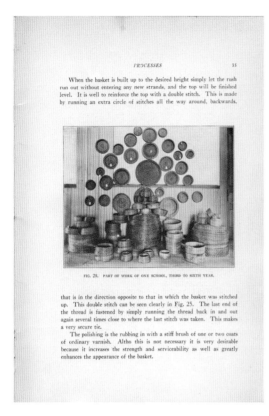

Fig. 5. William S. Marten, "Part of Work of One School, Third to Sixth Year" in *Inexpensive Basketry* (Peoria, IL: The Manual Arts Press, 1912), page 35.

skills and, perhaps more importantly, "judgment in the use of the eye and the hand." Finally, the economic value of basket making stemmed from the "varied and practical uses for which the baskets are made." Marten reasoned that when children drew from local materials, they realized "how to master their own environment;" to make something of value out of materials without value in themselves; and to produce a "commercially viable article" to support the community. Basket making rooted students in their local communities, cultivated their artistic sense, and prepared them for the workforce. It conjoined intellectual growth, bodily discipline, aesthetic judgment, and responsible citizenship.

The pedagogical utility of handcraft and the ubiquity of basketry in modern life also influenced the emerging profession of occupational therapy. While not formally organized until the return of shell-shocked soldiers after World War I, it evolved from the Arts and Crafts movement and the concept of work as therapeutic. Physician Herbert Hall's book, *The Work of Our Hands: A Study of Occupations for Invalids* (1915), proposed a "science of work" that studied the possibilities and "effect of productive work on each patient" for both its "therapeutic and economic" value.[15] That same year, another leader of the movement published a proposed course for nurses that suggested activities and crafts they could introduce to their patients, ranging from puzzles to string work, gardening to metal work, nature study to needlework, and card games to basketry.[16] As historian Jennifer Laws writes, "Through a return to traditional crafts such as basket-weaving and pottery-making, the early occupational therapists thus sought to rescue a restorative work ethic both from the degrading practices of factory work and from the quiet despotism of bed rest and, in doing so, to rescue the soul of the patient."[17] Some of the most enduring images of the era were photographs of recuperating soldiers weaving baskets in military hospitals (figure 6).

Traditional craft and modern industry also influenced the schools charged with assimilating Native and African Americans into modern American life. In the early twentieth century, Estelle Reed, the superintendent of Indian schools, developed the "Native Industries" curriculum. While not part of most government-funded Indian schools, most notably Carlisle Indian Industrial School in Pennsylvania and Hampton Normal and Agricultural Institute in Virginia, its goals were similar: to prepare students for citizenship, economic self-sufficiency, and industrial production. In her 1901 book *Course of Study for the Indian School of the United States*, Reed presented her approach to Native industries in a section entitled "Basketry and Caning."[18] Its goal was to maintain Native traditions that were "fast becoming a lost art" and to meet the demands of a global marketplace, since "demand for [basketry] is great everywhere." Despite Reed's admonishments to hire teachers from basket-making tribes, she cited a number of books about Native American basketry written by European American authors as useful guides. And despite her desire for students to employ

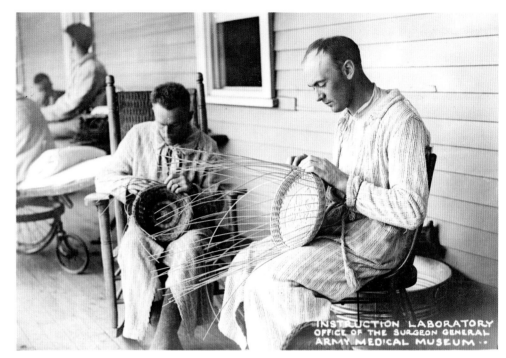

Fig. 6. *Basket weaving for physical therapy, Walter Reed General Hospital, Washington, DC, circa WWI.* Photograph. *Courtesy of Otis Historical Archives, National Museum of Health and Medicine (Reeve 000286).*

traditional materials and dyes, she suggested imported raffia as a material for the classroom. Echoing so many of her contemporaries, Reed considered baskets carriers of tradition that also met the demands of the marketplace. They maintained Native American identity, and at the same time, incorporated Native peoples into the industrial workforce.

Like the Native industries curriculum, the Penn Normal, Industrial, and Educational School in St. Helena Island, South Carolina, encouraged basket making to preserve cultural heritage and to support economic development. Northern abolitionists Laura M. Towne and Ellen Murray arrived on St. Helena Island in the early 1860s and formed the Penn School for freed slaves.[19] In the opening decade of the twentieth century, the school introduced industrial education into the curriculum, including the manual arts of basketry, blacksmithing, carpentry, cobbling, and wheelwrighting. The school proudly announced in its 1905 annual report that the "demand for the Island baskets of rush and palmetto" led them to hire native teacher Alfred Graham to provide "instruction to thirty-three boys."[20] Five years later, it proclaimed that Graham learned the art from his African father and that native island baskets "brought from Africa in the early slave days" belong "as truly to the Negro as the Indian baskets belong to the Indian."[21] Although administrators promoted the preservation of tradition as a vital reason for the program, another was economic. Beginning that same year, the school started selling the baskets through mail-order and retail outlets, and by 1913, through arts and crafts stores in Charleston, Philadelphia, and Boston. For northerners, coiled basketry preserved the African heritage of the islanders and integrated them into American culture.

## Tradition and the Advent of Modernism

The national distribution system, a product of the Industrial Revolution, created new markets and audiences for traditional baskets. While every cultural encounter has its own history, most followed a similar trajectory. European American cultural entrepreneurs "discovered" a basketry tradition and introduced it to American audiences. Basket makers, in turn, altered their production to meet the demand of the marketplace and used the opportunity for economic advancement and aesthetic expression. The relationship was by no means equal. The works of "primitive" cultures were appropriated into Western models of commodity production, altering the conventional uses of baskets. Baskets were absorbed, too, into the Western European system of art, particularly its burgeoning emphases on formal criteria and attention to the individual, aesthetic object.[22] Finally, historical baskets from all regions and traditions were absorbed into an aesthetic lineage of modern art that artists, critics, and curators considered truly American.

Tourism produced new markets for traditional baskets. The Fred Harvey Company forged a partnership with the Atchison, Topeka, and Santa Fe Railway in 1878. Ten years later, it managed and operated every restaurant and hotel along the railroad west of the Missouri River, catering to middle- and upper-class clientele. The "Indian craze," which reached its peak between 1880 and 1920, ensured that most of the tourists traveling west sought Indian curios as souvenirs.[23] The Fred Harvey Company "sold Indian art in their shops, arranged for Indian artists to 'perform' weaving or jewelry making in train stations, and ran special excursions to Indian communities where tourists could purchase artifacts from their makers."[24] Between 1894 and 1904, the Harvey Company increased its sale of Indian art more than 1,000 percent.[25] An early twentieth-century postcard of the Fred Harvey Indian Building in Albuquerque, New Mexico, shows an assembly of handcrafts from a variety of Native American traditions. Items were made by artisans in the building, which was intended to verify their authenticity (figure 7).

The Native American curio trade was stimulated by tourism as well as the sale of Native goods at department stores and mail-order catalogs. Collectors at all price points and degrees of familiarity with Native arts learned how to display their finds from articles in the popular press. In the "Home Notes" section of *Pearson's* magazine, for example, the writer displayed little interest in the origins or uses of Native baskets, but rather, encouraged readers to arrange "picturesque" items such as Navaho blankets, tomahawks, and moccasins in their homes.[26] *Papoose*, a journal published in New York for European American enthusiasts of Native cultures, combined romantic rhetoric and design advice with ethnographic description. In "The Basketry of the Northwest", the author began by linking aesthetics and consumption, ethnographic study and ownership, by declaring that "Indian basket collecting" combines "the study of aboriginal habits and customs with the acquisition of beautiful and rare specimens of native North American handiwork." The author cited Mrs. Alice Palmer Henderson, a "Tacoma lady and noted ethnologist":

Fig. 7. Indian Building, Albuquerque, New Mexico, Fred Harvey, 1906. Printed postcard. *Courtesy of Kristin Schwain.*

9902 INDIAN BUILDING. ALBUQUERQUE. N. M.    FRED HARVEY    COPYRIGHT 1906 BY FRED HARVEY

> I don't believe in making either a museum or a junkshop of one's home . . . Indian baskets, especially Northwestern weaves, are wonderfully durable and adapted to all sorts of uses. Could anything be more dainty or convenient than this beautiful covered hamper? It was an Indian woman's trunk, but a Gibson girl would seize upon it for her shirtwaists. It would solve the problem of what to give him (for his dress shirts), and it would make a unique wedding present for your swellest friend.[27]

Native handcrafts were simultaneously ethnographic artifacts, household commodities, collector's items, and aesthetic objects for expanding numbers of middle- and upper-class consumers.[28]

Many Native Americans embraced these new markets, reviving traditions that had become dormant with mass-production and using them as sources of economic development.[29] Although Native Americans and Europeans had a rich history of intercultural exchange going back at least three centuries, promoters of Native crafts marketed them as timeless artifacts of authentic cultural traditions uncontaminated by commercial life. For example, in 1895 Abe and Amy Cohn purchased baskets from Louisa Keyser, a Washoe basket weaver, and soon became her sole distributors.[30] The Cohns meticulously cataloged, marketed, and sold Keyser's baskets, and in return, covered her and her husband's expenses. A contributor to *Papoose* praised the Cohns for controlling Keyser's "entire artistic output" and sequestering her from "civilization," thereby preserving "the Washoe art unmixed with influence of the commercial order." Despite the mythology spun around her and her baskets, Keyser was a contemporary woman. She popularized *degikup* baskets, a rather simple utilitarian basket often used in ceremonies (see pp. 68–69). Keyser, however, transformed the *degikup* into a fine art object sold to collectors and museums. She altered its shape and produced large, sculptural forms with a flat base and small opening. In addition, she invented some designs and found inspiration for others in Pomo and Miwok weaving.[31] Keyser's baskets were modern creations, products of the commercial world her collectors sought to escape.

C-8—*Weaver of Baskets, Cherokee Indian Reservation, Cherokee, N. C.*

PHOTO BY CARLOS CAMPBELL

Fig. 8. Carlos C. Campbell, *Weaver of Baskets, Cherokee Indian Reservation, Cherokee, North Carolina*, n.d. Postcard. Standard News Agency (Knoxville, TN). *Courtesy of Kristin Schwain.*

In addition to individual Native artists, entire communities embraced new forms of marketing to increase tourism and sales.[32] For instance, the first annual Cherokee Fair took place in Cherokee, North Carolina, in 1914.[33] Although the Eastern Band's tribal council had been considering an event of this kind for almost fifty years, the construction of railway systems facilitated transportation through the mountainous region. Arts and crafts competitions were held in two categories: Ladies' Work, which encompassed quilting, weaving, embroidery, tatting, and needlework, and Arts and Crafts, which included river cane and white oak-basket making, pottery, woodworking, mask making, and beadwork. The fair, which continues today, promoted tourism in the Cherokee area and enabled artists to show and sell their work. This undated promotional postcard, intended to increase attendance at the fair and tourism more generally, shows basket maker, Nina Standing Deer (figure 8). Surrounded by trees, she sits and weaves a basket as a young child, presumably her son, stands at her side. The basket appears to be a miniature cradle board geared toward tourists, since those used by the Cherokee would have been larger and would not have been woven in the round. The description on the back supports this assessment: "Mrs. Nina Standing Deer was a feature of the Cherokee Indian Fair as she wove her baskets before interested groups. Baskets were bought faster than they could be woven, and customers waited eagerly as they watched the finishing touches put on."

African American coil basket makers in coastal Georgia and the South Carolina Lowcountry also sought to sell their products directly to consumers. The tradition arrived on American soil through the transatlantic slave trade, and male slaves created tools that facilitated agricultural work as well as containers for storage and domestic use. By the end of the nineteenth century, however, women took over the weaving once done by men. Baskets became smaller and more decorative, and their functions changed as they became souvenirs and *objets d'art* for tourists and collectors in Savannah and Charleston. While many entrepreneurs encouraged women to produce "show baskets" and sold their works through mail order and retail stores, many of the basket makers took control of their labor by establishing stands on the heavily traveled Highway 17 in Mount Pleasant, South Carolina, to reach their customers directly (figure 9).[34]

The anthropological description of baskets that permeated popular books, catalogs, and periodicals at the end of the nineteenth and early twentieth centuries took two forms: One was ethnographic, introducing audiences to the myriad roles baskets played in native and rural life; and the other was aesthetic, focused on basket materials, forms, and design elements. The latter introduced basketry as a fine art. Wharton's *Indian Basketry*, for example, opens with chapters on basketry in legend and ceremony, then proceeds to discuss the materials, colors, weaves, and forms. Later, he focuses on specific examples, including an Apache basket:

Fig. 9. Bluford Muir (1913-1990), *Roadside stand on Highway 17 in Mount Pleasant, South Carolina*, circa 1930s. Photograph. *Courtesy of US Forest Service.*

The apparently unsystematic ornament is indeed very regular. Four lines of black sewing of different lengths proceed from the black ring of the center. From the end of all these radiating lines sewing is carried to the left in regular curves. Then, the four radiating lines are repeated, and the curved lines, until the border is reached.[35]

Wharton's intense focus on formal elements mirrors the attention paid to the aesthetic object by fine artists and critics alike, including pioneering art educator Arthur Wesley Dow.

Dow's book, *Composition: A Series of Exercises in Art Structure for the Use of Students and Teachers*, first published in 1899, was the standard textbook in art education for fifty years. He encouraged artists not to copy nature but to "build up" harmony using the elements of line, mass, and color. His admonition to approach art through the lens of *structure* rather than *imitation* established what he deemed as two essential skills: The cultivation of judgment and an understanding of design principles.[36] Dow provided a series of exercises to teach students the elements of composition using arts from around the world in multiple media, including Japanese prints, Peruvian textiles, and Native American pottery. Dow's refusal to distinguish between the fine and decorative arts resonated with Arts and Crafts enthusiasts. His endorsement of individual expression rather than the copying of nature and art history resonated with contemporary artists. And the primacy he placed on a work's formal qualities echoed the writings of anthropologists, ethnologists, reformers educators, and art critics, all of whom helped forge modern art criticism.[37]

Wharton and Dow's attention to single works in their books served as textual equivalents to aesthetic and commercial display models that spotlighted individual objects. For example, the Appalachian Craft Revival was forged in the 1890s by an informal network that linked craftspeople with settlement schools and national markets. Allanstand Cottage Industries, organized by Yale-educated Frances Goodrich, displayed and sold its goods at an Asheville shop as well as through mail-order brochures distributed by the Presbyterian Church.[38] A professional and promotional photograph from the early 1900s displays a series of baskets on a cloth-covered table with pedestals against a painted backdrop (figure 10). The baskets are isolated from one another, allowing viewers to attend to specific objects and pay close attention to their manufacture. At

Fig. 10. Herbert W. Pelton (1879-1961), *Allanstand Cottage Industries Product Display*, early 1900s. Photograph. *Courtesy of the Archive of the Southern Highland Craft Guild.*

the same time, their careful arrangement leads the gaze from one object to another, emphasizing the variety of products available. By separating the baskets from the makers and their cultural contexts, the photograph suggests that the works speak for themselves. The ability to embody an entire people and cultural history is suggested further by the background, which was probably used in formal portraits produced at a local commercial studio. The Allanstand Cottage Industries display was by no means unique; it relied on the same exhibition models employed by department stores, museums, and world's fairs, the three most important heralds of America's modernization.[39] It also reflected the photographs included in catalogs, annual reports of industrial and settlement schools, and art education textbooks.

Dow's attention to pure design and focus on the modern aesthetic object did not negate a commitment to tradition. As early as 1891, Dow campaigned for the preservation of his hometown of Ipswich, Massachusetts, by asserting, "The day is dawning when America will have an art of her own founded upon her own history and character."[40] His call took on greater import in interwar years, which were distinguished by a widespread search for an authentic national culture. In his influential essay of 1918, literary critic Van Wyck Brooks called on intellectuals to "discover, invent a usable past," to create a storehouse of "apt attitudes and adaptable ideals," of cultural traditions and spiritual resources, that contemporary artists could draw upon to forge a collective American identity.[41] For many Americans, one of the primary sources was Native American art, most known through basketry. Dow and other "artists, teachers, and critics associated with the development of American modernism" were not only inspired by Native art in their art production, but also "included Native handicrafts in their own exhibitions, and used them as models in courses in fine art and design."[42] In 1922, art historian and critic Holger Cahill propagated this idea in an essay entitled "America Has Its 'Primitives'": "We great Machine People, who have carried ugliness well-nigh to apotheosis in the fairest of lands . . . may forego the conqueror's pride and learn wisdom from our humble brother of the pueblos, who has made the desert bloom with beauty."[43] Importantly, Cahill did not consider the primitive a stage in human and cultural development, as it had been for so many turn-of-the-century Americans seeking an antidote to modernity. Instead, Cahill defined it as a source of authenticity, originality, and heterogeneity, all essential for the creation of a uniquely American art.

Native American art was not the only source for a truly American art. Curators, collectors, and artists also embraced folk art, broadly defined as the unconscious expression of the common people. Folk art was central to this nationalist enterprise because it was perceived to present both the innate characteristics and the evolution of a race; it embodied a people's spiritual essence and exemplified its historical progress.[44] Thirteen years after his essay on the American Primitive, Cahill directed the Federal Arts Project, which included the massive *Index of American Design*. The *Index*, which focused primarily on the nation's Western European inheritance, sought to provide a comprehensive visual record of the nation's usable past that could also serve as a sourcebook for contemporary designers.[45] It was composed of exquisitely rendered watercolors and drawings of material culture deemed exemplary of regional traditions (such as an Appalachian buttocks basket) as well as baskets from many utopian communities, including the Shakers (New England and the Midwest), the Amana Colonies (Iowa), and Zoar Village (Ohio).[46] Like Native American art, these baskets and other objects were uniquely American and established a national aesthetic distinct from that of Europe. Other art-world luminaries, including Edith Halpert and Abby Aldrich Rockefeller, shared Cahill's enthusiasm for American folk art. Together, they "established folk art firmly as an art rather than as history or ethnology."[47] By elevating folk art from historical artifact to fine art, art-world leaders established traditional basketry as thoroughly modern and uniquely American.

## The New Basketry

America's success in World War II launched its Golden Age. The center of the modern art world—now fully commoditized, institutionalized, and professionalized—shifted from the old world (Paris) to the new (New York). The dominance of representational art waned as Abstract Expressionism flourished. The horrors of World War II prompted people to wonder whether humanity was inherently reasonable and capable of self-determination. Artists responded to this broad cultural question in their work, reshaping the art world as they did. The embrace of textiles by the fine arts, the rise of the American studio craft movement, the women's movement's celebration of "women's work," and the later embrace of environmentalism as a critique of the nation's consumer culture all facilitated the rise of basketry as contemporary American art.

The art world's emphasis on abstraction, personal expression, and the potential of materials to create meaning opened the door for basketry, due in no small way to the growth of fine arts programs in higher education. In 1944, President Franklin D. Roosevelt signed into law the Servicemen's Readjustment Act, popularly known as the G.I. Bill. While the bill provided a host of services for veterans, one of the most successful included cash payments for tuition and living expenses to attend university, high school, or vocational programs. Enrollment in universities increased dramatically as former soldiers enrolled in art programs. Ceramicist Peter Voulkos and basket artist Charles "Ed" Rossbach took advantage of the G.I. Bill and went on to make vital and transformative contributions in their respective media. Voulkos helped lead what became known as the California Clay Movement and American Clay Revolution, while Rossbach, considered the most influential textile educator in America, led the development of the New Basketry.[48]

Fine art programs gained an even stronger foothold in higher education with the introduction of master of fine arts degrees (MFAs) in the 1950s.[49] The Bauhaus ideal of the artist-designer-craftsman, embraced as the foundation of fine arts programs, helped institute the studio craft movement.[50] Craft courses were introduced into curricula, and as a result, craft media were discussed and evaluated as contemporary art. The resulting work was more personal and linked to individual expression.[51] According to critic Laurel Reuter, craft materials, craft techniques, craft ideology, and craft makers invaded and subsequently democratized contemporary art in the second half of the twentieth century. They helped collapse the historical hierarchy that privileged painting and sculpture over all other media and neutralized the hierarchy of materials, making textiles and other nontraditional materials part of the fine artist's toolbox. Basketry's roots in weaving and three-dimensional form played seminal roles in what Reuter calls the "crafting of art in America."[52]

When weaving entered the fine art curriculum in the 1950s, many artists studied the history of textiles and embraced the artistic potential of fiber. They viewed woven textiles as utilitarian but also as aestheticized objects as they explored new concepts and modes of production. They began free experimentation on and off the loom, incorporated a variety of media, and introduced everyday materials into their work, creating an environment in which artists were freed from the history of both fine art and textile traditions to invent new, personal ways to express themselves.[53] By 1960, this new art movement reached maturity and its practitioners considered themselves artists rather than craftspersons. Indeed, in less than a decade, many artists, including those initially trained as painters or sculptors, chose fiber-, thread-, and textile-based construction as their materials and processes of choice.

Artists of the era reacted to the narrowly defined modernist aesthetic promoted by influential critic Clement Greenberg by blurring the boundaries of all media and making connections across disciplines. While still focused on individual expression, they turned to a variety of materials to make art. In 1955, for example, Robert Rauschenberg produced his groundbreaking *Bed,* in which he applied quilts and decorative traditional patterns onto the canvas like paint. Sculptor Robert Arneson created works in clay that appropriated popular culture and scatological objects, drawing attention to their revelatory potential.[54] Rossbach explored popular imagery using traditional patterns and techniques with recycled, urban-foraged materials, a practice that became commonplace in a few short years.[55]

Fine artists trained as weavers paved the way for the New Basketry, perhaps even unwittingly. For example, Sheila Hicks and Claire Zeisler sought to win recognition for fiber as a material with the expressive power attributed to painting and sculpture (figure 11).[56] They employed fiber to create nonwoven, three-dimensional forms that liberated the medium from the loom and released their works from the confines of fiber's historically subordinated position in the art world. Ruth Asawa, also trained as a weaver, was one of the first artists to blend media and expand upon the use of materials. She crocheted aluminum, brass, iron, or copper wire, devising complex forms vaguely recalling fish-trap baskets, sea creatures, and seed forms. Their structural openness engaged the surrounding space with filigree shadows, furthering their sculptural impact. Textile historians and artists Mildred Constantine and Jack Lenor Larsen identified Asawa's work as "America's first monumental art fabrics" and "an unequivocal success."[57] Asawa worked with textile processes but viewed herself as a sculptor. Her work challenged categorization and set the stage for the New Basketry.[58]

Rossbach joined the faculty at the University of California–Berkeley in 1950.[59] He inspired Lillian Elliott and JoAnne Segal Brandford, two other pioneers who taught at UC Berkeley. Under his guidance, this program became the training ground for influential artists Gyöngy Laky, Pat Hickman, Joan Sterrenberg, Barbara Shawcroft, Nance O'Banion, and others, making the West Coast a hotbed of innovation in fiber and basketry during the 1960s and 1970s.[60] According to Rossbach, the new baskets he and his students explored were:

Fig. 11. Martine Franck (1938-2012), *Photograph of Sheila Hicks*, circa 1970. Photograph. ©Martine Franck/ Magnum Photos.

> Abstract compositions of constructed volumes and planes, with attention given to implied spaces, all the relationships of open and closed, of penetrating forms, of inside and out. The new baskets suggest that structural problems are being solved for the first time, that materials are being used for the first time, that forms are evolving for the first time.[61]

Rossbach and his disciples married fiber and dimensionality to forge the New Basketry movement, using basketry materials and techniques to build structures and create expressive sculptural objects.

The New Basketry, while primarily housed in university art departments, was supported and expanded by craft schools, community-based programs, workshops, journals, and professional organizations. Penland School of Crafts, Arrowmont School of Arts and Crafts, and many other schools founded in the early twentieth century continued to flourish, offering intensive workshop opportunities for anyone who wanted to enroll. Fiberworks, a Center for the Textile Arts (1973–1987), was an alternative program founded by Gyöngy Laky in Berkeley that further democratized the movement. Artists creating in all media experimented together, soaking up the passion and knowledge of their colleagues about historical and inventive textile production. In addition, independent workshops were taught by artists and authors, including Dona Meilach, whose *Basketry Today with Materials from Nature* (1979) served as a how-to manual organized by technique. She mixed and matched materials and processes, encouraging artists to look at both in new, inventive combinations.[62]

New Periodicals, associations, and galleries furthered the New Basketry. The journal *Craft Horizons* (now *American Craft*) came onto the scene as early as 1942, and the now defunct *Fiber Arts* magazine devoted issues specifically to contemporary basketry, helping to propagate the work of emerging and established artists. As organizations such as the International Surface Design Association and Handweavers Guild of America devoted to fiber and textiles emerged on the national scene, they also published journals and sponsored juried exhibitions of contemporary work. Finally, the burgeoning craft gallery scene in the 1980s, supported by the promotional work of the American Craft Council and the Rosen Agency, established wholesale and retail sales opportunities for contemporary basketry.

Shereen LaPlantz played a particularly important role in cultivating a community of basket artists to share their work, learn new techniques, and publicize the New Basketry. She traveled the country teaching workshops and wrote books on techniques that continue to be used today. She also founded a bimonthly journal, *The News Basket*, which served as a precursor to the National Basketry Organization's *Quarterly Review*. It offered historical, instructional, and photographic essays by leading figures, guild pages, and advertisements for conferences, supplies, and schools from across the nation. LaPlantz also forged a canon of basketry through the annual publication of *Basketry Round-up*, which highlighted the entire spectrum of contemporary production, and through a basket-artist-of-the-month club she sent six slides of work by a single artist to members in order to disseminate the great revivalist and sculptural work being done. While Rossbach and his colleagues established the philosophy behind the New Basketry, alternative schools, conferences, workshops, journals, and professional organizations established the structures necessary for it to become a national movement.

The New Basketry also found support in larger cultural movements of the late 1960s and 1970s. The Baby Boom generation challenged long-held American values and rebelled against the "normative standards of popular culture."[63] This resulted in two significant cultural movements that expanded the role of basketry in contemporary art: the women's movement and the back-to-the-land movement. The women's movement provided opportunities and support for women in the fine arts who employed basket techniques and materials. Feminist artists and historians promoted work made by women and legitimized female aesthetic expression. Inspired by the hallmark work of Judy Chicago and Miriam Schapiro on *Womanhouse*, women embraced their ability to create art that came from their personal experience.[64] They also elevated the status of what had been historically dismissed as the decorative arts, hobbyist activities, women's work, and folk art.[65] Many of the women artists involved in the movement also made baskets. By 1985, American women working in contemporary basketry had permeated the art scene and were featured in major national and international exhibitions. For example, Jane Sauer, Lillian Elliot and Pat Hickman, and Carol Shaw-Sutton exhibited at the International Lausanne Biennial, one of the most prestigious events and venues in the world. Their large-scale, basket-influenced sculptures were constructed with knotting, knitting, braiding, crochet, and many variations of basket-making techniques. Although a number of men have played critical roles in the New Basketry—Rossbach, John McQueen, and John Garrett among them—the movement has been heavily influenced by women artists and remains so today.

The back-to-the-land movement had a similar effect. Craft practices were so fundamental to the 1960s ethos that they became synonymous with basketry. Craft appealed to many because it involved a direct encounter of the maker with a material, drew upon America's pioneer roots, and rejected the homogenizing pressure of industrial mass production and commercial motivation. Craft practices supported the ideals of self-realization and self-sufficiency. Craft critic Rose Silvka asserted that "the hero is no longer the man who makes the money but the man who has values beyond money—the artist, the intellectual—and the work he does to which he transmits value."[66]

## The Contemporary Landscape of American Basketry

The contemporary basketry movement is composed of three distinct but interrelated practices. Artists who engage living traditions create baskets based on historical designs, materials, and processes that honor their utilitarian origins. Others treat baskets as vessels. Their works suggest functionality, but they employ particular iconographies, materials, and techniques for their potential to make meaning. They reference the basket as a container that embodies interior and exterior facets for its conceptual, metaphorical, and narrative potential. Finally, some artists go beyond the basket. They employ basketry materials and techniques to create architectural forms and sculptures that deny functionality and explore broader conceptual and aesthetic concerns. Regardless of the arena in which they work, all contemporary basket artists create aesthetic objects that are valued for their formal qualities and work as poetic ruminations on theoretical concerns or incisive responses to cultural debates. These artists have forged a truly American art form and, at the same time, contributed to and helped shape the contemporary art world.[67]

### *Living Traditions*

In the late 1960s, many European traditions of basket making were on the brink of extinction. As curator Nicholas Bell describes it,

> The basket was sufficiently removed from everyday life to challenge its fusty stature. From a distance the basket was not just old; it was unusual, even a riddle, with the potential for a nostalgic return. The gap in baskets' use provided this new perspective, which was critical to engineering the craft's comeback.[68]

Traditions were revived and infused with new life by "the politics of a generation with no previous ties to the field."[69]

During the 1970s and 1980s, many Americans rebelled against American capitalism and imperialism at home and abroad. Influenced by the environmental movement and nostalgia for what they perceived as the simplicity of rural life, Baby Boomers formed communities that attempted to live off the land. They had a financial and philosophical need to supplement their income and lifestyle with a creative outlet. Although they were not as geographically isolated as their seventeenth- and eighteenth-century predecessors or as formally trained as their Arts and Crafts precursors, some turned to basketry for similar reasons. The materials came from local, self-harvested sources, were inexpensive to produce (aside from the time and sweat equity necessary to prepare them), and were environmentally friendly. At the same time, there was a market for their wares. Many basket makers followed the burgeoning retail and wholesale craft show circuit, others sold work in local outlets and galleries, and still others became well-known professional artists.

The extent of the 1970s revival of traditional basket making and its impact on contemporary basket making was highlighted in Bell's recent exhibition, *A Measure of the Earth* (2013), at the Renwick Gallery of the Smithsonian American Art Museum. While makers produced utilitarian baskets that could be used in everyday life, they often became aesthetic objects appreciated by collectors and featured in museums. Indeed, Stephen Cole and Martha Ware's donation of their traditional basket collection provided the impetus for the Renwick exhibition, which highlighted the work of artists also in this catalog: Darryl and Karen Arawjo (see p. 132), JoAnn Kelly Catsos (see pp. 124, 126), Katherine Lewis (see p. 126), Leon Niehues (see pp. 120, 158), Joanne Russo (see p. 142), Polly Adams Sutton (see p. 141), Cynthia Taylor (see p. 128), Leona Waddell (see p. 127), Aaron Yachim (see p. 129), and Stephen Zeh (see pp. 128, 130–131). Most of these traditional basket makers share Bell's conviction that baskets be both functional and strong and that "their connection to place and the ritual of gathering natural materials is of equal importance."[70]

While many contemporary basket makers come from the American studio craft movement, artists who maintain traditional practices epitomize three alternative and overlapping educational methods. The first is apprenticeship. Some basket makers grew up in families that passed the craft from generation to generation. Appalachian basket maker Waddell, who received a National Heritage Fellowship from the National Endowment for the Arts in 2016, learned how to make split white-oak baskets from her mother in Kentucky. Yachim grew up in Appalachia surrounded by basket makers and learned to make baskets from his neighbor, fifth-generation basket maker Oral "Nick" Nicholson in the late 1970s. In contrast, Yachim's partner, Taylor, became enamored with basket making after living in China and seeing baskets so integral to daily life. Starting in 1982, she studied with well-known Appalachian basket maker Rachel Nash Law. Their relationship led to the extensive documentation of baskets and makers throughout central Appalachia in *Appalachian White Oak Basketmaking: Handing Down the Basket*.[71] In still another example, married couple Beth Hester and Scott Gilbert apprenticed with Lestel (1927–2010) and Ollie (1930–2003) Childress from Hart County, Kentucky. Hester and Gilbert have become well-known basket makers and advocates for the tradition as proprietors of *The Basket Maker's Catalog* and as contributors to the ongoing work of the Kentucky Folklife Program. They do not consider themselves traditional basket makers because they did not receive their knowledge from their families. Instead, they call themselves "bearers of the tradition."[72] The foundation of their evolving

Fig. 12. Beth Hester (b. 1956) and Scott Gilbert (b. 1953), *Bhutan Dzong*, 2015. White oak: 24" × 16" × 16". *Courtesy of the artists.*

work continues to reflect the skills and techniques they learned from a vibrant community of local and global artists, as is evident in this work in which they apply traditional Appalachian materials and weaving to an Asian-inspired design. In *Bhutan Dzong*, they apply traditional Appalachian materials and weaving to an Asian-inspired design (figure 12).

In addition to apprenticeships, traditional basket makers learn the craft through workshops and independent study. For example, Lewis from Mount Vernon, Washington, has traveled throughout the United States and Europe to learn techniques from basket makers committed to the functional tradition. One of the few basket makers today who cultivates and processes her own willow, she creates handsome, functional baskets in the European style. Still others reverse engineer historical baskets, which serve as "silent teachers."[73] Others learned from books: Arawjo learned to split white oak from a *Foxfire* book, a how-to series published in the 1970s and 1980s that sought to preserve a traditional Appalachian lifestyle by instructing readers how to build a log cabin, preserve fruit, cure and smoke hogs, and make a basket out of white-oak splints. Niehues took up baskets after reading a 1077 booklet published by the University of Arkansas Cooperative Extension Office.[74]

The functional basket revival is not limited to European American traditions. Native basket makers also work within their tribal traditions while pursuing individual expression, taking their place among other Native American artists who participated in the push for a more multicultural, mixed-media American art.[75] Lisa Telford is a Gawa Git'anee Haida weaver who learned from her aunt, Delores Churchill, a well-known Haida basket maker. *Summer Night's Do* (see p. 160), like most of Telford's work, is composed of traditional materials and techniques. However, it takes the form of a dress, an artifact of contemporary life.

Pat Courtney Gold revived the tradition of Wasco basket making by studying traditional baskets in museum collections. She painstakingly transcribed their designs on graph paper (a relic of her earlier career as a mathematician). Her baskets illustrate two interrelated iconographies. One is predicated on historical baskets, as in the traditional "sally bag" with ancestral petroglyph faces inspired by a basket in the Peabody Museum at Harvard University (figure 13). The other updates tradition and comments on issues facing contemporary Native peoples. *Yuppie Indian Couple* (see p. 125) features a couple in two guises: on one side, they appear "Indian" according to the traditional iconography of Native life; on the other, they flaunt the urban style they acquired after leaving the reservation, obtaining a college education, and accepting a good-paying job. The pairs are linked by a design that juxtaposes a historic Californian condor with a modern airplane, reinforcing Gold's examination of the many elements, both traditional and contemporary, native and non-native, that

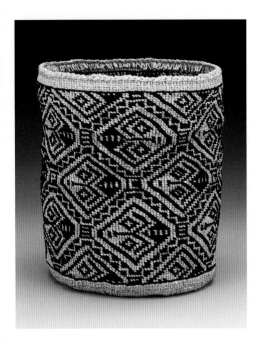

Fig. 13. Pat Courtney Gold
(Wasco tribe, b. 1939), *Traditional
Wasco basket (sally bag) with
ancestral petroglyph faces*, 2016.
Split cattail leaves, dyed raffia.
Photograph by Bill Bachhuber.
*Courtesy of the artist.*

fashion Indian identity. Like so many contemporary artists, Telford and Gold call on their personal and cultural histories to create works that speak to multiples audiences and their individual and communal experiences of American life.

### *Basket as Vessel*

The pliability and variety of materials and the structural possibilities inherent in basketry inspired Rossbach's fiber constructions. Traditional techniques became tools for contemporary artists to generate concept-driven sculptures. The resulting objects, many of which retained the vessel form and references to functionality, participated in several art world trends; the emphasis on materials and techniques as signifiers of meaning, the appropriation of popular iconography, and the reintroduction of subject matter into the work.

Like artists working in other media, the basket makers of the 1960s and 1970s challenged Greenberg's emphasis on the purity of media by investing materials with cultural significance. As art historian Elissa Auther argues, artists since Rossbach, Brandford, and Elliott have incorporated a "radical new use of materials, redirecting the work's value away from the utility of its technique toward a 'useless' aesthetic appreciation of such materials."[76] Meaning, in other words, is created by the repurposing of materials, leading viewers to look at it new ways. For instance, Karyl Sisson's *Mixing Bowls* (see p. 121) are composed of common seamstress tape measures used to measure both curved and flat surfaces. Referencing food preparation through a series of nesting bowls, the materials measure time and imbue domestic labor with value, as American culture equates time spent with economic remuneration. Sisson's thoughtful imbrication of form and material makes a poignant statement about the physical labor performed by women that remains invisible and uncompensated but nonetheless celebrated as a romantic ideal.

In contrast, John Garrett used tools he found cleaning out his deceased father's garage in his *Builder's Basket* (see p. 149), constructed in memory of his father. As an electrician, his father accumulated a variety of mechanical objects that differed from the sorts of things Garrett himself salvages from thrift and antique stores. By using materials found in his father's workshop and collaging them into a form associated with his work, Garrett commemorated his father's life through the "stuff" he left behind, integrating his father's life with his own.

Other artists employ specific techniques to further a work's impact. Norma Minkowitz crochets and shellacs cotton in *Final Resting Place* (see p. 119). The open-weave vessel embodies dichotomies of soft and hard, internal and external, transparent and opaque. The interplay of light and line complicate any easy binary; as soon as a visible element disappears a new form emerges from the shadows. *Final Resting Place* casts doubt on a definite separation of life and death, since presence continues to exist, even in absence.

Christine Joy, on the other hand, randomly weaves willow she harvests every fall. By slowly integrating one branch at a time, Joy develops a dialog between and among the materials, the technique, and the form (see p. 153). These aesthetic choices situate both her and her work within the rhythms and cycles of the natural world. She writes that her willow sculptures "resonate with the land. They are dynamic linear forms that speak of clouds, mountains, water and fields. The density and movement of each piece evokes the rhythm of seasons and cycles."[77] They suggest the windswept Montana landscape from which they emerge.

Just as materials and techniques are carefully selected for their aesthetic and cultural significance, so too is iconography. Rossbach translated traditional techniques like coiling and plaiting into containers composed from the consumer detritus of contemporary urban life. And, like Andy Warhol on the East Coast, he appropriated popular iconography to challenge viewers' perception of what constitutes fine art and social import. In his well-known *Mickey Mouse Coil Basket* (see p. 122), he wove the famous Disney icon into the piece to elevate the cartoon character into the realm of fine art and to critique the low status given to craft media by many in the fine art world. "It's not that I'm so fond of him," Rossbach said, "but he's a statement of our present condition in the crafts."[78] Approximately thirty years later, Kate Anderson, a former painter, appropriated 1960s Pop art in her work. In *Mickey Mouse Teapot/Warhol-Haring* (see p. 143), she did not depict the Disney character, but rather, painstakingly knotted Andy Warhol's silkscreen of Mickey Mouse on one side and "Andy Mouse," Keith Haring's portrait of Warhol as Mickey Mouse, on the other. The lid's knob and the body's handle reiterate the fine art connections, composed of a stainless steel cutout of Mickey in text and four Haring-inspired figures, respectively. By quoting Rossbach, Warhol, and Haring, Anderson calls attention to the critical issues they raised regarding the hierarchy of materials and the intimacy of fine art and popular culture. By painstakingly weaving the teapot, constructing it stitch upon stitch, she adds gender to the conversation, calling attention to artistic media historically associated with women as well as their domestic role as consumers.

Iconography and the appropriation of visual culture are two ways that basket artists introduce narrative into their work. Others introduce content through historical references and the tactility and familiarity of forms. For example, Cherokee artist Shan Goshorn addresses the history of Native and European American encounters in *They Were Called Kings* (see p. 138). Plaited with watercolor paper rather than the traditional river cane, each piece presents a photograph of a contemporary member of the Warriors of the Anikituhwa—originally the first line of defense for the community and now ambassadors for the Eastern Band of the Cherokee Nation—wearing eighteenth-century-style clothing. The interweaving of past and present takes a narrative turn on the interior, which features printed accounts by Europeans of a 1762 visit of three Cherokee Warriors to England. Together, they show how European American representations of Native peoples, established over two hundred and fifty years ago, continue to dominate popular perceptions.

While Goshorn references historical artifacts in contemporary materials to establish the subject matter of her work, Ann Coddington does so through the tactility and visceral familiarity of her forms. In *Fingerprints* (see p. 147), she twined fifty hand-sized vessels out of waxed linen to evoke memories, both intentional and visceral, of the psychological and physical power of touch. Each basket calls attention to itself individually, embodying specific emotions or events, but also interacts with the others, revealing that life is composed of intimate moments and sensory experiences. She writes that she employs "the technique of twining from the traditional craft of basketry to create a sculptural expression of my beliefs and experiences and how they are sensed by the body."[79] Indeed, she wants viewers to respond to her work emotionally, not just conceptually, because she seeks to make them more aware of the relationship between the conscious and unconscious, the mundane and the sublime, in the quotidian world.

*Beyond the Basket*

Some contemporary artists push beyond basketry's traditional association with form and function to such a degree that they no longer look like containers. Nevertheless, they rely on one or more elements of traditional basketry: its forms, materials, patterns, or techniques. They engage with the language of materials, the hierarchy of value, and the drive to make. For example, artist John McQueen's installation at the Racine Art Museum, *Table of Contents* (see p. 89), presents a series of tensions that tells the story of American basketry more generally. He built scaffolding from willow twigs that ran the forty-eight-foot length of the gallery, mounted the large grid on orange-painted shipping crates, and suspended from it 172 sketches of small, everyday objects. McQueen took digital photographs of items in his home, ranging from eyeglasses to a Windsor-styled dining chair, from a camera to a plunger, and created their outlines in willow and fastened them together with wax-coated string. Using natural materials that he found on his farm in upstate New York and employing traditional weaving techniques, McQueen amplified the rich history of American basketry. By creating a site-specific installation that called attention to the role of consumption in American life as well as to the hierarchy of objects that appear (and do not appear) in museum settings, McQueen joined the fine art world's avant-garde lineage. *Table of Contents* is rooted in the natural world but responsive to contemporary concerns, attentive to the idea of containment but resistant to its borders and boundaries, and carefully crafted but theoretically conceived. Put differently, McQueen's work complicates any easy distinction between local and global, craft and art, basket and sculpture, traditional and contemporary—all the dualisms that have framed the history of American basketry for more than one hundred years.

The depth and breadth of work by North Carolinian Bryant Holsenbeck shows how the materials employed by an artist often carry ideological meanings that animate an entire career and have the potential to transform lives. She began as an urban basket maker using natural materials to produce functional and sculptural baskets in the late 1970s (figure 14). Holsenbeck's deep concern for the ecosystem led her to use the detritus of consumer culture to produce both small-scale objects and installation work. A self-proclaimed environmental artist, Holsenbeck weaves bottle caps, credit cards, plastic bags, and chopsticks, as well as other remnants of mass production to create works that represent the natural world. For example, *Bottle Fall* (see p. 98) was an installation at Bucks County Community College in Pennsylvania composed of 20,000 bottles that were collected and cut by college and community members. The result was a twenty-foot waterfall that flowed from the gallery ceiling to the floor and into the hallway. This important work called attention to how plastic water bottles are actually polluting and destroying our waterways, and it altered the power relationship between artist and viewers by actively involving community members in the creative process. Holsenbeck embraces a new role for the contemporary artist, one advocated by critic Susi Gablik, who asserts that, unlike modern art, contemporary art *should* play a vital role in community-building and serve as a catalyst for social and political transformation.[80] *Bottle Fall* illustrates how the waste of a single community has long-term repercussions, and highlights how individuals can make a difference and initiate change just by drinking from a reusable container.

Fig. 14. Bryant Holsenbeck preparing for an art fair, circa 1970s. Photograph. *Courtesy of the artist.*

Emerging artist Aron Fischer is part of a growing group of self-proclaimed makers who have graduated from MFA programs and are keenly aware of art's history and their role in it. At the same time, they exhibit a do-it-yourself ethos and a desire to "make stuff." Fischer's *Work* (see p. 149) is composed of a Shaker-style peg board holding a series of handcrafted implements made from historical and contemporary materials: ebonized white oak, walnut, leather, synthetic reed, Egyptian paste, and steel. At first glance, it appears to be a historic installation celebrating the Shaker ethos, articulated by Mother Ann Lee: "Put your hands to work and your hearts to God." However, an examination of the tools does not clarify their utility. For what were they used? Are their functions no longer known by contemporary viewers who purchase their tools at home improvement emporiums? Or are they useless but for their beauty and craftsmanship? In *Work*, Fischer questions the concept of handcraft. He employs traditional materials and techniques to pay homage to "tinkerers," a word he uses to reference his father and others like him who invented new tools to facilitate their work and become more efficient. He calls attention to the romantic glow of the handmade, while reminding us that even the Shakers employed the assembly line and catalog marketing to meet the needs of consumers.

Fig. 15. Aron Fischer (b. 1980), Display of items sold through *FacturedGoods*, 2016. Photograph. *Courtesy of the artist.*

Fischer produces fine art and, at the same time, is the proprietor of the international wholesale business FacturedGoods, which features handmade, functional items intended for everyday use (figure 15). He is part of the most recent incarnation of a craft revival, one that embraces contemporary materials and traditional techniques and that produces functional goods with aesthetic qualities at affordable prices. These two aims—to create fine art and produce utilitarian goods—have, throughout the last one hundred and fifty years, been seen as both complimentary and at odds. Fisher and his contemporaries deliberately create works that function and enhance our lives. They are heirs of the Arts and Crafts movement and the history of Modern art, bringing the ideals of both to bear on an increasingly global and digital world. Like the generations that preceded them, they confirm that basketry is continuously rooted, revived, and reinvented.

CHAPTER 2

# NATIVE AMERICAN BASKETRY
# FROM THE MULTICULTURAL SOUTH:
## Craft, Labor, and Heritage

*by Jason Baird Jackson*

THE BASKETRY of the Indigenous peoples of the American South is a testament to continuity and change. Its consideration also provides insight into themes of labor, heritage, and the interconnectedness of Native societies as well as their longstanding relationships with non-Native communities.[1] Native peoples used cane baskets as fishing traps, for sifting and processing corn and other foods, for gathering and hauling goods and raw materials, for the storage of seed and of other household goods, and for sleeping and work mats. Because of the variety of forms that developed among Southern Native groups, river-cane basketry is considered a quintessentially Native craft by the region's Natives and non-Natives alike. While Native and non-Native basket makers create white oak baskets, only Natives have a river-cane tradition, and because each native nation developed its own variations on the regional style, their baskets are powerful emblems of national identity and tribal tradition. Once ubiquitous, such baskets are scarce today. As the ability to make river-cane baskets has become increasingly rare over the past century, possession of this highly specialized knowledge is a point of pride for native craftspeople and their families.

Fig. 1. Rowena Bradley (Eastern Band Cherokee, 1922-2003), *Double-woven Basket and Lid*, circa 1973. River cane. *Courtesy of Mathers Museum of World Cultures, Indiana University.*

Before the arrival of Europeans and Africans, the Indigenous peoples of the American South fashioned their baskets from river cane (*Arundinaria gigantea*), a bamboo-like plant native to the region. River cane was ideal as basketry material because it was readily available; it could be worked with native tools and techniques; it lent itself to incorporation into a wide variety of forms; and it is both extremely durable and water-resistant. This last characteristic was especially beneficial in the hot, humid South. While not related to Southern Native basketry in terms of shared cultural histories, these basic characteristics also underpin the similarly made cane/bamboo basketry traditions of the Indigenous Amazon and of East and Southeast Asia.[2]

While all river cane baskets in the South are created using plaiting techniques, there is considerable variety among different communities, for instance, in the manner in which rims are treated. Among the most significant variations is the distinction between "single-weave" and "double-weave" baskets.[3] As illustrated by a double-woven basket and lid made in the early 1970s by Cherokee craftswoman Rowena Bradley (1922–2003), double-woven baskets are essentially two baskets integrated into one, with the elements woven into a basket of double thickness in which the shiny, highly water-repellant outer surface of the cane splints faces both inward and outward (figure 1). In contrast, a single-woven Mississippi Choctaw gathering basket collected by ethnologist William C. Sturtevant in 1958 has the shiny surface of the cane facing outward; the rougher inner surface of the splint is visible on the inside (figure 2).

River cane basketry is seen throughout the region as quintessentially Native by Natives and non-Natives alike because of its antiquity and because it took a variety of forms central to the customary lifeways of Southern Native groups.[4] This sense is amplified in a context in which only Native Southerners have made such baskets; that is, the making of river cane baskets is not a practice shared (as, for instance, white oak baskets are) with non-Native people in the South. Because each Native nation developed its own variations on the regional style, such baskets are also often powerful emblems of national identity and, because the skills needed to make them are no longer widespread, possession of such knowledge is an understandable point of pride for individual craftspeople and their families. While they once carried a lot of literal weight, as when pack baskets were used to transport corn harvests from field to village, today river cane baskets carry symbolic weight as key expressions of regional, tribal, and family identities. Once ubiquitous, such baskets today are rare and special. As we will see, the same is true for the plant out of which they are made.

Fig. 2. Mississippi Band Choctaw, *Single-woven Gathering Basket*, circa 1958. River cane. Photograph by Jason Baird Jackson. *Courtesy of National Museum of Natural History, Washington, DC.*

Baskets formed from wood splints, most often from strips of white oak, constitute a second major basketry tradition in the Native South. White oak baskets were also plaited, but the process of converting a standing oak tree into wood splints ready for basket making requires considerably different skills and tools and creates distinct forms.[5] While river cane baskets point to a deep history preceding European colonization and the Middle Passage endured by enslaved African peoples, white oak baskets and related forms became important among some of the region's Native communities after contact with these groups and the adoption of associated metal tools and European basketry techniques. White oak baskets are best known from among the Cherokee in North Carolina, where they continue to be a vital and popular craft. They are made and sold today in a regional craft market in which broadly similar baskets made by European and African American craftspeople can also be found. These baskets—like the famous foodways of the American South—speak to intercultural contacts, convergences, and combinations.

Like river cane baskets, the forms that wood splint baskets take are rooted in everyday labor practices of the past. Today, they are also symbols of cultural tradition, the individual skills of their makers, and the taste preferences of those who buy, collect, and display them. Rarely today is a white oak basket made by a craftsperson of the Native South used for practical labor, even though that labor determined its canonical forms: baskets for collecting eggs or berries, for harvesting corn or cotton, for hauling laundry, for sewing supplies, or for holding a worker's lunch. If a Cherokee white oak basket is going to be put to a work task, it is likely to be, as with Julia Taylor's (1902–1991) fruit basket, a task inside rather than outside the home. Such baskets

Fig. 3. Julia Taylor (Eastern Band Cherokee, 1902–1991), *Fruit Basket*, circa 1973. White oak. *Courtesy of Mathers Museum of World Cultures, Indiana University.*

increasingly fill roles as decorative objects, as valuable collectibles, and as expressions of cultural heritage (figure 3).

In the newer—but no longer new—basketry of the region, the historical utility of baskets and the canonical forms they generated give way to forms that are less designed to address technological need and more designed to appeal to aesthetic sensibilities, especially those of tourists and non-Native collectors. The coiled basketry of the Florida Seminole is illustrative of these trends.[6] Like other Native American peoples of the South, the Seminole people plaited workbaskets in many forms, including low walled trays and sifters used in processing corn and other food plants (figure 4). Among the Seminole who remained in Florida after the majority were forced into exile in Indian Territory (present-day Oklahoma), a tourist trade arose as the Florida frontier transitioned into a contemporary travel destination. A new Seminole basketry practice arose, one that focused on the production of a marketable craft item aimed at non-Native visitors to the state. These baskets are coiled rather than plaited. They are made of sweet grass (*Muhlenbergia filipes*) and sometimes incorporate palmetto (*Serenoa repens*) fiber. Unlike the similar coiled grass baskets of the African American (Gullah) peoples of the Sea Island region of coastal South Carolina, the coils in Florida Seminole baskets are joined together with commercially manufactured embroidery thread rather than with strips of palmetto frond. Although they provide a fine place to store small household items, these Florida Seminole baskets are decorative and often have forms that echo ceramic bowls, trays, and vases (figure 5). Craftswomen found ready buyers for works that combined a lidded basket form with a doll-head handle on the lid (figure 6). The handle matches the form and appearance of heads found on dolls, another key craft produced for the tourist market. These dolls wear a distinctive and iconic Florida Seminole women's hairstyle, which brands the dolls and baskets as unmistakable works of Florida Seminole craftspeople.

The Florida Seminole are not the only Indigenous makers of coiled basketry in the region. The Coushatta people of Louisiana and eastern Texas use similar coiling techniques to make pine needle baskets (*Pinus palustris*) in a range of animal effigy forms, including turkeys, alligators, frogs, and armadillos. These baskets sometimes incorporate pieces of pinecone and other decorative elements native to the region and are designed to appeal to non-Native consumers and their presumptions about Native crafts and culture. While oriented towards the marketplace, such baskets have become increasingly integrated into local cultural life over the last few decades, becoming meaningful expressions of local Native culture and identity.[7] Coushatta influence has also spread, as in the coiled chicken basket made by Choctaw-Biloxi weaver Rose Jackson-Pierite (figure 7).

Fig. 4. Florida Seminole or Miccosukee, *Riddle Basket*, circa 1950. Palmetto. *Courtesy of Mathers Museum of World Cultures, Indiana University.*

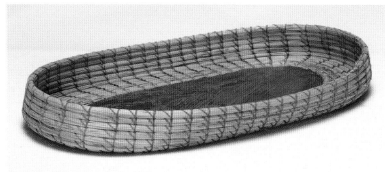

Fig. 5. Florida Seminole or Miccosukee, *Tray*, circa 1950. Sweetgrass, palmetto fiber, cotton or cotton-blend embroidery thread. *Courtesy of Mathers Museum of World Cultures, Indiana University.*

Fig. 6. Florida Seminole or Miccosukee, *Basket and Lid*, circa 1950. Sweetgrass, palmetto fiber, cotton or cotton-blend fabric, glass beads, cardboard. *Courtesy of Mathers Museum of World Cultures, Indiana University.*

Fig. 7. Rose Jackson Pierite (Choctaw and Biloxi), *Chicken Effigy Basket*, 20th century. Pine needles, raffia. Photograph by Jason Baird Jackson. *Courtesy of National Museum of Natural History, Washington, DC.*

Among the Cherokee in Oklahoma, a parallel market-oriented basket tradition arose using buckbrush (*Symphoricarpos orbicalates*) (figure 8). Buckbrush is related to another basketry plant in the native Southeast—Japanese honeysuckle (*Lonicera japonica*). Western Cherokee (Oklahoma) baskets of buckbrush, like honeysuckle baskets among the Eastern Cherokee, are formed using twining techniques (figure 9). Buckbrush vines are larger in diameter than delicate honeysuckle vines, but in both cases, baskets are made in rounded shapes that result from twining.[8]

Like the most durable river cane baskets, twined-vine baskets can be double-woven. The technique is very different from the double-weave plaiting used with river cane, but the basic idea is the same in each instance. The maker produces two connected layers of basketry, one directly inside the other. Plaited (vine-runner) baskets of this type have become equally popular in tourist and collector markets. However, there are some significant differences between river cane and honeysuckle baskets and the materials used to make them. River cane is an ancient basketry material and river cane baskets—with their affecting aesthetic quality and incredibly skillful execution—originated to meet practical needs related to storage and physical labor. River cane was once abundant, but it and the habitats that support it are now rare and endangered. Paralleling this environmental change, much of the everyday work once done with baskets is handled with plastic buckets, metal bins, machines, and mass produced tools. In contrast to river cane, honeysuckle is an abundant and invasive species and its use in basketry is relatively new. It thrives in disrupted and degraded landscapes. Native people have had to learn to live with it, but resourcefully realized its potential as raw material for their craft. For entirely different but not unrelated reasons, baskets made from both materials have become an expression of cultural heritage.[9]

The sale of baskets to tourists and other collectors was once related to the needs that Native people had for cash. During the twentieth century, tourist-oriented basketry was one of a small number of occupations through which native women—especially among the Eastern Cherokee, Mississippi Choctaw, and Florida Seminole—could help contribute to the economic wellbeing of their households. Today, economic life has shifted again and basketry is rarely a cost-effective business for most weavers. New employment opportunities have contributed to a repositioning of basketry as art, contemporary craft, and cultural heritage. Native people in the South increasingly make baskets because they enjoy doing so and because doing so connects them in a very conscious way with the cultural traditions—the heritage—of their communities or families.

The linkage between river cane ecology and cultural preservation among the Native people of the South is most evident in the work that Indigenous people and their federally recognized governments are doing to protect and re-establish river cane growth in its historical habitats. Recent years have seen the Eastern Cherokee and Mississippi Choctaw in particular becoming very active advocates in such efforts, often in partnership with conservation groups and Federal land managers. In gatherings such the 2009 Rivercane Symposium, hosted by the Mississippi Band of Choctaw Indians and Mississippi State University, basket makers stressed the deep cultural significance of

Fig. 8. Eastern Band Cherokee, *Basket*, 20th century. Buckbrush. Photograph by Jason Baird Jackson. *Courtesy of National Museum of Natural History, Washington, DC.*

Fig. 9. Lucy N. George (Eastern Band Cherokee, 1897-1978), *Vase-shaped Basket*, circa 1973. Honeysuckle, white oak. *Courtesy of Mathers Museum of World Cultures, Indiana University.*

basketry practices and the necessity of robust river cane habitats. In connection with access to a range of basketry materials, the same themes were stressed by weavers participating in the 2002 Southeastern Indian Basketry Gathering.[10]

Conservation and restoration efforts relating to river cane, longleaf pine, and other key materials run in parallel with an increased emphasis in Southern Native communities on formal instruction in basketry techniques; on the bestowing of special recognition on weavers; and on creating opportunities for them to showcase and sell their work. While such efforts can be found in many Native communities, the situation of baskets and basket makers among the Cherokee in Oklahoma is illustrative. In the capital city of the Cherokee Nation, Tahlequah, Oklahoma, the Cherokee Heritage Center offers a regular program of cultural classes focused on introducing and teaching Cherokee crafts, including basketry. These four-hour courses are offered on Saturdays and bring established craftspeople into contact with eager learners, some of whom go on to become skilled and active basket makers themselves.[11]

Since 1988, the Cherokee Nation bestows the title of "Cherokee National Treasure" on individual Cherokees to recognize their accomplishments in the "visual arts, music, language, technology, and mathematics." As of 2015, eighty-four such Cherokee citizens had been so recognized. Testifying to the importance accorded to basketry, basket makers comprise a prominent proportion of those named and include: Bessie Russell, Betty Frogg, Rachel Dew, Shawna Cain, Ella Mae Blackbear, Rosie Chewie, Kathryn Kelly, Mary Foreman, Jennie Sapp, Marie Proctor, Maxine Stick, Anna Huckaby, Nadine Wilbourn, Lena Blackbird, Thelma Forrest, and George Fourkiller.[12] As in Korea, Japan, and other nations with similar systems of heritage recognition for individual traditional artists and craftspeople, the Cherokee National Treasures program serves to highlight the enduring importance of arts and crafts rooted in the long cultural history of the Cherokee people. Designation

Fig. 10. Mississippi Choctaw, *Hamper*, circa 1958. River cane. Photograph by Jason Baird Jackson. *Courtesy of National Museum of Natural History, Washington, DC.*

as a National Treasure also impacts the stature and marketability of work produced by individuals so designated.

Another innovation in the service of tradition that touches on Cherokee basket making in Oklahoma is the rise of organizations, such as the Oklahoma Native American Basket Weavers Association, that have formed to "preserve, promote, and perpetuate traditional basketry and culture of Native American tribes through educational programs in Oklahoma." Cherokee weavers are prominent in this and other organizations active in this field, including the Cherokee Heritage Center and the Five Civilized Tribes Museum. The latter two museums regularly host competitions and exhibitions that highlight basketry among other regional arts and crafts practices. Newer events, such as the now annual Cherokee Art Market, function to provide markets and encouragement for Cherokee citizens eager to continue working in basketry.[13]

The rise of heritage practices relating to Native basketry in the South—environmental conservation efforts, national treasure/master designations and other awards, the development of formal instruction programs, the hosting of craft and art fairs, the holding of specialized conferences and gatherings—are signs of how important baskets and basketry are to many Native southerners. In the language of this volume, some of this work is rooted deeply in history. However, even the oldest traditions—river cane baskets, for instance—have been continually revised over time. This is illustrated clearly in the vibrant commercial dyes adopted by some Mississippi Choctaw weavers of river cane basketry (figure 10). This is the normal transformation of culture that happens even when rootedness is a priority. Adaptation and change keep tradition vibrant. The theme of revival is also present when native people of the South possess a desire to connect with their people, or the region's basketry, but lack family members or community members to instruct them. The rise of classes and organizations and other formal means provide a pathway to the continuity of the form, helping those with the greatest interest become connected with those possessing basketry skills and the willingness to share them. These transformations have made recent decades a particularly vital time in the history of Native basket making in the multicultural South.

CHAPTER 3

COILED BASKETS
OF THE SOUTH CAROLINA LOWCOUNTRY:
Who Knew the Art World Would Embrace
Baskets as Works of Art?

*by Sybil E. Gohari*

WHO KNEW THE ART WORLD would embrace baskets as works of art? As it turns out, many people did, more than a century ago. We can even pinpoint the moment when coiled baskets of the South Carolina Lowcountry came to be regarded more for their decorative and aesthetic functions than their utilitarian purposes.[1] During the eighteenth century, coiled baskets were used on rice plantations in the southeastern United States as tools for processing rice. A conscious divide between work and "show" baskets emerged in the early decades of the twentieth century that correlated to their marketing and sales. This viewing of baskets in a new light accelerated throughout the twentieth century, culminating from the 1970s to the present, with the art world simultaneously embracing artists previously excluded from the art historical canon and recognizing the need to broaden its definition of what constitutes a work of art. The art world's gatekeepers—critics, curators, gallerists, and art historians alike—increasingly regard sweetgrass baskets as fine art. Through it all, basket makers continue honing their craft, producing a range of finely detailed baskets that often serve multiple functions simultaneously.

Fig. 1. *Mulberry plantation rice field worker winnowing rice with a sea grass basket,* 1918. Photograph. *Courtesy of Margaretta Childs Archives at Historic Charleston Foundation.*

After examining the early utility of coiled basketry in the southeastern United States, the changing uses and perceptions of coiled baskets are discussed along with the subsequent new approaches to basketry design. This transition is viewed through analysis of the works and reception of influential artist Mary Jackson (b. 1945). Finally, a look at the contemporary landscape of coiled basketry underscores a variety of uses for diverse audiences. By considering baskets in relation to their cultural functions, the varied ways that socioeconomics and politics have shaped the modern art world become clear.

Historically anonymous in nature, coiled basketry was utilized across the rural southeast starting in the eighteenth century.[2] The technique of weaving coiled baskets arrived at the southeastern coast of the United States with the importation of slave labor from Africa.[3] On rice plantations in the southern US, slaves used their knowledge of basket making to create tools that facilitated the processing of rice, as well as the carrying of clothing and infants.[4] Smaller baskets were also woven on plantations to store various household items.

The early significance of baskets on plantations is demonstrated by their utility in cultivating rice.[5] So vital were baskets for the production of rice that historian Dale Rosengarten, an authority on the history of Lowcountry coiled basketry, asserts, "Rice could not have been processed without a particular coiled basket called the 'fanner.'"[6] These round baskets generally have an approximate diameter of twenty inches with an extending lip and were used to clean rice; rice was thrown in the air, time and again, until the breeze removed dust and dirt (figure 1). In contrast to many contemporary baskets, which boast more detailed, intricate designs, the fanner had no room for decoration, which would have impeded the basket's integral function.[7]

In the late nineteenth and early twentieth centuries, basket makers continued to produce smaller baskets used in domestic spaces as storage for private household items. However, their status as handmade objects introduced them with new meaning during a period of heightened industrialization and consumerism. It was not long before enterprising parties became interested in these and other Southern crafts. The evolution of this shift in usage, from a technology of rice production and domestic utility to an *objet d'art* of European American middle-class homeowners, has grown exponentially over time.[8]

As basketry's focus increasingly became the aesthetic value of the product, so too did the makers shift from primarily males to primarily females. Although some women created baskets on plantations in the Lowcountry prior to the Civil War, it was considered African American men's work. Men collected the materials and coiled the baskets.[9] However, by the twentieth century, women were encouraged to produce decorative show baskets to take advantage of the growing market.[10] These objects differed from traditional work baskets in several ways: first, in the use of palm leaf rather than palmetto; second, in the development of varied decorative styles; and finally, in the basket makers' appeal to buyers, including bread trays, purses, table mats, and wall pockets.[11] Increasingly, basket makers shifted their focus to meet the consumer demand, leading to artistic and product innovation.

In fact, Dale Rosengarten explains that during this period many basket makers outsourced their wares to intermediates. For example, Charleston merchant Clarence W. Legerton established the Sea Grass Basket Company (later known as Seagrassco) and bought large quantities of baskets from basket makers. Legerton purchased the baskets in substantial volumes at low prices, and sold at high prices in dime stores and via mail-order.[12] However, Gerald Davis notes, "The basket makers seem to be less worried than their 'concerned white friends' who purchase the baskets outside the city and sell them for inflated prices in Charleston and, now, around the country. The basket makers themselves were prohibited from selling their products on Charleston streets by an ordinance enacted sometime between 1939 and 1941."[13] There is an important distinction between the meaning made by "concerned white friends" and the basket makers. This clearly prejudicial ordinance excluded those who produced the baskets from any access to the buyers, thereby handing over complete market power to the middlemen and alienating the makers from their own work product. Although many basket makers continued to utilize the convenience of retail shops, wholesalers, and middlemen for the sale of their works throughout the 1930s, others opened stands of their own to sell directly to buyers. They did so along Highway 17 in Mount Pleasant, South Carolina (figure 2). In fact this

Fig. 2. Bluford Muir (1913-1990), *Viola Jefferson at her family's basket stand on Highway 17, Mt. Pleasant, South Carolina*, 1938. Photograph. *Courtesy of US Forest Service.*

Fig. 3. Mary Jackson, 1980. *Courtesy of the John D. & Catherine T. MacArthur Foundation.*

part of the highway is so important to the rise of sweetgrass basketry in South Carolina that the Seven Mile section of Mount Pleasant is commonly referred to as "Sweetgrass Basket Makers Highway."[14]

Marketing became an increasingly important function in developing and communicating the artistic value of the baskets to a newly created and continually expanding target audience. It became apparent that the historical narrative associated with the baskets attracted potential buyers. Even today, historian Patricia Jones-Jackson explains, baskets "are displayed in educational centers and museums of art throughout the United States and elsewhere, and are purchased by art collectors the world over as survivals of an ancient African craft."[15]

Thus, the reception of coiled basketry has undergone a multi-part historical process. First, in the late nineteenth and early twentieth centuries, emphasis on basketry as tool transformed into focus on basketry as commodity, as middlemen realized that there was a market for these objects. These businessmen sold the baskets as decorative art forms rather than work tools and created a new market for coiled baskets. Gradually, these objects were increasingly valued for their aesthetic qualities, thus ushering in the second part of the evolution of baskets, in which their uses expanded into pricey decorative pieces. Basket makers attempted to gain control of the end-to-end process of making and selling the baskets during this second phase; they started directly selling and marketing their works.

Today many basket makers take creative license and create elaborate objects from sweetgrass. These baskets are intricate objects that are increasingly viewed as sculpture and considered part of the contemporary art scene. Mary Jackson is an artist whose works illustrate this new fine art use; she creates delicate-looking objects with nuanced design and pattern (figure 3). While still in coiled basket form, these objects' presence as works to be viewed, as opposed to works created for a primarily utilitarian purpose, becomes increasingly apparent as viewers analyze her work through a formal artistic lens. This adds another layer to the reception of coiled baskets of the South Carolina Lowcountry. Works by Jackson, and those similar in style and function, mark an important, contemporary path of sweetgrass baskets—an exploration of the aesthetic potential in general, and that of the materials in particular. Starting in the latter half of the twentieth century, art world gatekeepers recognized the necessity to revamp previously accepted definitions of art to include the breadth and diversity of art produced particularly by women artists, artists of color, and artists working outside traditionally accepted media.[16] Art historians, gallerists, and other tastemakers increasingly look to a range of media and art forms to incorporate into the canon of great art, including sweetgrass sculpture.

South Carolinian Jackson, a 2008 MacArthur Genius Award Fellow, learned to weave baskets at the age of four.[17] The artist explains, "My goal has been constant—to produce simple, yet unique and finely detailed sculpture, in which the patterns and symmetry complement each other."[18] Jackson's design impetus reflects the prevalent artistic idioms of the 1960s, a period that marks the early days of her professional career. Throughout the decade, she traveled to New York and viewed a broad range of artistic output. Pop, Op, and Minimalist idioms were readily available for viewing.[19] In fact, juxtaposing Jackson's works with those of Op artists such as Bridget Riley (b. 1931) reveals a similar focus on undulating rhythm and overlapping form (figure 4). Both artists create abstracted works of art that stand as highly refined, stylized formal expressions. The curving, rhythmic nature of line, its push and pull that leads the eye around the objects, further underscores a related sensibility. Jackson and Riley share an interest in the formal properties of their artistic creations. Furthermore, both employ a minimal palette: while Riley's works are often comprised of blacks and whites, Jackson utilizes browns and creams. The visual similarities are striking, with Riley creating a three-dimensional woven effect on a flat surface and Jackson creating three-dimensional woven objects.

Fig. 5. Blanche Watts (b. 1927) and members of her family, *Sweetgrass Basket*, n. d. Sweetgrass, rush, palmetto fronds, pine needles. *Courtesy of Margaret Fairgrieve Milanick.*

The art world's reception of Jackson's work often employs modernist (formalist) language:

A master of design, Jackson has developed a vocabulary that emphasized form, volume, silhouette, and line. Her baskets, confident in their deceptive simplicity, are richly enlivened with patterns of lights and darks. French knots boldly punctuate surfaces; sweetgrass sprays provide decorative extension of lines. Mary Jackson's creations are a high point in the contemporary basket movement.[20]

Reception of her work also focuses on the history of Lowcountry coiled basketry. For example, the MacArthur Foundation describes Jackson as a "fiber artist translating practical designs into intricately coiled vessels that preserve the centuries-old craft of sweetgrass basketry and push the tradition in stunning new directions."[21] Recognized for the expressiveness of her work, the role of tradition in her production, and her knowledge of contemporary art movements, the MacArthur Fellows program notes, "Her innovations include the dramatically arched handle . . . and the spray of unbound grass . . . as if suspended in mid-assembly . . . While preserving the culture and history of her ancestors, Jackson infuses this inherited art form with a contemporary aesthetic and expressiveness all her own."[22]

Thus, the appeal of Jackson's work is broad—many collectors and museums have added her sculpture to their collections. Author Susan Sully writes, "What makes Jackson's baskets so special is that she treats them as abstract works of art . . . she also gives her new designs names that indicate their value."[23] Here, Sully incorporates Jackson's sculpture into an art historical narrative. Concurrently, in an interview with Joyce Lovelace, a contributing editor to *American Craft* magazine, Jackson notes, "I always wanted to keep the tradition in mind, to respect what was passed down to me . . . I just wanted to bring it to another level."[24] And as she gained recognition for her innovations, she noted, "I'm amazed and thrilled that all this recognition has come . . . but I see it as something that is benefiting to everyone—not just my work or my tradition, but other artists from all over the country who have this passion for baskets."[25]

Analysis of Mary Jackson's reception indicates that in order for sweetgrass baskets to be considered primarily for aesthetic value, there are a number of criteria that needed to be adopted. Careful analysis of this shift reveals at least five qualities onlookers had to observe: (1) The artist needed to be seen as a key innovator. Once established, Jackson's work and that of other basket makers was included in a variety of prestigious exhibitions throughout the United States; (2) Art world gatekeepers recognized the skill and expertise required to weave show baskets; (3) The terminology reserved for baskets shifted to art and sculpture; (4) The investment potential of these objects was established by their acquisition for museum collections, including the Renwick Gallery, Smithsonian American Art Museum, the Museum of Arts & Design, White House Collection of American Crafts, and the Museum of Fine Arts Boston. One brochure, for instance, notes that sweetgrass baskets are "a proud tradition, a valuable investment;"[26] and (5) Creators of baskets now sign and often title their work. This act has been instrumental in baskets' insertion into the art historical canon, while simultaneously identifying basket makers as artists, no longer anonymous creators. It also emphasizes that these objects are not mass-produced but one-of-a-kind objects, also part of the lineage of fine art. Some makers sign the baskets directly, often with permanent marker, to reinforce their position in the history of signed art objects. Others opt to disseminate business cards containing their names and other pertinent information to accompany the sale of the baskets (figures 5 and 6).

Increasingly evident is the stratification within coiled basketry that has emerged over the past 40 years. On the one hand, there are those who produce collectible sweetgrass baskets and represent a category of basketry made and sold primarily as decorative household objects that could also be used in everyday life. On the other, a cohort of makers like Jackson are singled out by the influential art world elite as artists whose collectible sweetgrass baskets sell in measures comparable to art

Fig. 6. Blanche Watts (b. 1927) and members of her family, *Sweetgrass Basket* (detail), n.d. Sweetgrass, rush, palmetto fronds, pine needles. *Courtesy of Margaret Fairgrieve Milanick.*

forms such as printmaking, drawing, and painting.[27] Former Renwick Gallery Curator-in-Charge Kenneth Trapp notes of Jackson, "She is a consummate designer and a superb craftswoman, and I think those two combined create an art that is timeless and beautiful."[28] Such a description of Jackson amplifies this growing hierarchy within the genre of basketry in general.

Despite the national success of sweetgrass basketry as art form and collectible, production, and even preservation, remains closely tied to South Carolina. In fact, state officials and organizations have a lot invested in maintaining a market, including materials and the long-term health of sweetgrass basketry. In 2005, the *Post and Courier*, Charleston's local paper asserted, "S.C. may designate sweetgrass basket as official 'state handcraft,'" and it became the official state Lowcountry handcraft in 2006.[29, 30] The development of local sweetgrass festivals has promoted basketry, often explaining that sweetgrass basketry is a "dying art."[31] Indeed, due to ever-expanding real estate development, many of the raw materials required for production have been destroyed. Consequently, many Lowcountry institutions have intervened. The Charleston Museum's Dill Sanctuary and the Historic Foundation's McLeod Plantation have planted sweetgrass sprigs to replenish the raw material. However, others are not as generous. Along Highway 17 in Mount Pleasant, various entities have contributed to the closing of basket stands citing concern for basket makers' safety during construction. In many instances, representatives of private corporations falsely lead the makers to believe they are not permitted to remain in certain areas, when in fact they are on state, not private, property.[32]

The history of coiled basketry in South Carolina provides an important lens through which to examine the journey of African heritage in America. What started as a utilitarian tool taken from the shores of Africa to South Carolina and Georgia during the slave trade later gave birth to a craft during the post-Civil War era and early twentieth century increasingly valued for its handmade, decorative qualities, and sold by profiteering middlemen who dominated the landscape. Over time, as this creative endeavor shifted in use to decorative object and eventually art/sculpture, basket makers were able to expand their control over their own work product. Today the most abstracted, broadly conceived of these objects are included in major art exhibitions and collections. Examining coiled basketry within this historical context provides a nuanced understanding of its manifold and changing functions.

CHAPTER 4

THE OAK-ROD BASKETS
OF BROWN COUNTY, INDIANA

*by Jon Kay*

Fig. 1. Frank Hohenberger (1876-1963), *Motherless Home*, 1929. Photograph. *Courtesy of the Lilly Library, Indiana University, Bloomington, Indiana.*

**FOR MUCH OF THE NINETEENTH** and early twentieth centuries, members of the Hovis and Bohall families in Brown County, Indiana, made oak-rod baskets for their neighbors to gather, carry, and store everyday items. Locals gathered corn in bushel baskets and carried smaller ones to the woods to collect nuts and berries (figure 1). These sturdy baskets were also used to transport food to church dinners and family gatherings and to carry grocery items home. As the economy of the region transitioned from subsistence farming to industrial labor, this distinctive craft became obsolete as an agricultural implement. Nevertheless, as many raced toward all things modern, others became concerned about the "vanishing" way of life in the Midwest. It was within this new context that oak-rod baskets changed from commonplace containers to desirable souvenirs and emblems of the region's idealized pioneer past. This essay traces the history of oak-rod basket making in Indiana and demonstrates how these everyday objects changed from routine tools into ready-made antiques, heirlooms, and art objects.

## Work Baskets

Like other types of white oak baskets, rod baskets are made from rived oak; however, in this tradition, they are rendered round by pulling lengths through iron dies. The rounded rods look similar to the willow used in some basket traditions but have the advantage of being stronger and more durable.[1] Henry Hovis (1810–1896) brought this distinctive tradition to Brown County when he emigrated from Ohio in 1848. The son of a basket maker, Henry had grown up in York County, Pennsylvania, a nineteenth-century hub of oak-rod basket making. Although remembered as a farmer, gunsmith, and fiddler, Henry also taught his sons Jacob, John, Henry W., and Lewis his techniques and patterns for making oak-rod baskets.[2]

Listed in the 1900 census as a basket maker, Henry Hovis's oldest son Jacob married Deborah Ping, and may have made the baskets shown in a photograph of the Ping family gathering hickory nuts (figure 2). Taken around 1900 by local photographer Otto Ping, this photograph pre-dates the rise of tourism and is perhaps the earliest known image of oak-rod baskets being used as agricultural tools in Brown County.[3] While these baskets would continue to be made and used for decades, they would become less common over time, and these domestic and agricultural tools would be replaced with mass-produced wares. Jacob's brother, John, also grew up helping his family make baskets but moved to Martin County, Indiana, after he married. While the 1880 census listed him as a

Fig. 2. Otto Ping (1883-1975), *Gathering Hickory Nuts*, n.d. Photograph. *Courtesy of the Indiana Historical Society, P075.*

Fig. 3. Frank Hohenberger (1876-1963), *Alex Mullis and George Allen Turner at Grindstone*, 1922. Photograph. *Courtesy of the Lilly Library, Indiana University, Bloomington, Indiana.*

Martin County basket maker, by 1900, his occupation was recorded as "day laborer." It is difficult to know why he abandoned basket making as his primary occupation, but it is likely that increased industrialization was a contributing factor. Mass-produced slat baskets, buckets, and other containers quickly replaced traditional baskets in the early twentieth century. A 1922 photograph shows Brown County shingle-splitter Alex Mullis sharpening a tool at a grinding wheel. In the foreground is an oak-rod basket, and in the background, hidden in plain sight, sits a metal pail (figure 3). The photograph records the brief moment when handmade baskets and mass-produced buckets co-existed, reflecting the passage from agrarian to industrial culture. As the demand for woven baskets waned among Indiana farmers, makers discovered a new market for their wares—handicraft enthusiasts and tourists.

## Souvenirs from Brown County

In 1904, *Indianapolis News* illustrator and cartoonist Frank McKinney Hubbard created the cartoon "Abe Martin of Brown County."[4] A rural sage and country wisecracker, Abe commented in rural dialect on the rapidly changing world. By locating his Abe Martin character in rural Brown County, Hubbard helped shape a perception of the county as a backwards community and stoked urban interest in this peculiar place. In 1907, several artists made a sketching trip to the county and discovered its rolling hills, log homes, and rural people. Artists T. C. Steele and Gustave Baumann were among the first to make the county their year-round home, and by the early 1910s, Brown County had emerged as a major art colony.[5] The *Brown County Democrat* reported in 1914, "The advent of the artist[s] excited general interest and of late years a great number of outsiders have been attracted [to the county]." Fueled by Hubbard's syndicated comic as well as the emerging art colony, urban elites from Chicago, Indianapolis, and beyond began to view the residents of Brown County as an isolated remnant of Indiana's early settlers.[6] As anti-modern sentiment swelled in the 1920s and 1930s, carloads of tourists arrived. By 1941, the belief that Brown County was a "perfect cameo of pioneer life," that it remained "unspoiled and untarnished by the march of time" was so entrenched in the popular culture of the state that influential congressman Louis Ludlow proposed designating the county as a cultural preserve.[7] Basket making was material evidence of the county's rural and rustic nature, and artists and tourists purchased the baskets as both art objects and souvenirs.

Fig. 4. Frank Hohenberger (1876-1963), *Henry W. Hovis, Basketweaver*, 1928. Photograph.*Courtesy of the Lilly Library, Indiana University, Bloomington, Indiana.*

Photojournalist Frank Hohenberger promoted this nostalgic view of Brown County in his weekly *Indianapolis Star* column, "Down in the Hills of Brown." His photographs of rural craftspeople weaving rag rugs and making homemade brooms fueled tourist interest in local handicrafts, and few images captured the attention of outsiders like those showing the making of oak-rod baskets.[8] In 1928, Hohenberger photographed Henry Hovis's middle son, Henry W. (1840–1935), who was then eighty-six years old, nearly blind, and living in the county poorhouse (figure 4). Born in Richmond, Ohio, Henry W. had moved with his family to the Grandview area of Brown County when he was six, and by age twelve he was making baskets with his father and brothers. He married Elizabeth Bohall and was an uncle to the Bohall brothers, who made a variety of oak-rod baskets for tourists, which they sold through gift shops in Nashville, Indiana, from the 1920s through the 1940s.[9] Henry W., however, continued to weave the traditional forms of baskets he had learned from his father.

Fig. 5. Frank Hohenberger (1876-1963), *Basket weaver [William Bohall] pulling reeds*, n.d. Photograph. *Courtesy of the Lilly Library, Indiana University, Bloomington, Indiana.*

The Hovises were not the only basket makers in Brown County. In fact, locals still call oak-rod baskets, "Bohall baskets," after the other basket making family in the region. Family tradition maintains that the Bohall family made willow baskets in England, long before immigrating to Indiana. Henry W. may have introduced the technique of using white oak to the Bohalls when he married into the family. Nevertheless, Henry W.'s brother-in-law, James Bohall (1848–1918), was a prolific basket maker in Jackson County, Indiana, who along with his five sons made thousands of oak-rod baskets for both local and distant markets.

In 1924, Hohenberger visited James's son, Joseph "Josey" Bohall (1872–1960), in Story, Indiana, in southern Brown County. The basket maker gave the photojournalist a tour of his basket-making operation, and Hohenberger photographed Josey's son William (1904–1977) pulling rods for his father (figure 5). Years later, when describing the image, William described the strenuous process:

> What I was doing see, I was pulling those strips through a steel plate that we always had to draw [the splits] through to make them round. Because you see they came out almost as big as a pencil square and we had to work those out with a knife by hand. I'd pull them one at a time, and you think that's not time consuming—it is. You'd have to reach over if there wasn't someone there to feed your machine. Why you'd have to reach over there and slide some on through . . . You put a point on them with your knife when you pull them out you see, so they're ready to go through the machine. Then you get them with your pliers and pull them through . . . You just walk backwards and forwards real fast. Just as fast as you could get up there and get another'n' and walk back.[10]

Fig. 6. Frank Hohenberger (1876-1963), *Basket weaver, John [Josey] Bohall*, n.d. Photograph. *Courtesy of the Lilly Library, Indiana University, Bloomington, Indiana.*

As William recalled, the process of making rod baskets from the second-growth white oak that they harvested from area forests was difficult and time-consuming, but he and Josey were weaving about a hundred baskets per month in their "factory," which was an old barn behind their house where they pulled rods and wove baskets.

Hohenberger wanted to photograph Josey, but the basket maker was reticent, concerned that Hohenberger might use it to "make fun" of him. While many, including Hohenberger, had made fun of the rustic lifeways of Brown County locals, many also celebrated the skills and talents of its artisans.[11] Josey finally conceded to a photograph. The image shows him seated, holding a newly made basket (figure 6). His coveralls are patched and worn; he stares out at the camera with a little apprehension in his eyes. The image was one of Hohenberger's favorites. He included it in an exhibit at A. J. Rogers's Old Country Store in 1953, which included more than thirty portraits of local residents taken in the 1920s and 1930s, including Iva Lucas, a rag-rug weaver; Handy Bill Hamblen, an old-time fiddler; and Valentine Penrose, a one-hundred-year-old foxhunter.[12]

Fig. 7. Frank Hohenberger (1876-1973), *John Bohall at work*, 1927. Photograph. *Courtesy of the Lilly Library, Indiana University, Bloomington, Indiana.*

Where Josey was wary of having his photo taken by Hohenberger, his brother, John Bohall (1878–1936), was well prepared when the photojournalist visited him. Wanting to look his best for his photograph, John Bohall wore his dress clothes for the photographer; however, it is important to note that the basket maker was not the only one shaping the image (figure 7). Hohenberger set up the scene to make it look as if John was at work, but upon closer inspection, viewers can see that the basket he is holding is already completed—the handle is wrapped with oak-rods, the final step in the basket making process. In addition, Hohenberger placed oak splits and several finished baskets at the weaver's feet, which would not have been part of the natural basket making workflow.

Besides Hohenberger, other journalists were interested in the basket makers of Brown County. Victor Green visited another Bohall Brother, Levi (1885–1957), who lived and worked near Belmont, Indiana. Green notes that Levi harvested white oaks that "range from five to twelve inches in diameter at the base" and that an average oak could supply enough rods to make "fifteen large corn baskets or thirty-five small baskets."[13]

Though similar in form and shape to those made of willow, the rod baskets made by the Bohalls and Hovises were stronger and sturdier. Nevertheless, a few basket makers in Indiana continued to weave willow through the 1940s. For example, Dearborn County farmer William Berbrick cultivated willow on his farm for making clothes hampers, baby beds, and sewing baskets that he sold in Indianapolis.[14] However, oak-rods were longer and stronger than willow and weaving was faster, more uniform, and resulted in a much stronger basket. Levi noted: "They just don't break, they wear out. Two Columbus men loaded one up with bricks and I offered to give them an extra one if they could break it. It held all they could lift and wasn't hurt. As they season, they get tighter and stronger, instead of weakening."[15] Levi made baskets not just for local use, but also filled custom orders. While his father, James, taught him to make "large corn baskets," Levi explains that he figured out how to make several other patterns of baskets. Green writes:

> Indianapolis people order many by picture or by description, Bohall explained, and he experimented until he copied their picture or made something that satisfied customer instructions . . . "There are a lot more orders than I can take care of usually, in spite of working at it all year round." The weaver said, "Why I don't even have any for myself. If I wanted to go plant potatoes or something I'd have to borrow a basket to use."[16]

As outside interest increased in Brown County baskets, the traditional forms began to change. Levi added looping, decorative rims to his baskets to make sewing baskets and began staining some of his baskets to make them conform to customer desires and expectations.

Fig. 8. Frank Hohenberger (1876-1963), *Loads of baskets and chairs from Nashville, Tennessee*, 1928. Photograph. *Courtesy of the Lilly Library, Indiana University, Bloomington, Indiana.*

## Trade and Wholesale Distribution

While articles and photographs by journalists such as Green and Hohenberger stimulated outside interest in Brown County baskets, there were other factors that contributed to their popularity, not the least of which was the growing number of gift shops and roadside stands that sold baskets and other handmade items. Tourists had purchased handicrafts at local stores and from artisans since the early 1900s, but by the 1920s, an infrastructure of shops and tourist-related services emerged in the county. Hohenberger described the growing tourist trade in baskets this way: "Dozens of baskets may be seen dangling from the store fronts almost any day and the visitors deplete the stocks very rapidly, especially on Sundays."[17] While tourist demand for baskets soared in the 1920s and 1930s, prices remained low and the work demanding, and shops struggled to keep baskets on hand for tourists to buy. By 1928, truckloads of handmade baskets were imported from Cannon County, Tennessee, to Brown County to help satisfy the demand for handmade items (figure 8).[18]

Fig. 9. Theodor Jung (1906-1996), *Restaurant and shop in Nashville, Brown County, Indiana*, 1935. Photograph. *Courtesy of Library of Congress, Prints & Photographs Division, FSA/OWI Collection, LC-USF33-0045054-M3.*

During the Depression, Portia Howe Sperry began promoting "native" handicrafts through her Brown County Folks Shop, which was located inside the Nashville House, a popular inn and tourist destination. Alongside rag dolls, homemade rugs, and sorghum candy, Sperry sold baskets made by local men.[19] In addition to Sperry's shop, Joshua Bond's Rustic Inn Restaurant offered oak-rod baskets and a variety of other souvenirs in addition to serving fried chicken, fancy candies, and cold drinks to its patrons (figure 9).[20]

As tourism increased in the county during the 1920s, so did opportunities for residents to find work in nearby cities. Many Brown County residents relocated to Indianapolis, Bloomington, or Columbus, Indiana in search of better wages. For example, William Bohall quit basket making and took a job in a furniture factory in Indianapolis, where he could earn steady wages. When the factory closed during the Depression, however, he returned to making baskets. He did not sell to tourist shops, but rather traded his wares to farmers and stores for groceries. He recalls:

> We'd take that Ford Roadster and we'd go down [to southern Indiana] loaded with baskets, different types, different kinds you know—little ones and big ones, all kind of types. And those farmers down there, they liked those baskets, you know. And they was hard for money in the Depression like that. They'd trade us meat or maybe chickens or flour and meal, and stuff like that. And maybe the grocery store would trade me sugar and stuff like that for baskets. And I'd come back with a carload of groceries. See that was better than the cash then.[21]

Fig. 10. Frank Hohenberger (1876-1963), *Display of woven baskets at Bill Schnepp's*, 1949. Photograph. *Courtesy of the Lilly Library, Indiana University, Bloomington, Indiana.*

Besides selling to farmers and grocery stores, both William and his father sold baskets to Bill Schnepp's Curio Shop in Nashville, which actively marketed "Brown County Baskets," as a sign advertised outside his shop. However, a 1949 image shows a display of baskets in front of his shop and mixed among several locally produced rod baskets were fancy baskets from western Kentucky (figure 10).[22]

Some makers sold baskets to wholesale distributors as well as to local farmers and tourists. Folklife researcher Warren Roberts discovered that the Van Camp Hardware and Iron Company in Indianapolis advertised "Brown County" oak-rod baskets in their catalogs in the 1930s, describing them as "round oak splint; braided; capacity about one bushel."[23] While before World War II makers produced baskets for a variety of markets, change was coming.

Frank Hohenberger observed that, while the gift shops in Nashville had once sold many locally made baskets, by 1955 local oak-rod baskets were a "rarity." Retailers wanting to continue to capitalize on the anti-modern interests and the aesthetics of tourists sought other makers to supply their stores. Hohenberger relates: "One shopkeeper when asked whether his baskets were native-made would point southward and say they were made back in the hills, and those hills were in Kentucky and Tennessee—that's where most of the hand-woven baskets come from."[24] Despite the influx of baskets from the South, members of both the Bohall and Hovis families continued to sell baskets to local shops. As the older generation of basket makers passed, however, younger makers, like William Bohall, moved to nearby cities where they could work for day wages. In the 1940s, William supplied several baskets to the Curio Shop; but he quit fulltime basket making in the 1950s when he took a job as a dispatcher for the Campus Cab Company in Bloomington, Indiana. William and others periodically wove baskets for tourist shops, but by the mid-1970s, Howard "Bruce" Hovis, Henry Hovis's grandson, and Reuben Morgan, a Jackson County basket maker, were the only active oak-rod basket makers still working in southern Indiana.[25]

## Conclusion: The Last Basket Maker

In the fall of 1973, an Indiana University student interviewed Bruce Hovis about the baskets he made (figure 11).[26] The elder's family had practiced the craft for generations. "Well it goes from the tree to the fro to the knife and then to soak," he summarized; "then to the drawing irons and then I soak them again before I weave them—it makes them real soft and easy to bend and weave." Bruce then rived a length of white oak with a fro.[27] Using a knife, he split the wood into a workable size; as it separated, he coaxed it apart with his hands. After soaking it, he pulled the oak stock through a drawing iron, a metal die with a series of graduated holes punched in it. The irons rounded the splits and reduced the diameter of the rods (figure 12). "Three times, I pull each split through the irons," he explained; "a lot of these irons are what my father had made originally and some are my grandfather's."

After pulling several rods, the elder took the student down to the creek behind his house and showed her how he soaked them. As the two walked back to the workshop, she asked how long it takes to make a basket. He replied, "Well, about an hour just to weave a bushel basket. Let's go back to the shop and I'll show you how I start them." The student watched as the basket maker made the cross-shaped bottom, wove the randing pattern, and poked rods into the bottom of the basket to form its sides.[28] After her fieldwork session, the undergrad went home to transcribe her interview, and Bruce went on quietly making baskets as he had done for decades. Cynthia Clark's paper captured insights into a craft tradition that was nearing its end. Howard "Bruce" Hovis (1904–1991) was one of the last traditional oak-rod basket makers from Brown County, Indiana.[29]

Bruce learned the craft in 1919, when his father Lewis Hovis unexpectedly died of blood poisoning, leaving a widow and a large family. Bruce's uncle Henry W. came to live with them for several months to help them farm and to teach his nephews to make baskets, so they could help support the family. The youngest, just fourteen when his father passed, Bruce had already helped his father with the basket

Fig. 11. Gary Stanton (b. 1946), *Bruce Hovis weaving an oak-rod basket*, 1975. Photograph. *Courtesy of Traditional Arts Indiana and the Mathers Museum of World Cultures, Indiana University.*

Fig. 12. Gary Stanton (b. 1946), *Bruce Hovis pulling rods*, 1975. Photograph. *Courtesy of Traditional Arts Indiana and the Mathers Museum of World Cultures, Indiana University.*

making process by poking splints through the drawing irons; nevertheless, it was under the guidance of his uncle that he learned the ins and outs of the basket maker's trade. He recalled, "Well my father he taught me quite a bit and at the same time though not too much. So my uncle he came after my father passed away. Then I was just fourteen years old and he was also a basket maker. And he showed me how to make them from start to finish."[30] Young Bruce learned to make traditional harvest baskets, such as bushel, two and three pecks, as well as the laundry and egg basket forms; and though his brothers would pursue other careers, Bruce continued to make baskets throughout his life.

Once grown, Bruce moved to Rugby in neighboring Bartholomew County, but frequently returned to Brown County to harvest his basket making material and sell his wares. When he was young, he made baskets for area farmers and hardware stores, but in 1950, Brown County postman and entrepreneur Clarence Aynes agreed to purchase as many baskets as Bruce could make. The Aynes Family operated a popular roadside stand at the crest of Schooner Hill, a scenic overlook between Nashville and Bloomington, where auto tourists stopped to take photographs and buy gift items including baskets.[31] For several years, Bruce and other makers produced baskets for this roadside stand. Local basket makers would weave all winter to make enough baskets for the Aynes Family to sell during the summer and autumn tourist seasons.

By the 1970s, Bruce produced most of his wares for the Basket Shop in Danville, Indiana. This unique store featured handmade baskets and related items from around the world (figure 13). Where once the Hovis family made baskets for neighbors and area farmers, by the 1970s, oak-rod baskets competed not just with Appalachian crafts, but also handmade goods from Europe, Asia, and other distant lands. It is unknown when Bruce made his last oak-rod basket, probably sometime in the early 1980s. Virtually destitute and having no family, Bruce spent his last years in the IOOF Home in Greensburg, Indiana. When the elderly basket maker passed in 1991, it seems that Indiana's tradition of making oak-rod baskets ended.

Today oak-rod baskets occasionally show up at area flea markets and antique stores with little evidence as to who made them, how they were used, or the symbolic meaning once invested in them. A few enthusiasts collect the baskets, usually out of interest in local history and crafts, rather than any personal connection to a maker. In the fall of 2015, aiming to illuminate the complex cultural history of this once local craft, Indiana University's Mathers Museum of World Cultures produced the exhibition, *Working Wood: Oak-Rod Baskets in Indiana*. The artifacts, photographs, and oral histories in this exhibition placed oak-rod baskets at the center of a complex story of industrialization, markets, and regional identity. While unique to Brown County, the shifting uses and meanings of oak-rod baskets reveal the impacts of tourism and popular culture as well as the politics of craft marketing on the history of twentieth-century basketry.

Fig. 13. *Oak-rod baskets at a Danville basket shop*, circa 1970. Photograph. *Courtesy of Traditional Arts Indiana.*

CHAPTER 5

FASHIONING NANTUCKET MINK:
From Nantucket Lightship Basket
to Friendship Purse

*by Margaret Fairgrieve Milanick*

THE NANTUCKET FRIENDSHIP PURSE is a unique object in the history of basketry. From a local basket-making tradition came a fashion icon so popular that it is said a woman leaving a crowded Paris subway noticed a purse similar to hers being carried into the subway. Lifting her purse high above the crowd, she called out, "Nantucket?" and received a big smile and the answer, "*Oui*, Nantucket!" The friendship purse signified membership in an elite international community, instantly recognizable as something more than just a basket. But at its root, it *is* a basket with a story that touches upon geography, commerce, and maritime and fashion history as it weaves from past to present through the eyes of an artist who had a vision for its revinvention.

The name Nantucket derives from the Wampanoag word that translates to "land far away at sea." The Wampanoag were the first people to inhabit the island thirty miles off the coast of Massachusetts and lived there when the first English immigrants settled it in the 1640s. By 1763, only 358 Wampanoag remained, and between August of that year and February 1764, 222 died of "Indian sickness." Scholars today have made an educated guess that it was a louse-borne relapsing fever brought to Nantucket by sick crewmembers of an Irish trading ship.[1] At that time, the whaling industry had made Nantucket the leading whaling port in the world. By the beginning of the 1800s, however, profitable whaling had moved to the Pacific, and voyages often lasted three to five years to compensate for the financial loss.[2] To fill the tedious weeks, months, and years on the ship, seamen worked with their hands creating unique objects, among them baskets and scrimshaw, from materials they found on board. Because longer voyages required that whale blubber be rendered into oil in transit, constructing barrels to store that oil became central to the enterprise.[3] Barrels had hardwood bottoms and hardwood staves that fit into them. To hold the barrel together, hoops, first made of wood but later of metal, were riveted to the staves. These barrels were likely the template for what would later be known as the Nantucket lightship basket (figure 1).

The close, tight weave of the body of the Nantucket lightship basket comes from a material readily at hand aboard whaling ships—rattan—procured from trade with East Asia where the climbing palm grows. Rattan (*Calumus*), also called cane, is a versatile material used for many purposes in its native environment. It would have been wrapped around bales of anything shipped in large quantities.[4] Rattan had become popular for caning chairs in America, too, and was therefore part of the Pacific trade exchange network in which whaling ships participated. Whalers used rattan for baskets because it was pliable, strong, and required minimal processing. Rattan was often used instead of hardwood for staves and hoops in early ship-crafted baskets.[5] If a handle was required, typically it was a bail or swing handle carved from hardwood, soaked to become pliable, bent into shape, and then riveted to carved wooden ears. The earliest baskets were made freehand, not over a mold, and as a consequence were not very regular in shape.[6]

Fig. 1. Stanley E. Roy (1910s-1960s), *Old South Wharf covered with barrels, with the three-masted schooner* Nantisco *docked alongside*, circa 1930. Photograph. *Courtesy of the Nantucket Historical Association.*

Fig. 2. Captain Thomas James (1811-1885), *Open, round lightship basket*, 1896. 6.5" × 4". *Courtesy of Nantucket Lightship Basket Museum.*

In 1823, New Bedford surpassed Nantucket as the leading whaling port. Larger ships were required to make voyages around Cape Horn and into the Pacific, and they could not enter Nantucket's harbor because of its geology. This drawback, as well as the Great Fire of 1846 that burned down much of the wharf area and central commercial district, caused the demise of profitable whaling in Nantucket. As whaling on Nantucket Island began to fade as a viable industry, basket creation moved to the studios of ex-whalers who sought supplementary and eventually alternative incomes.[7] For baskets to become profitable, however, producers needed a market and a standardized manufacturing process. The market was provided by the rise in tourism and summer residency of America's wealthy in the second half of the nineteenth century.[8] Visitors were eager to buy souvenirs of their restful time in Nantucket (figure 2). The use of molds in the creation process decreased production time and enhanced uniformity (figure 3). Standardization of size and shape made it possible to sell nests of three, five, or seven baskets, and a modification of the ears to which the bail handles were attached made them stackable.[9] Production time decreased further when the bottoms, as well as the molds, were made on a lathe.[10] Hardwood bottoms were nailed to the molds to begin weaving, creating a hole in the center. Since these baskets continued to serve utilitarian purposes, strength was a sought-after quality. Therefore, staves and hoops were made of hardwoods such as oak, hickory, or maple instead of rattan.[11]

Fig. 3. Example of a mold used to form lightship baskets. *Courtesy of Nantucket Lightship Basket Museum.*

Fig. 4. *View of No. 1 New South Shoal Lightship,* circa 1890s. Photograph. *Ken Black Collection. Courtesy of James W. Claflin.*

Former whalers from Nantucket Island also found new income from serving as crew members on the South Shoal Lightship, first commissioned by the federal government in 1853 (figure 4).[12] In the 1850s, New York Harbor became the busiest port in America and the treacherous shoals off Nantucket Island represented a threat to commerce, as the approach into and out of New York Harbor lay just to the south (figure 5).[13] Lightships served as lighthouses where no lighthouse could be built, patrolling waterways and dropping anchor to warn ships away from navigational pitfalls. Eleven men manned the lightship thirty miles southeast of Nantucket and spent long periods at sea alternating with long periods on shore leave.[14] Given the isolation and tedium of life at sea, many crewmen brought their basket-making supplies aboard ship, resulting in their long association with lightships. For about fifty years, this level of production fed the tourist trade and supplemented the meager salaries the Lightship Board paid its crews.[15]

In the early 1900s the Lightship Board itself became a casualty of standardization. Deemed an inefficient committee, it was transferred from the Department of Treasury to the Department of Commerce, and its governance was streamlined and professionalized.[16] The lightship service was no longer locally controlled and the crews were no longer islanders. Although the Nantucket lightship baskets were no longer physically associated with lightships, the name stuck since their profitability depended on that relationship. The Nantucket basket industry almost met the same fate as the Lightship Board, virtually disappearing during the Great Depression as cheaper paper and plastic bags and boxes replaced handmade items and tourism declined precipitously. By World War II, basket making was no longer profitable.[17]

Along came José Formoso Reyes, whose mixed-race family settled on Nantucket after World War II because of its ethnic diversity (figure 6). Although Nantucket may appear an unlikely destination, its historical participation in world trade networks and tourism enticed settlers from around of the world. Reyes was born in the Philippines, but graduated from high school in Portland, Oregon. He met Mary Elizabeth "Betty" Ham, a native of Cambridge, Massachusetts, when they were undergraduates at Reed College. They married in 1933, the same year Reyes graduated with a master's degree in education from Harvard University. He and Betty settled in the Philippines.[18] Reyes taught English and art at the University of the Philippines in Padre Faura, and then accepted a position as chair of the Department of Languages and Social Arts at the Philippine Military Academy in Baguio. He held the chairmanship until early 1941, when, as the Japanese invasion became imminent, he joined the Philippine Army and was appointed Secretary of the General Staff. After the fall of Bataan and Corregidor, Reyes went underground gathering intelligence for the US Army. He was given US citizenship upon discharge from the Army

Fig. 5. *Map of the Shore Line Railroad route between New York and Boston, showing its railroad and steamboat connections with New York, New Haven, New London, Stonington, Providence, Newport, and Boston,* 1860. *Courtesy of the Library of Congress, Geography and Map Division.*

with the rank of captain. Like many immigrants to the US, Reyes was forced to accept work neither in keeping with his education nor his past experience. He began with house painting in summer and repairing cane and rush chairs in winter, but soon met Clinton Mitchell "Mitchy" Ray, a third-generation lightship basket artist and one of the few surviving makers. They became good friends and Ray taught Reyes the art of making Nantucket lightship baskets. It was a natural fit because basket making with rattan was a skill Reyes had learned as a boy in the Philippines. He later inherited many of Ray's molds that dated back to lightship days.

Fig. 6. Louis S. Davidson (1891-1983), *Lightship basket maker José Formoso Reyes seated in his workshop, beginning a new basket,* circa 1940s. Photograph. *Courtesy of the Nantucket Historical Association.*

Reyes's reinvention of the Nantucket lightship basket as the Nantucket friendship purse in 1948 resulted from an astute reading of the postwar economy. To keep the American people working and to avoid another depression, industrial war output was reconfigured for domestic production. Women were reassigned to the domestic sphere as household managers and consumers.[19] As labor-saving appliances freed women from some of the drudgery of housework, advertisers exhorted them to spend their leisure time shopping. Magazines, movies, and television allowed viewers to see what others were purchasing, and as advertisements continually reminded them, "to see it is to want it."[20] *Life* magazine was one of the most important disseminators of fashion advice, and according to some accounts, Reyes saw a basket with a cloth top in a 1948 issue and appropriated the idea for his reinvention.[21]

Reyes revived the Nantucket lightship basket tradition by reinventing it as a consumer product with communal identity that allowed for personal expression (see p. 127). He did this by keeping all the features that connected it to its origins, including the wooden bottom, staves, riveted hoop, tightly woven body, and swing handle. However, Reyes made certain adaptations since, as a ladies' handbag, it was carried as a fashion accessory. He lightened the weight by using rattan for the weavers as well as the staves and hoops, reverting to the baskets' earliest iterations made aboard whaling ships. He added a domed lid that mirrored the construction of the body.[22] Reyes replaced basic hardwood with a rare luxury material, ivory from African elephant tusk. A carved ivory clasp secured the lid. Reyes dispensed with the wooden "ears" of lightship baskets and pinned the handle to the outside of the hoop with carved ivory knobs that allowed the hinged lid to be easily raised while adding another decorative flourish.

The changes Reyes made to the lightship basket were calculated to keep the "look" that connected it to Nantucket's communal identity and, at the same time, to create a unique consumer object that conveyed personal status. Reyes typically signed every basket he made with his name. He also included the incised outline of the island of Nantucket and the words "Made in Nantucket." In a 1975 interview with the Nantucket Historical Association, Reyes spoke about the baskets' potential to bestow status when he revealed, "The ladies vie with each other to put ivory on top (on the lid of the purse). [The friendship purse] has become a status symbol. In other words, the more ivory you have, the more money you spend, the more affluent you are, and the more they recognize you are affluent. The ladies call it 'Nantucket mink.'"[23]

Reyes never advertised in the traditional sense; he had more work than he could handle through word of mouth. He told an interviewer in 1958 that shortly after he made his first purses he could "hardly make enough to meet the demand of the market." Legends grew up around the purse, passed on orally and recorded in all publications describing it. These stories became advertisements, creating desire for the purse and enhancing its value. One story connected the purse to status by invoking royalty. A group of British expatriates living on Nantucket reportedly ordered a purse from Reyes for Her Royal Highness, Queen Elizabeth II, as a gift for her coronation in 1953.[24] In terms of

Fig. 7. José Formoso Reyes, *Nantucket friendship purse,* interior detail of owner's signature, 1961. Oak, reed cane, ivory. *Courtesy of the Nantucket Lightship Basket Museum.*

American royalty, the *Wall Street Journal* reported that islanders could not stop gossiping about how Frank Sinatra bought three on a vacation visit to the island in 1973.[25]

Importantly, the legend that opened this essay about women forging a friendship through their shared taste in accessories took place in Paris, linking the purse to the world of fashion. The evolution of the Nantucket lightship basket mirrored the development of the fashion industry as it moved from *haute couture*, or handmade originals, to mass-produced fashion.[26] Originally, couturiers designed dresses that were hand-sewn and modeled individually to prospective customers. The customer bought that specific dress, a unique creation. After the war, designers began to create fashion "lines," pricing the items according to the degree of handwork used in their production. They advertised the top of these lines in two extravaganza shows a year calculated to excite desire.[27] Similarly, Nantucket lightship baskets started out as unique creations by whalers on long voyages for loved ones at home, but in the new postwar consumer economy, they transformed into easily individualized fashion objects. The most expensive were handmade by the designer on the island of Nantucket; exhibited the finest quality standard features of the lightship basket; and included add-ons created from luxury materials such as ivory, ebony, mahogany, and scrimshaw. Reyes's price list allowed for adding features separately to facilitate personalization and status building (figure 7).[28] By doing so, he followed the same retail model as the American automobile industry, in which a consumer picked a basic model and then selected accessories or refinements that made it a personal expression.[29]

Fig. 8. Louis S. Davidson (1891-1983), *Gathering at an auction at the Kenneth Taylor Galleries in the Macy Warehouse,* circa 1950s. Photograph. *Courtesy of the Nantucket Historical Association.*

The association of the friendship purse with French fashion is not limited to their shared economic models. As Reyes started producing purses, the French fashion designer Christian Dior unveiled a fashion revolution called the "New Look" on the runways of Paris in 1947, reviving and reinventing the French fashion industry. The New Look emphasized differences between women and men, since it required a tightly fitted waist, curving hips, and accentuated breasts.[30] This shape could only be achieved through significant substructure of corsets, girdles, stays, bones, ribs, and hoops similar to those used in the construction of the friendship purse. Advertising women to "consume beautifully," both the New Look and the friendship purse created the polished appearance a modern woman was expected to maintain in her role as household manager (figure 8).[31]

The fashions of the 1950s indicated the wearers' conformity to certain expectations of womanhood in the postwar consumer economy. This included marriage. In her book *Wife-Dressing*, fashion designer Anne Fogarty admonished women to dress first and foremost for their most important role as wife.[32] Not surprisingly, the name Reyes chose for his reinvention of the lightship basket connects the purse with facilitating relationships. Several stories reinforce this association. On a transatlantic voyage, a woman met the man who would become her husband because he recognized the purse she carried came from Nantucket and struck up a conversation.[33] It led to a shipboard romance and ultimately, marriage. Another story casts the purse as a token of friendship. Many Nantucket basket artists placed a penny in every purse to prevent the severing of a relationship. From a practical point of view, the penny solved the problem of how to cover the hole in the wood bottom created during its construction, but the story added a relational feature women appreciated. Still another story relates that every girl who graduated from Nantucket High School received a friendship purse as a graduation gift, cementing her relationship to the island.[34]

Reyes's friendship purse perpetuated the Nantucket lightship basket tradition and put it into a new and highly desirable context. The shift of its name from lightship basket to friendship purse connects the object to how women, as opposed to men, are defined by relationships. In recasting the basket as a purse, Reyes created something a woman could carry with her that would be recognizable enough to signal membership in an elite community but personalized to confer individual status. At the same time, the materials and construction of the purse reinforced a connection to history and the larger world (figure 9). Reyes celebrated the international character of his baskets when he related to his customers that the rattan for weaving was from Java or Malaya, the wood for the bottoms was from Honduras or Brazil, the decoration on the covers was from Africa, India, and Norway, and the white oak for the handles was from America. And with a bit of humor, he would add, "And the maker of the friendship basket is imported from the Philippine Islands."[35] Not surprisingly, Reyes's enterprise has had a lasting legacy: A gentleman who was asked if he knew Nantucket replied, "Oh, you mean that island where all the ladies carry little baskets?"[36]

Fig. 9. John McCalley (1912-1983), *Guests at the Shipwreck Ball on Nantucket Island,* August 3, 1973. Photograph. *Courtesy of the Nantucket Historical Association.*

# BEYOND SUMMER CAMP AND MERIT BADGES:
## The Studio Craft Movement, Education, and the American Basket

*by Perry Allen Price*

THE INDUSTRIAL REVOLUTION and the processes of modernization fundamentally changed the production, distribution, and transmission of work in all craft media, but basketry best exemplifies the changes in craft education in the twentieth century. While studio craft education in the United States preserved the instruction of basket making, it also expanded the range of acceptable materials and forms, resulting in the development of highly individualistic contemporary basketry alongside the maintenance of traditional forms and techniques. Workshops and classes across the country sustained and disseminated European American basket traditions, supplementing or replacing the apprenticeship experience. In the academy, led by influential and charismatic artists such as Ed Rossbach, basketry was subject to the same pedagogical shifts and market forces that shaped developments in other craft media. While Native and African American basket weaving traditions continued to be transmitted through traditional means, they were impacted by developing markets and the studio craft movement as well.

Perhaps one of the most paradoxical, uncomfortable, yet ultimately liberating realities about baskets in the contemporary moment is that they are largely superfluous while remaining a ubiquitous part of our material culture. For example, in the 1980s and 1990s, strawberries were sold in square baskets of translucent green injection-molded plastic, designed to mimic the diagonal or vertical plaiting of what many remembered as a berry basket (figure 1). These plastic baskets are *skeuomorphs*, or objects that mimic the design of similar artifacts produced in a different material. In the 1986 edition of his book, *The Nature of Basketry*, Ed Rossbach commented, "Only for a brief time these replacements are imitating baskets until new forms are found and old forms are forgotten."[1]

Fig. 1. Evan Mitchell, *Plastic berry basket*, 2011. Photograph. *CC by 2.0.*

A visit to any grocery store confirms Rossbach's prediction: Berries are now sold either in clear plastic clamshells or open-topped boxes made of molded, pulped fibers that optimize shipping quantities without any visual reference to basket weaving. In a generation, no one will have any idea what a berry basket is, and they will likely not associate the form with the craft of basketry at all.

## Popular Conceptions of Basket Weaving

As the traditional role of baskets has changed throughout the twentieth century, the craft has become popularly associated "with summer camps and merit badges, and with the therapy in mental institutions."[2] Basketry continues to be a subject of study for the Boy Scouts, with the possible award of a basketry merit badge after the successful identification of coiled and ribbed baskets and the production of three weavings: a round basket, a square basket, and a stool seat (figure 2). Because the connection between basket weaving and calming handwork for wards of mental institutions has an historical foundation, it is a familiar enough image that Rossbach's comment in the mid-1980s required no explanation. And, as anyone who has explored non-canonical academic subjects can attest, "underwater basket weaving" is a derisive term often used to describe courses viewed as impractical by mentors and parents overseeing an education.[3]

Fig. 2. Boy Scouts of America Basketry Merit Badge, Type C, 1936-1939, and Girl Scouts of America Campcraft badge, 1955-1956. *Private collection.*

The use of kits to introduce and instruct the populace in basket weaving also contributed to the reputation of basket making as a rudimentary or hobby activity. Early in the twentieth century Deerfield baskets—raffia baskets with pastoral rather than geometric patterns made popular after the publication in 1915 of the monograph *Raffia Basketry as Fine Art* in Deerfield, Massachusetts—presented the hobby of basket weaving as an appealing artistic diversion rather than a production method for utilitarian objects (figure 3).[4] Raffia and rattan were popular among amateur basket makers who imitated Native American basket techniques during this same period.[5] These baskets lacked all of the material and production knowledge that typified Native basket forms; the fundamental substitution of raffia for the grass, bark, needle, willow, and other fibers prepared for weaving according to particular practical and cultural norms resulted in mere approximations of the originals and were justifiably criticized, no matter how faithfully the colors, patterns, and forms were executed. Without widespread examples to the contrary, the basket as an art form became associated with the amateur.

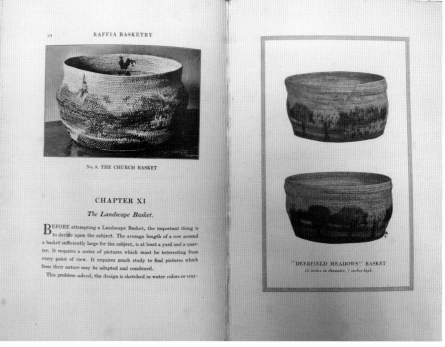

Fig. 3. Gertrude Porter Ashley and Mildred Porter Ashley, "The Landscape Basket" in *Raffia Basketry as a Fine Art* (Deerfield: Montague Press, 1915), pages 24–25.

Native American basketry was concurrently affected by the popular cultural perception of basket making. Interest in basket weaving was predicated in part on the growing awareness of and appreciation for the basketry of numerous western Native American groups and the expanding production and sale of those baskets and other trade work to non-Native consumers. In 1904 George Wharton James published his survey, *Indian Basketry*, which sought to catalog and preserve the forms, materials, and uses of Native basketry. Despite its colonialist language, it remains a common reference text today. James lamented the inferiority of baskets made for sale to non-Natives and stressed the importance of training and educating successive generations of Native basket weavers.[6] However, the market had already begun to influence the Native artists James admired. The Washoe basket weaver Louisa Keyser, for example, produced many of the pieces that James described as masterpieces under contract with Abe and Amy Cohn for their Carson City, Nevada, store (figure 4). Her iconic *degikup* form, a spherical open-top basket in willow with decorative patterns composed of bracken fern, was a contemporary invention marketed by the Cohns as traditional, as was Keyser's assumed name, Dat So La Lee (figure 5).[7] The idea that various forms of Native American art and material culture, including baskets, remained static rather than continually developing, ignored the frequency with which Native American art included creative developments that occurred as the result of friction between cultures. For example, Mi'kmaq and Onondaga artist Gail Tremblay has, since the 1980s, woven baskets made from recycled photographic film stock, a medium noted for its use to disseminate misinformation and stereotypical depictions of Indigenous Americans, instead of traditional weaving materials (figure 6). Even the stitch patterns Tremblay uses are selected to allow the Mi'kmaq and Onondaga elements to evoke larger commentary on the subjects of her contemporary pieces.[8] Tremblay's baskets are comparable to Keyser's in that neither conform to traditional Native American art or history as it exists in the popular imagination. In fact, both address contemporary issues, concerns, and pressures using traditional methods and non-traditional materials or vice versa.

## Centers of Studio Craft Education

American Studio Craft has its roots in the Arts and Crafts movement of the late nineteenth century. While Studio Craft inherited the Arts and Crafts movement's emphasis on the handmade, and both movements stressed the mastery of skill and technique, Studio Craft placed greater import on the unique expression of the individual maker and encouraged the production of one-of-a-kind objects (or possibly work in a series). Both movements shared a philosophical commitment to the handmade fabrication of functional objects, yet the functionality of the studio craft object is not the exclusive or even primary motivation of the maker.

The development and expansion of Studio Craft is due to parallel developments in other centers of education that taught craft disciplines. Three overlapping yet unique pedagogical perspectives shaped craft education: the Manual Training Movement, the immersive craft school, and academia.

Fig. 4. *Washoe squaw and baskets*, circa 1899. Photograph. *Courtesy of the Library of Congress, Prints & Photographs Division, LC-USZ62-117637.*

Fig. 5. Louisa Keyser (Dat So La Lee) (Washoe, 1835-1926), *Degikup* basket, circa 1918. Willow. *Courtesy of Granger, NYC.*

Fig. 6. Gail Tremblay (Onondaga-Mi'kmaq, b. 1945), *An Homage to Wild Strawberries*, 2003. Discarded 35mm ethnographic documentary film with green and red leaders. *Courtesy of Michigan State University Museum.*

Very much in line with the progressive education movement of his day, Calvin M. Woodward founded the St. Louis Manual Training School in 1880 and authored *The Manual Training School* seven years later. He advocated for instruction in drawing, wood, and metals in addition to Latin, mathematics, the sciences, and English. He designed a three-year course of study for young men ages fourteen to eighteen based on the Swedish educational model known as *slöjd* ("craft" or "hand skills") popularized in Europe by Otto Salomon as an adjunct to the common teaching methods of rote memorization and recitation. Rather than instruct pupils in preparation for a trade, *slöjd* philosophy proposed "its purpose is not to turn out carpenters, but to develop the mental, moral and physical powers of children."[9] Craft education was not meant to produce better potters, but better people. As Woodward wrote, "The finest fruit of education is character; and the more complete and symmetrical, the more perfectly balanced the education, the choicer the fruit."[10]

The tenets of the Manual Training Movement were widely accepted, and by the 1930s, woodshop, metal shop, and home economics courses were required of middle and high school students until the close of the twentieth century. Generations of students were introduced to the work of the hand without a commitment to a trade, something expressly advocated by Woodward, who wrote, "To make the production of articles the main object, and the learning of principles and methods incidental, would be to choose the shadow rather than the substance; to destroy our school by converting it into a factory."[11] With no expectation of practical application, the goal of shop class was to familiarize individuals who might never have a career requiring manual dexterity with the skills and pleasures of craftsmanship, and it seeded generations of amateur craftspeople, from woodworkers to basket weavers, throughout the twentieth century.

The Manual Training Movement reinforced the romantic ideal that to work with one's hands was personally enriching to the maker and superior to the industrial production of consumer goods. This model helped establish and maintain a marketplace for handcrafted items. In the 1960s and 70s, when the anti-establishment proclivities of American youth led them "back to the land," it spawned another craft revival as individuals sought new means of economic and aesthetic opportunity. As Nicholas Bell points out in *A Measure of the Earth: The Cole-Ware Collection of American Baskets*, many of the basket weavers responsible for this revival of American basket forms, techniques, and practices had no prior training in basket weaving or connection to historic basket making traditions.[12] Often reverse-engineering baskets from antique examples or working from the scant texts available, the resurgence of basket weaving may not have been possible without some basic familiarity with handcrafting or the notion of its intrinsic value instilled by the Manual Training Movement.

The same progressive education reform that helped foster the Manual Training Movement also provided fertile soil for the establishment of immersive craft schools, such as John C. Campbell Folk School, the Haystack Mountain School of Crafts, and the Penland School of Crafts. Lucy Morgan, or "Miss Lucy," came from Chicago to the community of Penland, North Carolina, in 1920 to teach at the Appalachian School. She immediately saw the benefits that weaving could have for local women personally and economically (figure 7). Morgan's weaving workshops soon outgrew their facilities, and by 1935, the school began to construct its own buildings and expand its workshop offerings to include bookbinding, ceramics, jewelry making, and soap making in addition to weaving. Three years later, the Penland School of Handicrafts was registered as a non-profit corporation.[13]

Penland arose from a vocational form of craft education as a means of economic empowerment. Its weaving program was one of many in the region that provided instruction and, just as importantly, established small-scale production for a consumer market. As Penland began to adopt other disciplines, the emphasis on folk skills, handicrafts, and the Appalachian craft revival remained. However, the pedagogy of the immersive craft school changed as the Studio Craft movement developed. For instance, Penland's second director, William J. Brown, took over from Miss Lucy in 1962. He received an MFA from Cranbrook Academy of Art and taught for a decade at the Haystack Mountain School of Crafts on Deer Isle, Maine. Haystack, founded in 1950, was itself partially inspired by the Penland experience of its supporting founder, Mary Beasom Bishop.[14] Brown was given complete autonomy in running Penland, and he soon began to offer workshops: small, short-term classes with focused educational goals taught by artists for whom teaching was not a full-time endeavor (although media-based studios could be overseen by an individual for whom it was a full-time occupation).

The workshop model promoted by Brown was a fiercely egalitarian environment, open to anyone with the time, interest, and money to participate. Like shop class in secondary school, it was neither skill-based nor product-oriented. In fact, workshops were often introductory experiences for craftspeople. The workshop template was repeated at other notable craft schools founded in the mid-twentieth century, including Anderson Ranch Arts Center in Colorado, Peters Valley Craft Education Center in New Jersey, and Arrowmont School of Arts and Crafts. Workshops served as a complement, if not an outright counterpoint, to craft training provided in higher education.

## Craft in the Academy

In the decade that followed the establishment of the Servicemen's Readjustment Act of 1944, otherwise known as the G.I. Bill, more than two million veterans used their benefits to attend colleges and universities.[15] These veterans bolstered the number of students in academic art programs, which were established or expanding at a rapid rate. At the same time, craft media were becoming

Fig. 7. Bayard Wooten (1875-1959), *Basketmaking, Penland School of Handicrafts*, circa early 1930s. Lantern slide. *Courtesy of the Penland School of Crafts Archives.*

more and more common in academia. The Studio Craft movement was driven in no small part by the many graduates of higher education art programs.

The large numbers of students in the post war period stretched the capacity of many art programs and many artists celebrated today discovered craft media as an alternative to painting and sculpture. Two convenient examples are Warren MacKenzie and Peter Voulkos. Although the two could not have forged more divergent paths over their careers (MacKenzie became a critic of Abstract Expressionism for which Voulkos was ultimately celebrated), they both began as ex-servicemen in art departments.[16] Voulkos attended Montana State University after his discharge from the Air Force in 1946, studying commercial art before committing to painting. He resisted registering for ceramics until he was told he could not graduate without completing the course.[17] MacKenzie registered at the Art Institute of Chicago in 1941 to study painting. Drafted into the army, MacKenzie served as a cartographer and was sent to Occupied Japan after the end of the war. He was discharged in 1946, but on his return to the Art Institute of Chicago found no openings to resume his painting courses. He registered for ceramics instead.[18]

Another important change in the role of craft media in academic art departments was the effect of foundational courses. The pedagogy of the German Bauhaus school in particular precipitated the shift in American art education. The Bauhaus, founded in 1919 by the architect Walter Gropius, sought to create a holistic school for art, connecting the crafts, industrial design, painting, sculpture, and eventually architecture. Students, faculty, and lecturers of the school helped to spread the Bauhaus approach in the United States, especially after the closing of the German school in 1933 under Nazi rule. Black Mountain College in western North Carolina was led by Bauhaus instructor and artist Joseph Albers, who along with his wife, Anni, immigrated to the US when the Bauhaus school closed.[19] In Chicago, architecture and design were heavily influenced by the architect Mies van der Rohe, contemporary and compatriot of Bauhaus founder Gropius and by the Hungarian painter and Bauhaus professor László Moholy-Nagy. The foundation courses espoused by the Bauhaus and adopted by art programs emphasized training in abstract composition in both two and three dimensions, color theory, and design principles before advancing on to courses in specific media. While craft has always been a way of thinking through process and materials, foundational courses emphasized creativity over vocational training and blurred the boundaries between craft and fine art media.

At the same time, craft associations began to exert greater influence in higher education, aided and abetted by outside individual or organizational patrons. The American Craft Council, then the American Craftsman's Educational Council and itself only two years earlier formed from an aggregate of craft advocacy organizations, was an initial sponsor of the School for American Craftsmen at Dartmouth. The school welcomed its first student in 1944, a Marine discharged after he sustained combat injuries. The school moved to the Rochester Institute of Technology in 1949. In 1975, Boston University inaugurated its Program in Artisanry, a unique and self-contained department in ceramics, wood, metals, and fiber independent from the other arts taught at the university. Ten years later, the program was absorbed into the University of Massachusetts Dartmouth's College of Visual and Performing Arts and exists today in a more conventionally academic framework.[20]

More common than entire departments or divisions dedicated to craft was the integration of craft media into art programs, which affected the Studio Craft movement in a number of important ways. First, it placed new emphasis on graduate education. In the 1940s some of the first recipients of masters of fine arts (MFA) degrees preceded or accompanied the wave of students that flooded college courses under the G.I. Bill. These artist educators influenced the rise of the Studio Craft movement and its expansion, serving as "movers and shakers" in the field. Ceramist Daniel Rhodes, for example, received the first MFA to be awarded by the New York State College of Ceramics at Alfred in 1943.[21] Rossbach, who taught at the University of California Berkeley for more than thirty years, received an MFA in weaving and ceramics from Cranbrook Academy of Art in 1947.[22] Rossbach was perhaps the Studio Craft movement's most significant teacher and investigator of basketry. In his own work, in the classroom, and in his impressive amount of writing in books and articles, Rossbach was instrumental in the development and expansion of contemporary basketry in the twentieth century. Rossbach was a continuous experimenter who, according to scholars Janet Koplos and Bruce Metcalf, "felt that to truly understand a method he had to do it himself."[23] Many of Rossbach's explorations in fiber, such as the use of ephemeral materials, research and revival of technical processes in weaving, and the use of the basket as a starting point for sculptural forms became essential to contemporary basket weaving and found a ready audience among his students in the classroom and the many inspired by his writing. Artists like Rossbach provided basketry and other traditional craft media a platform for innovation and education that severed contemporary craft from its applied arts origins as perhaps no other development could.

## Studio Craft, Fiber Art, and the Basket Weaver

The Studio Craft movement radically altered what it meant to make a basket. As with clay, wood, glass, or metal, fiber provided fertile ground for experimentation that altered traditional conceptions of craft as manual and occupational training. While traditional basketry continued to flourish, the emergence of a new basketry coincided with the educational and marketplace shifts precipitated by the Studio Craft movement.

One important result of craft education in colleges and universities was the expectation that graduates of MFA programs would go on to teaching positions themselves.[24] To hold positions or receive tenure in academia, craftspeople were subject to the same career markers and achievements as their peers in painting, printmaking, and sculpture. Gallery representation, museum exhibitions, and inclusion in public collections had greater significance than production work. For example, Rossbach benefited from the freedom and flexibility afforded by his academic post. He rarely if ever worked in series, declined occasions for commissions and sales, and produced a diffuse body of work over his career.[25] Rossbach's work was part of a shift in fibers in the twentieth century that he concurrently recorded and interpreted in his writings. He called it "The New Basketry."[26]

Throughout the 1970s and 1980s there was a struggle to reconcile the new basketry with the old. Rossbach viewed the new basket as "less of a development than it was a reinvention," a practice inspired by but certainly disconnected from the forms, traditions, and preoccupations of the past.[27] Jack Lenor Larsen, himself an accomplished weaver for both art and industry, saw a parallel in fiber's turn to the basket as vessel as similar to clay, glass, and turned wood's shift from functional forms to "a ritual object with function more implied than real."[28] Exhibitions of this period explored the connection between the utility of the historic basket and the sculptural form of the contemporary vessel.[29] Curator Ulysses Grant Dietz poetically describes the ceramics collection of the Newark Museum in his book *Great Pots* as beautiful pots, useful pots, wise pots; it is an astute lens that avoids the contortions often required to root the new basket in the traditions of the past.[30] Once the function of the historical basket was supplanted by other forms or materials, traditional baskets were free to be read and understood in the same manner as the new baskets of the Studio Craft movement. Indeed, the baskets of weavers like Louisa Keyser were never intended for utility, but because of history and cultural expectations were examined as functional objects first.

In 1976 Rossbach said, "The new basket makers are not attempting to revive traditional basket making, although they certainly are stimulating a new appreciation and awareness of the old. Nor are the new baskets made to replace those that are disappearing."[31] Today, the basket holds a unique place in contemporary material culture. Traditional baskets and new are divorced from functional utility, described as objects of contemplation (as though the only function of a work of art is contemplation, a reactionary and regressive simplification). The basket is romanticized and eroticized, as shown in Elissa Auther's examination of the work of Harmony Hammond, who uses the symbol of the native basket as a stand-in for "alternative, authentic artistic expressions" disassociated from academic art.[32] The basket maker now enjoys an unparalleled resurgence of traditional basket-making processes, materials, and techniques, many maintained against all odds by adherents and revivalists, as well as a half-century of experimentation and innovation among makers of the "new" basket. The contemporary art world currently favors artists with an emphasis on materials, so fibers and ceramics are having a moment in the sun.[33] Whatever the immediate future holds for the basket, it is now safely outside the realm of summer camp crafting and merit badges, a living and evolving representative of the confluence of humanistic education, studio crafting, and the imperatives of academia.

CHAPTER 7

NEW BASKETRY BEGINNINGS:

1970–1990

*by Patricia Malarcher*

A GIGANTIC IMAGE of a splint basket, rendered in black and silver metal, surrounds the riders in one of the elevators at the new Whitney Museum in New York City (figure 1). There is irony in artist Richard Artschwager's homage to a humble woven container on the walls of a cube for carrying people. A passenger attuned to fiber art might see in this a twenty-first-century extension of the contemporary basketry movement.

The new basketry's early stirrings took place in the 1950s, as evidenced by Ed Rossbach's 1957 vessel of palm fronds and plastic reproduced in the book *Beyond Craft: The Art Fabric*.[1] But it was in the 1970s that, as an outgrowth of the radical reinvention of textile studies, basketry attracted a critical mass of practitioners. Rossbach, a visionary professor in the Design Department at the University of California in Berkeley and a prime mover in the field, described fiber as an art medium without conditions.[2] Viewing textile construction as structural language freed from conventional usage, artists cast aside long-held precedents for materials, process, and scale. Rope, wire, plastic, seaweed, and other linear substances were applied to weaving, knitting, and crocheting. Techniques formerly used exclusively for basketry—especially twining, coiling, and plaiting—offered previously unexamined possibilities for expressive form.

Various aspects of basketry, including its use of linear elements shorter than the continuous threads on a loom, prevent its application to industrial production. Thus, many types of baskets were unknown apart from local usage in remote places. Rossbach's seminal book, *Baskets as Textile Art*, a worldwide survey of traditional basketry published in 1973, introduced a previously unseen range of innovations.[3] By analyzing basketry from the perspective of visual art, Rossbach departed from ethnological or instructional approaches to the subject. He did not discuss how baskets were made or how they were used, but rather the aesthetic effects of phenomena such as the proportional relationship of a form to a handle or how the character of a natural material influenced a form.

In the introduction, Rossbach recalls his assignment during World War II to an army post in the Aleutian Islands, a volcanic archipelago off the southwest coast of Alaska. Although the native Aleuts had been evacuated, he mused on how they survived in their desolate environment. It was apparent to him that the use of local plants for basket making was central to their culture. Rossbach quickly abandoned his own attempt to fashion a form from a few strands of grass, but his interest in basketry followed him into later teaching and artwork. The baskets he made then departed from the traditional practice of using indigenous natural substances. Nevertheless, in turning to materials that proliferated in his urban environment—for example, newspapers and images from pop culture—he followed the precedent of using what was at hand (figure 2). (His frequent use of difficult processes to depict a famous rodent refuted dismissive appraisals of weaving and basketry, sometimes referred to as "Mickey Mouse" courses.) (See p. 122).[4]

The San Francisco Bay area became an energetic hub of fiber activity. According to Joan Sterrenburg, who studied with Rossbach at Berkeley, basketry was not part of the curriculum but was "simply in the air" with a strong community of advocates.[5] Joanne Segal Brandford, a textile

Fig. 1. Richard Artschwager (1923-2013), *Six in Four - E4*, 2012-2015. Elevator at the Whitney Museum. Stainless steel and powder-coated metal: dimensions variable. Whitney Museum of American Art, New York; Commissioned by the Whitney Museum of American Art 2015.159.4. © 2015 Estate of Richard Artschwager.

Fig. 2. Ed Rossbach (1914-2002), *Newspaper*, 1976. Mixed media: 7" × 24" × 24". © Tom Grotta. *Courtesy of browngrotta arts.*

Fig. 4. Lillian Elliott (1930-1994), *Troy*, 1993. Pressed paper, gesso, acrylic paint: 29" × 34" × 20". Photograph by Scott McCue. *Private collection.*

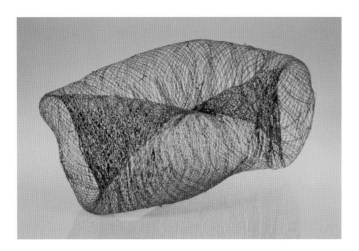

Fig. 3. Joanne Segal Brandford (1933-1994), *Sojourner*, 1992. Dyed rattan and nylon sprang: 13" × 30" × 16". Photograph by Joanne Segal Brandford. *Courtesy of Family of Joanne Segal Brandford.*

historian with an appreciation of baskets as art, was Rossbach's colleague at Berkeley (figure 3). Lillian Elliott, who had studied ceramics but became known for adventurous two-dimensional works in fiber as well as for basketry, intermittently taught there and at the California College of Arts and Crafts (now the California College of Art) in Oakland (figure 4). Elliott was also an instructor at the Pacific Basin School of Textile Art, an independent center started by graduates of CCAC. That school, along with Fiberworks in Berkeley, provided dynamic fiber education for about a decade. Gyöngy Laky, Fiberworks' founder and a former student of Rossbach, was known for environmentally conscious constructions, including basket-like vessels from pruned woodcuttings (see pp. 92, 118). She later joined the art faculty at the University of California at Davis. Sylvia Seventy, whose vessels of handmade paper and grids of sticks alluded to basketry, directed the education program at Fiberworks.

Disregarding craft associations, artists critiqued their work in the language of contemporary art. Elliott, for example, said baskets require "attention to form, structure, inner shape, and surface planes."[6] To solve spatial or structural problems, she investigated materials, whether thread, bark, or a discarded section of a woven cane chair, to find what forms they could take.[7] She said, "I do not copy the old baskets, neither do I use traditional techniques and materials. Rather, I explore this form, that idea, and push it as far as I can."[8]

Brandford's initial focus was research, but with Elliott's encouragement she began creating structures in sprang and other forms of netting. Disassociating her efforts from those of the historical basket makers she admired, Brandford typically started by constructing a flat plane of fabric, then coaxing it into three dimensions. Delicately poised in the space they occupied and frequently alluding to figures, her baskets usually held the memory of a searching hand. Drawing on her deep knowledge of textiles, Brandford made insightful observations on her work. For example, she noted that netting allowed room for air to pass through it; she referred to her baskets as "breathing."[9]

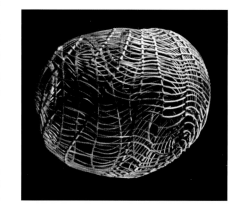

Fig. 5. Lillian Elliott (1930-1994) and Pat Hickman (b. 1941), *Romany*, 1985. Mixed materials: 5' × 8'2" × 6'7". Photograph by Scott McCue. *Courtesy of Pat Hickman.*

When Brandford relocated to Massachusetts, she held a textile history seminar at the Cambridge Adult Education Center that included field trips to the nearby Peabody Museum. Pat Hickman, who had developed an interest in traditional textiles while in Turkey teaching English, was one of her students. Hickman then moved to Berkeley, and at Brandford's recommendation, pursued fiber studies with Rossbach and Elliott. While viewing an exhibition of ethnic clothing in San Francisco, Hickman became intrigued by the translucent quality of gut parkas made in Alaska.[10] Seeking to capture the same effect, she began experimenting with the animal membrane (sausage casing) that became her signature material. Her first trials were small two-dimensional pieces, but a conversation with Elliott pulled her into basketry. Elliott had expressed a desire to cover a particular form with a surface; Hickman suggested the membrane as a solution. Thus was launched a series of collaborative works that continued for more than a decade. Hickman stretched her material over Elliott's skeletal armatures to give them taut, skin-like surfaces. The project culminated with a monumental basket created for the 12th International Biennial of Tapestry in Lausanne, Switzerland, in 1985, the first time textile sculpture was a theme for that exhibition (figure 5). Hickman's influence on basketry continued when she left the Bay Area to chair the Fiber Department at the University of Hawaii.

As others who studied basketry in the Bay Area moved around the United States, they spread enthusiasm for the burgeoning art form. Sterrenburg, for example, launched a basketry program at Indiana University in Bloomington when she joined the textile faculty there. This inspired another generation of students—among them Diane Itter, Diane Sheehan, Lissa Hunter, and Gary Trentham—who further imagined basketry's potential as twentieth-century art. Sterrenburg's own richly textured baskets, drawing inspiration from traditional textiles of Africa, Asia, and the Americas, reflected the emphasis at Berkeley on anthropological artifacts as aesthetic resources.[11] Suellen Glashausser, a Berkeley graduate whose baskets and other structures echoed Rossbach's fearlessly playful approach to materials, coauthored an authoritative book on plaiting with Carol Westfall, her colleague at Montclair State University in New Jersey.[12] This augmented a stream of books being published to meet the surge of interest.

Fig. 6. Joan Austin, *Containment Series: No. 8*, 1971. Natural rattan: 9" × 12" × 9". Photograph by Joan Austin. *Courtesy of Jonathan Austin.*

Fig. 7. Carol Shaw-Sutton (b. 1948), *Our Bones Are Made of Stardust*, 1986. Willow, pigment, and waxed linen: 18' × 10' × 10'. Photograph by Gene Kennedy. *Courtesy of the artist.*

In southern California, another lineage of basketry artists, many under the tutelage of Joan Austin at San Diego State University, emerged independently (figure 6). Austin, like Rossbach and Elliott, graduated from Cranbrook Academy of Art. Her interest in basketry, however, predated her academic career. As the daughter of a tuna fisherman, Austin spent much of her childhood on her father's boat, helping him repair nets and observing sea life. Her artwork included reed constructions inspired by fish traps and aquatic organisms.

Carol Shaw-Sutton, a graduate of San Diego State, recalls Austin's interest in unfamiliar materials, as when she returned from Japan with a deepened understanding of bamboo's relationship to textiles. Focused on research and experimentation, Austin failed to develop a consistent body of work prior to her untimely death in her fifties. As a consequence, her influence is often overlooked.[13]

Shaw-Sutton, too, was exposed to basketry early in life—as a Girl Scout craft and as a part of the Native American culture seen during family vacations in the American southwest. Knitting, also learned in childhood, instilled in her a love of process and the altered sense of time that sustained attention brings. Shaw-Sutton made her first art baskets, inspired by the mountainous environment in which she lived, before graduate school. While acknowledging that work in the Bay Area reinforced her interest in basketry, Shaw-Sutton identified more closely with "the vigor and flow of growth of all textiles and fiber as a material study" than with a movement.[14] She challenged the notion of baskets as static objects in works that spiraled off the wall into space, freed from the confinement of form (figure 7). Her *Spirit Canoes* are multi-layered grids that curve into arcs; in the catalog for the 12th International Biennial of Tapestry, she described them as "personal vessels of memory that store hour by hour, day by day, week by week, the rhythms of life" (figures 8 and 9).[15]

Austin's work was also the catalyst that launched Ferne Jacobs's lifelong commitment to basketry. Jacobs had studied weaving with Arline Fisch, Neda Al-Hilali, and other prominent artists around Los Angeles when she discovered Austin's baskets on exhibit. The notion of freestanding textiles, built without burdensome equipment, excited her. She taught herself coiling after viewing one demonstration and never stopped. Coiling is an open-end process that allows a form to build up organically as the basic linear element is bent back upon itself (figure 10). Repetitively wrapping

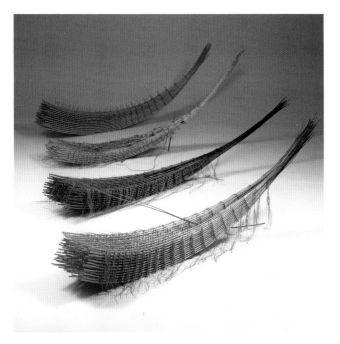

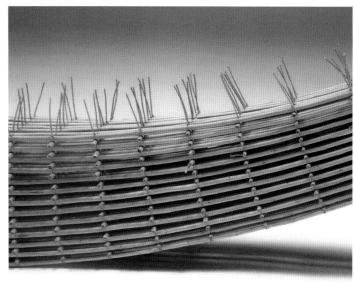

Fig. 8. Carol Shaw-Sutton (b. 1948), *Spirit Canoes* (4), 1982–1988. Lashed willow and waxed linen: 6' × 18" × 30". *Courtesy of the artist.*

Fig. 9. *Spirit Canoes* (detail). *Courtesy of the artist.*

waxed linen on a hemp core, Jacobs works intuitively with a meditative rhythm, relishing the slowness and labor-intensity of hand work, never certain of the outcome until a piece, which could be a tall cylinder or a baroquely sensuous form, has evolved.[16]

Prompted by the rapid growth and development of basketry as a studio practice, Rossbach's second book on the subject juxtaposed traditional and contemporary baskets. Experimental work reproduced in *The New Basketry* ranged from massive rope constructions to delicate pouches of seaweed.[17] Emphasizing the emergence of contemporary basketry from the study of weaving, the author observed that fiber artists tended to derive forms from a two-dimensional perspective rather than from an understanding of volume, as exemplified by a Pima basket, its pattern conforming to the curve of the walls, or a Zulu hut with skeletal arches as framework. Rossbach wrote that much of the new work seemed tentative, with structural problems being solved for the first time. He observed that softness remained a conspicuous reflection of weaving origins, but also that artists were starting to manipulate rigid materials, resulting in structures more akin to actual baskets.[18]

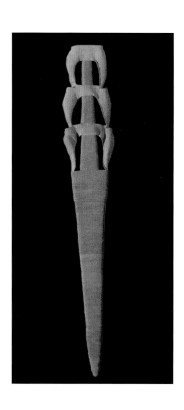

Fig. 10. Ferne Jacobs (b. 1942), *Arrow,* 1986–1988. Coiled and twined waxed linen thread: 68.5" × 10.75" × 4". *Courtesy of the artist.*

Fig. 11. John Garrett (b. 1950), *Pop Pod*, 1992. Aluminum drink cans, aluminum flashing, hardware cloth: 12" × 18" × 18". Photograph by John Garrett. *Courtesy of the artist.*

Shaw-Sutton was among those who early on turned toward reed and other stiff substances similar to conventional basketry materials. Others, like John Garrett, looked beyond fibers to industrial materials. Garrett's textile career began at the loom. He often made experimental three-dimensional forms from the fabric he wove and found that weaving with different materials, such as metal, increased the possibilities for manipulation. His early baskets of hardware cloth, folded and embellished with elements such as plastic, sequins, and beads, grew from those investigations.[19] For Garrett, synthetic materials served as expressive correlatives to the "glaring plastic world of every commercial street" in Los Angeles, where he continued to live after finishing an MA at UCLA. He described his basic basketry process as painting garish colors on fabric-backed vinyl, which was cut into strips and woven into the wire grids of hardware cloth.[20] Garrett's baskets from recycled metal components—some made of used beverage cans to invert the meaning of "trash basket"—anticipated the twenty-first century rediscovery of recycling and repurposing (figure 11).

Even as baskets were surfacing in craft shows and galleries that promoted contemporary fiber arts, a touring museum exhibition with a catalog dedicated to the genre was a rare undertaking. A notable exception was *Basketry: Tradition in New Form*, curated by Bernard Kester, a professor of textiles and textile design at the University of California in Los Angeles.[21] The nine exhibitors from across the United States included not only Garrett, Jacobs, and Shaw-Sutton, but also Kay Sekimachi, whose reputation as a weaver preceded her entry into basketry with bowls of handmade paper and boxes shaped on the loom; metalsmith Elliott Pujol, known for copper vessels; and Rina Peleg, who made basket-like sculptures from coils of clay. Thus basketry was allied with sculpture and vessels in other craft disciplines as well as with weaving. In his curator's essay, Kester set the new basketry in a historical context, citing originality as the characteristic that distinguished it from previous attempts at basketry art—in particular, imitations of Native American baskets that emerged from the early twentieth century Arts and Crafts movement. Opening at the Boston Institute of Contemporary Art in 1981, the exhibition traveled to the Cooper–Hewitt Museum in New York and the Greenville County Art Museum in Greenville, South Carolina.

As an offshoot of contemporary fiber, the new basketry played a minority role in a genre that already held minority status in the larger art world. In *The Art Fabric: Mainstream*, the 1985 book documenting a major exhibition of the same name, less than two pages of text are devoted to basketry.[22] Nevertheless, awareness filtered through educational institutions offering accredited and non-accredited courses; curators, gallery owners, and collectors who were passionate supporters; and documentation by publications such as *FiberArts*. Inevitably, exposure brought new waves of artists. Fresh interpretations of the genre ranged from intimate hand-held vessels to towering structures in an unlimited range of natural and fabricated materials.

Diversification generated questions about the definition of a basket. Was "basketness" determined by form, process, materials, scale, allusion to functional antecedents, or something else? Shereen LaPlantz, an artist and author of books on basketry techniques, guided collectors to three characteristics: function as a container; use of a basketry process such as twining, plaiting, or coiling; or plant fibers as materials. "An object must have two or more of them to be a basket," she wrote. With only one, "it's either not a basket or questionable."[23] Basket makers themselves have avoided definitions but concurred on one essential feature: interior space. In John McQueen's succinct words: "A basket is an empty space surrounded by a structure."[24]

Although Rossbach described fiber as an urban movement centered in universities and art centers, some artists found their way to basketry far from academia.[25] McQueen's eureka moment took place at a state fair in New Mexico, where a Pueblo basket large enough for its maker to sit in caught his attention. As an undergraduate, McQueen had studied welded sculpture, but was fascinated by the massive form coiled from fibers. He began to gather plant materials and build forms from them. Eventually, he enrolled as an MFA student at Tyler University in Philadelphia. Adela Akers, who headed the fiber program, offered him open-ended freedom to explore basketry.[26]

McQueen approached unprocessed natural materials with a keen understanding of structure and an unusual rapport with nature. For example, he once built a cube from a stack of flat woven squares sandwiched together with layers of burdock between them. With a nod to our throwaway culture, he sometimes used plastic fasteners or twist-ties to bind up linear elements, or he would translate the form of a commonplace object such as a corrugated carton into a finely plaited basket. Weaving words into baskets, embedding verbal equivalents of what was happening within the forms, pulled baskets into the realm of concrete poetry (figure 12). For example, a cylindrical piece might include a word referring to roundness, placed so that a viewer would have to circle the form in order to read it. McQueen's idiosyncratic inventiveness brought wide recognition from others in the field. Rossbach referred to him as "the outstanding basket maker" of his era.[27]

A daily gatherer of twigs, bark, and branches from the forest around his studio, McQueen perceived an analogy between a tree and the human body. This is vividly expressed in a two-piece sculpture, *A Tree and Its Skin*: one part consists of a segment of a tree trunk resembling a torso; the other, shaped from bark stripped from the same tree, is a hollow form with matching contours. This work could be identified as figurative sculpture, but McQueen chose to call himself a basket maker. "I liked that baskets were the original man-made objects and have a wider territory than pure sculpture, which just began in the Renaissance," he stated.[28]

Fig. 12. John McQueen (b. 1943), *To the Spreading Speech*, 1981. (Text: "Speech spreads down the side pushing out from next to far away moving the end to where it is.") White pine bark: 29" × 8" × 8". Photograph by Brian Oglesbee. *Courtesy of the artist.*

As some artists pushed the basket toward sculpture, others concentrated on maximizing the aesthetic yield from straightforward vessels. Kari Lønning had studied jewelry, ceramics, and weaving at Syracuse University, but none satisfied her desire to make large forms with predictable color. She found her medium at a basketry workshop taught by Carol Hart, who had investigated Eastern Woodland baskets while working with an Indian Studies Program and was writing a book on basketry made with natural materials and dyes.[29] Lønning's sturdily built rattan baskets evolved from that point on. Rhythmic patterning and double-walled construction enhanced their clean, classical forms. Eventually, reeds with long ends extending from the walls added "hairiness" as a textural element. Lønning's baskets allude to functional containers, but their primary purpose is to exist as strong formal statements, often enhancing interiors (see p. 118).[30]

Fig. 13. Nancy Moore Bess (b. 1943), *O-Seibo Baskets*, late 1980s. Twined raffia: 4.5" × 15" × 4". Photograph by D. James Dee. *Private collection.*

Traditional basketry forms offer insights into the cultures from which they came, such as how certain people stored or prepared food. As the work of Nancy Moore Bess illustrates, contemporary baskets also can be infused with cultural content. Bess worked with ceramics and wood while living in the Bay Area but bypassed basketry until she moved to New York. As the organizer of a craft program at a museum on Long Island, Bess met Virginia Harvey, whose book *The Techniques of Basketry* referred to the new basketry in its early stages.[31] While twining became her obsession, she was also intrigued by the Japanese packaging described in *How to Wrap 5 Eggs* by Hideyuki Oka.[32] An extended stay in Japan afforded a close encounter with a culture she had admired from afar. Inspired by details of daily life such as metal ornaments on newel posts, rope made of rice straw, and ingenious transformations of paper squares, Bess began to incorporate aspects of Japanese aesthetics into her work—for example, by creating formal arrangements of baskets in special boxes or tying untrimmed ends of a raffia warp—like a knot on a *furoshiki* bundle (figure 13).[33]

Initially an American phenomenon, the new basketry spread around the world as artists carried it to other countries. While Bess brought Japanese influence home to America, Hisako Sekijima took American basketry home to Japan. She had studied rattan basketry in Japan before a temporary relocation to New York. Having seen McQueen's work at the Hadler-Rodriguez Gallery, one of a few Manhattan venues then showing fiber, she promptly enrolled in his course at the Peters Valley Craft Center in New Jersey.[34] Within a short time, Sekijima found her own conceptual approach and gained recognition as a maker of innovative forms. In pieces embodying an uncommon structural intelligence, Sekijima emphasized the function of voids as spatial elements, equal in importance to the physical components of a basket. Upon returning to Japan, she introduced the new basketry as a challenge to deeply ingrained traditional forms in bamboo and other wood substances.

Fig. 14. Douglas Fuchs
(1947-1986), *Floating Forest*,
1981. Installation view in 2012
at Ararat Regional Art Gallery,
Ararat, Australia. Mixed media:
dimensions variable. *Courtesy
of Powerhouse Museum,
Sydney, Australia.*

Recognizing Sekijima's contribution to the basketry movement, Jack Lenor Larsen included her among some thirty Americans represented in *The Tactile Vessel*, an exhibition based on a basketry collection he assembled for the Erie Art Museum in the late 1980s.[35]

Another contributor to the global awareness of basketry, Douglas Fuchs, was an art instructor for disturbed adolescents when he took a basic basketry class to increase his teachable skills. In his studio, he wove reeds together to create a series of slender cylindrical forms, some taller than himself.[36] Granted a year-long residency in Australia, he expanded his practice dramatically while introducing the new basketry to local artists. Fuchs's residency culminated in *Floating Forest*, an ambitious fiber environment that occupied more than one gallery, versions of which were shown in three Australian states (figure 14). In addition to a cluster of tapering towers, the ensemble included a skeletal boat form in which a figure lies on its back, implying a mythical passage that seemed strangely prescient when illness and death cut short Fuchs's promising career. Nevertheless, a recent exhibition marking the thirtieth anniversary of *Floating Forest* at the Ararat Regional Art Gallery in Ararat, Victoria, confirmed his lasting influence on the Australian continent.[37]

In the mid-1980s, the United States Information Agency sent *The New American Basket*, an exhibition representing more than twenty artists, to several sub-Saharan countries in Africa, including Burundi, Rwanda, Tanzania, Zaire, and Zimbabwe. Under the title *The New Basket: A Vessel for the Future*, the exhibition was organized by Lucia LaVilla-Havelin, an independent curator, for the Brainerd Gallery at the State University of New York in Potsdam. It subsequently traveled to other venues in the United States.[38]

As paths leading to basketry widened or diverged, some artists chose directions more related to traditional basketry than to contemporary fiber art. Mary Jackson, for example, was discovering ways to enliven her heritage of sweetgrass baskets in coastal South Carolina. Others were developing fresh approaches to regional basketry traditions in natural materials such as willow and pine needles. Jane Sauer was a painter who sought a new way of practicing art after an injury prevented her from working at an easel. She was conversant with embroidery and weaving but found basketry compelling. Referring to the book *A Modern Approach to Basketry* by Dona Meilach, Sauer taught herself to coil by adapting the directions to left-handedness.[39] Once she had made a basket from waxed linen thread, she abandoned her paintbrush.[40] Sauer enrolled in a course at the St. Louis School of Architecture to study form. Her first baskets were built around ready-made Styrofoam solids like cylinders and cones, but her architectural studies pushed her toward the creation of original forms, still made of Styrofoam but with irregular curves and intricate excavations carved into them. Frequently, Sauer paired organic forms that embodied a tension evocative of human relationships (see page 121). As the forms remain within the "skin" built around them, the lack of interior space gave the work a hybrid identity between basketry and sculpture. Sauer's work in two solo exhibitions in St. Louis, one at a museum and the other at a gallery, appeared in the *New Art Examiner* in the mid-1980s. Of one show, Nancy N. Rice wrote, "The controversy of art versus craft, or even utilitarian versus non-utilitarian art, are non-issues in the case of Jane Sauer's work."[41]

The *New Art Examiner* was known for its non-hierarchical leanings and its independence from New York's art establishment. Elsewhere, as the last decade of the twentieth century approached, critical perspectives still separated the new basketry from the mainstream art world. Sculptor Carol Hepper's sticks-and-twine construction, for example, was described in *Arts Magazine* as "a large basket that has popped its bottom and sprouted stick wings."[42] Robert Gober's handwoven dog bed, its cushion printed with disturbing images, was critiqued as a one-time venture into basketry to serve a particular idea, rather than as a long-term dedication to process. In her 1993 essay for the catalog, *Baskets: Refining Volume and Meaning*, an in-depth representation of eleven artists at the University of Hawaii Art Gallery, Pat Hickman addressed a disparity she saw in the arts: "Isolation and marginalization are constant companions of the fiber world," she wrote. The results are "fewer exhibits, fewer critics addressing this work, fewer reviews, less interaction with other artists, less money for work and growth."[43]

Still, as the 1990s advanced, the new basketry seemed positioned to benefit from a sea change in the art world. Gradually that world was broadening to embrace a global community; artists from countries with honored textile traditions, basketry among them, were beginning to present work derived from those legacies in fine art galleries in New York and elsewhere. In addition, the cultural thrust toward environmental concerns brought attention to diminishing natural materials such as those used by many basketry artists and renewed appreciation of their value. Finally, divisions between art and craft began to erode as conceptual content, rather than materials, became the unifying core of "crossover" exhibitions that purposefully combined works in craft media with other disciplines.

Twenty-plus years later and moving forward in a new century, it no longer is surprising to find the structural language and materials of basketry applied to the expression of sculptural concepts. Yet, even in an elevated status, basketry constructions retain an identity connected to antecedents that, by serving everyday needs, contributes to the flourishing of human cultures.

CHAPTER 8

# DIVERSE STRUCTURES,
# DISSOLVING BOUNDARIES

*by Carol Eckert*

BASKETRY IS AN ANCIENT TECHNOLOGY, connected to humans' earliest days on earth. Collecting materials from their surroundings and assembling them into constructed objects, early makers experimented in order to build and survive in their environments, devising shelters, traps, armor, boats, ceremonial garments, fences, cages, spiritual implements, and all manner of storage containers, both large and small. These ancient makers had no historical precedents to follow; they invented freely, without patterns, rules, or constraints. They adapted and experimented, using their hands and simple tools to create whatever was needed, from architectural structures to vessels. Today's artists bring the same experimental approach to their own work, which ranges from large-scale, site-specific works to installations, wall pieces, and sculptural vessels. They refer to ancient techniques when it suits their purposes and invent new methods and processes when necessary.

Digital communication has enabled contemporary makers to remain tied to the traditional processes of their particular region or culture, but has granted them access to the many ways artists throughout the world are thinking about basketry, whether that be in a Russian village, a Belgian city, or an Alaskan homestead. Consequently, innovations are rarely restricted to one particular region or country. While there is a long tradition of sharing within the basketry field and a history of workshop/instructor exchanges, particularly among the United States, Australia, and the United Kingdom, that cross-pollination has been intensified in the internet era. Access to artist and gallery websites, blogs, image-sharing sites, and on-line museum collections creates a climate in which artists are less likely to be isolated by location or language, resulting in an expansive reframing of the field and collapsing boundaries between art, design, craft, and architecture.

Among the artists working with basketry processes in the United States today is a group of significant and influential makers from the contemporary basketry movement of the twentieth century. Many of these innovators originally referenced the vessel in their works but have branched out into wall works and large installations. John McQueen, one of the more influential artists associated with the basketry field, embraces sculptural forms of all kinds, including books, columns, wall pieces, and installations, all involving basketry processes, and most employing materials traditionally associated with baskets: twigs, bark, and vines, along with recycled plastics, zip-ties, and string. McQueen's *Table of Contents*, originally exhibited at the Racine Art Museum in 2004, filled the gallery with a forty-eight-foot-long architectural grid of willow scaffolding resting on fabricated wooden crates, surmounted with a frieze of willow images of everyday household objects—furniture, tools, personal items, and kitchenware (figure 1). *Continental Drift*, an elaborately patterned wall mural (also constructed of willow) extended the length of the crates, topped by a border of human and animal symbols. McQueen's unconventional use of willow in this conceptually and structurally complex installation was based in basketry.[1]

Fig. 1. John McQueen (b.1943), *Table of Contents* (detail), 2004. Installed at Racine Art Museum. Willow twig scaffolding mounted on shipping crates with 170 willow sketches of everyday objects: 48' long. *Courtesy of Racine Art Museum.*

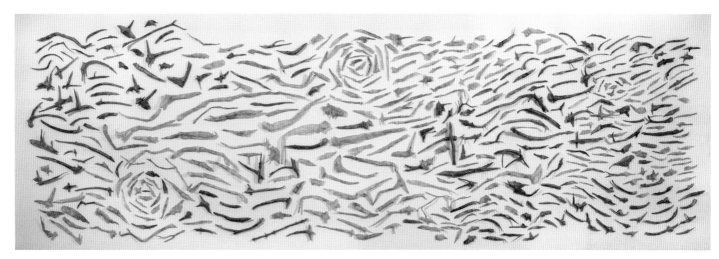

Fig. 2. Pat Hickman (b. 1941), *The River That Flows Both Ways*, 2015. Fragments of tree trunks from the Hudson River and animal gut: dimensions variable. Rockland Center for the Arts, West Nyack, New York. Photograph by George Potanovic, Jr. *Courtesy of the artist.*

Throughout her long career, Pat Hickman has explored numerous textile processes, becoming particularly well known for her work with animal membrane (gut), which she used in the construction of vessels, layering it over armatures. Recently, expanding upon innovative techniques she developed as a result of her scholarly and curatorial background in historic Inuit garments, Hickman executed large floor and wall installations comprised of constructed gut forms and gathered wood elements (figure 2). These pieces have an obsessive, repetitive quality that amplifies their time-intensive process in what Janet Koplos has referred to as "the *work* of art . . . an amount of labor that suggests that the doing itself is meaningful to the artist."[2] This commitment to process infuses Hickman's work, as do themes of loss, memory, time, and transience.

McQueen and Hickman, like many artists of the contemporary basketry movement, developed their studio work from backgrounds in textiles, drawing upon traditional basketry and textile techniques while engaging with new materials and imagery to transform the field, moving away from "baskets" and into "basketry" and, in the process, creating works that no longer fit neatly within the studio craft field. Inherent in the word "basket" is an allusion to the vessel or container,

Fig. 3. Martin Puryear (b.1941), *The Charm of Subsistence*, 1989. Rattan and gumwood: 84.6" × 66.5" × 10.5". Saint Louis Art Museum. Funds given by the Shoenberg Foundation, Inc. 105: 1989 © Martin Puryear. *Courtesy Matthew Marks Gallery.*

and many of the artists involved in the contemporary basketry field originally made pieces that, while innovative and experimental in approach, referenced those forms. "Basketry," however, is a much broader concept, encompassing a range of processes and ideas that can be employed in any number of disciplines. Indeed, the language of basketry permeates many areas of aesthetic practice, including architecture, sculpture, and design.

As elemental methods of construction deeply embedded in human history, basketry processes find their way into the work of a number of contemporary artists who would not necessarily define themselves as basket makers. Martin Puryear, Sopheap Pich, and Maria Nepomuceno are sculptors whose approaches to constructing forms are influenced by their early exposure to the basketry traditions of Africa, Asia, and Latin America. Martin Puryear's sculpture reveals his interest in the traditional craft processes he observed during his early experiences as a Peace Corps volunteer in Sierra Leone: "I make sculptures using methods that have been employed for hundreds of years to construct things that have had a practical use in the world" (figure 3).[3] Puryear sometimes incorporates basket-weaving techniques into his work, and his respect for these traditional processes, along with his affinity for natural materials, results in unique forms that appear both ancient and contemporary. Working primarily with rattan and bamboo, Cambodian artist Sopheap Pich constructs ethereal structures, at once both fragile and monumental (figure 4). Using the natural indigenous materials familiar to him since childhood and traditional Cambodian basketry techniques, Pich creates organic openwork forms imbued with a deep sense of memory and time.[4]

Finally, Maria Nepomuceno's large, fluid installations evoke basketry, hammocks, vining and trailing vegetation, umbilical cords, and strands of DNA. Spiraling forms of straw, rope, and beads, often vibrantly colored, reflect the environment of her native Brazil and the regional basketry traditions of her ancestors. One of her most ambitious works, *Tempo para Respirar* (*Breathing Time*), was commissioned by Turner Contemporary and installed in 2012 (figures 5 and 6).[5] Ropes became objects of connection, with the artist exchanging colorful new Brazilian ropes for used local fishing and sailing ropes. These swapped and donated ropes were incorporated into the construction of the piece, along with elements transported from Brazil. A complex sculpture of multiple parts, it extended across the floor of Sunley Gallery, crept up the walls, and dangled from the ceiling. Nepomuceno's practice often includes other people, and this installation involved many members of the local community. The artist trained a group of local volunteers for a three-week period. The Maria Nepomuceno Studio Group participated in the construction of the piece and continued to work after she departed, extending and expanding it. The visiting public also interacted directly with the work, resting in hammocks, scooping up beads, and sometimes rearranging elements within the composition.[6]

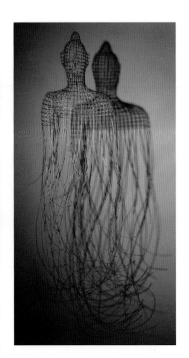

Fig. 4. Sopheap Pich (b. 1971), *Buddha 2*, 2009. Rattan, wire, dye: 100" × 29" × 9". Purchase, Friends of Asian Arts, 2012 (212-349). Image © Metropolitan Museum of Art. Image source: Art Resource, NY. *Courtesy of Sopheah Pich.*

Fig. 5. Maria Nepomuceno (b. 1976),
View of *Tempo para Respirar*
(*Breathing Time*), 2012. Ropes, beads,
fabric, ceramic, foam, braided straw,
resin, fiberglass, wood: 36' × 23' × 33'.
Installed at Turner Contemporary. ©
Maria Nepomuceno. Photography by
Stephen White. *Courtesy of the artist
and Turner Contemporary, Margate.*

Fig. 6. Maria Nepomuceno (b. 1976), View of *Tempo
para Respirar* (*Breathing Time*), 2012. Ropes,
beads, fabric, ceramic, foam, braided straw, resin,
fiberglass, wood: 36' × 23' × 33'. Installed at Turner
Contemporary. © Maria Nepomuceno. Photography
by Stephen White. *Courtesy of the artist and
Turner Contemporary, Margate.*

Fig. 7. Nathalie Miebach (b. 1972), *External Weather, Internal Storms* (sculpture), 2009. Reed, metal, wood, data: 33" × 40" × 60". *Courtesy of the artist.*

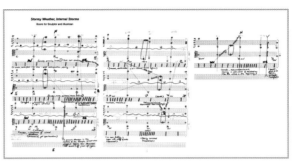

Fig. 8. Nathalie Miebach (b. 1972), *External Weather, Internal Storms* (musical score), 2009. Weather data: 11" × 26". *Courtesy of the artist.*

Environmental concerns are central themes to many contemporary basket makers, including Nathalie Miebach and Gyöngy Laky. Miebach considers the collection of data an integral and essential part of a practice that merges scientific and visual inquiry. A fascination with weather informs her work; patterns of weather in the Gulf of Maine or the stormy Atlantic conditions that produced Hurricane Sandy are transcribed into wild and colorful configurations of reed, wood, and bamboo.[7] Miebach's *Weather Scores* project is predicated on the same data, but it is transformed into a score that is interpreted and performed with composers and musicians (figures 7 and 8).

Gyöngy Laky, who refers to herself as an "artist participant," also addresses ecological and geopolitical issues.[8] The artist's additive process, along with her use of both natural and industrial materials, often positions her within basketry, but her body of work includes site-specific outdoor sculpture, vessels, and wall structures, and her wide-ranging practice encompasses craft, design, engineering, architecture, and agriculture.[9] Her recent work has been referred to as "organic typography"—word sculpture in which "the tangible nature of the letter becomes intertwined with its meaning as a recognized word" (figure 9).[10]

Fig. 9. Gyöngy Laky (b. 1944), *Globalization III: Red Ink*, 2005. Ash branches, commercial wood, paint, building screws: 32" x 97" x 4". Photograph by Bob Hsiang. *Courtesy of the artist.*

Laky's approach is one that resonates with many younger artists, who do not see themselves as defined by or restricted to specific categories. Doug Johnston's background in working with various textile processes, primarily knitting and sewing, is influenced by his experiences in architecture, fabricating spiral staircases and observing 3-D printing. He refers to his basketry process as "analog 3-D printing with a sewing machine," and he has explored the possibilities of coiling to produce a wide range of functional objects, including vessels, bags, and stools (figure 10).[11] Johnston's wide-ranging practice includes musical performances that can be downloaded from his website, Doug Johnston Studio. This site also features a shop that sells limited-edition and one-of-a kind hanging light sculptures and other coiled objects. His interdisciplinary practice is not unlike that of many of his contemporaries, and it seems likely that the future of basketry will be shaped by approaches like his. Basketry is inherently interdisciplinary, encompassing architecture, art, design, engineering, botany, and mathematics. It is a medium uniquely suited to an interconnected age and a global village.

Fig. 10. Doug Johnston (b. 1979), *Sash Cord Studies*, 2010–2016. Cotton or poly sash cord, polyester thread: dimensions vary. Photograph by Michael Popp. *Courtesy of Doug Johnston Studio.*

Prolific and innovative industrial designer Stephen Burks has been described as working in the "blur zone," and he predicts that the future will be "collaborative, composited, pluralistic, hybrid, and cross-disciplinary."[12] Through Aid to Artisans, he collaborated with South African artist Willard Musarurwa on a series of basket-like wire stools for retailer Artecnica. The work of his Brooklyn-based design studio, Readymade Projects, includes transcultural collaborations with traditional Senegalese artisans working in New York and Dakar, whose meticulous, colorful, coiled baskets of sweetgrass and plastic strips are transformed into sculptural lamps and imaginative furniture.

Contemporary basketry artists are not neglecting the rich potential of the physical landscape, either. In the environmental art movement, particularly in the United Kingdom and Europe, many artists use the materials and processes of basketry to construct large on-site sculptures, often gathering materials from the environments in which they are working, engaging with and participating in the living cycles of nature. Sandy Heslop of the University of East Anglia posits, "Basketry is a wondrous technology and is the interaction between human ingenuity and the environment."[13] Hers is a concept that can be applied to contemporary land art sculptors as well as ancient trap builders and boat makers. Early inventions grew out of an intense relationship with the natural environment that is shared by many land artists whose work is informed by a connection to place and respect for nature. At land art gatherings such as those at Grindelwald, Switzerland, and Humus Park, Italy, artists from various countries work in teams over limited time periods, creating ephemeral works that will eventually return to the forest (figure 11).

Fig. 11. Marie Hess-Boson (b. 1963) constructing a sculpture with Team Schweiz/Switzerland at LandArt Grindelwald, 2015. *Courtesy of Marianne Scheitlin Pfeiffer*.

Fig. 12. Chris Drury (b. 1948), *Time Capsule*, 2002. South Carolina Botanical Gardens. American beech, silver birch, serviceberry saplings. Photograph by Ernie Denny. *Courtesy of the artist*.

British artist Chris Drury is sometimes described as an environmental architect. He began making baskets after long, meditative walks in wild places. There he collected the simple materials at hand, which he later wove into baskets that became "containers of experience."[14] One of his earliest installations, at the Tranekaer International Centre for Art and Nature, consisted of a marking cairn enclosed in a large basket/shelter constructed of green hazelnut sticks that could be seen as an object from the outside or experienced from the inside.[15] Drury often works with materials he gathers on site. *Time Capsule*, constructed for South Carolina Botanical Gardens at Clemson in 2002, is on the border between indigenous woodlands and introduced species (figure 12). Live saplings surround two domes made of woven sticks. As the sticks decay over time, the living trees will take their place and the interior will change into a restricted and mysterious space. The artist frequently collaborates with scientists and ecologists and describes his work as "about place, culture, and connections across disciplines." "When you work with the land," he says, "you are making a political statement as well as an aesthetic one."[16]

Finally, some contemporary artists have turned to basketry as a catalyst for community revitalization. In the Russian village of Nikola-Lenivets, basketry has become "a technology for the resuscitation of the village."[17] Nikolay Polissky moved to the region, a nearly abandoned community with a failed collective farm, in 1989. There he constructs massive works that dominate the landscape. The village has become a center of creative activity and contemporary art with the an-

Fig. 13. Nikolay Polissky (b. 1957), *Beaubourg*, 2013. Birch sticks, twigs, metal frame: 72'. Nikola-Lenivets Sculpture Park, Russia. Photograph by Alexey Lukin. *Courtesy of the artist.*

nual Archstoyanie Land Art Festival. Polissky's monumental seventy-two-foot-high sculpture, *Beaubourg*, was constructed in 2013 in cooperation with Nikola-Lenivets Handicrafts, an organization of trained local artisans that provides employment for a number of residents (figure 13). Beautifully sinuous, constructed of logs, branches, and twigs with traditional basket weaving techniques, the towering structure, inspired in part by the exterior elements of the Centre Georges Pompidou in Paris and by Pollisky's interest in the origins of Russian culture, suggests mysterious rituals and ancient architecture.[18]

Fig. 15. Fiona Hall (b. 1953), *All the King's Men*, 2015. Knitted uniforms, wire, bone, horns, teeth, dice, glass, leather boxing gloves, pool ball. Installation: dimensions variable. *Courtesy of the artist and Roslyn Oxley9 Gallery, Sydney, Australia.*

Fig. 14. Fiona Hall (b. 1953) with the Tjanpi Desert Weavers, *Kuka Irtitja (Animals From Another Time)*, 2014. Tjanpi grasses, yarn, wool, raffia, wire, camouflage fabric, ininti seeds, feathers, button, camel teeth, burnt paper. Commissioned by TarraWarra Museum of Art. *Courtesy of the artist and Roslyn Oxley9 Gallery, Sydney, Australia.*

Central Australia is another region that has been revitalized by basketry. Tjanpi Desert Weavers was founded in 1995 as a social enterprise to provide livelihoods for women artists working in twenty-eight remote communities. Working with traditional and invented techniques and using gathered tjanpi grass, wire, raffia, and wool, the weavers produce vibrant, innovative, and constantly evolving creations based on their surroundings. They fashion helicopters and trucks, lizards, boats, birds, cameras, and a wide variety of fantastical creatures, both mythological and extinct.[19] In partnership with Australian artist Fiona Hall, Tjanpi Desert Weavers participated in the 2015 Venice Biennial. *Kuka Irtitja (Animals From Another Time)* included images of animals now vanished, except in the stories handed down and the likenesses the weavers create: banded anteater, golden bandicoot, and spotted quoll (figure 14). Hall, whose work explores sensitive political and ecological issues, worked at a desert camp with the weavers to construct parts of her installation, *All the King's Men* (2014–15), which included suspended woven masks made of strips of camouflage fabric (figure 15).[20]

The expansive field of contemporary basketry includes artists who are exploring the media, processes, and ideas of basketry from different points of origin and with different intentions. The limitless terrain encompasses a vast range of traditional concepts and contemporary approaches, materials made by nature and by humans. Basketry is a process both universal and particular, extant in almost every culture throughout history and accessible to artists working in tiny studios and large warehouses, in desert camps, forest parks, and urban workshops; in meditative solitude or exuberant collaboration; with ancient techniques or invented adaptations. The language of basketry is elemental, essential, and always current.

CHAPTER 9

THE SPACE BETWEEN

*by Jeannine Falino*

THE LANDSCAPE OF CONTEMPORARY AMERICAN BASKETRY is in flux.[1] Despite being far removed from its ancient, utilitarian, and ritual origins, modern makers are grappling with the form's inexorable pull as a primordial container for human needs and its inescapable reference to the human body, mind, and spirit. Influenced in part by a new generation of fiber artists, we are now in a transitional period during which the prevailing boundaries, expectations, and hierarchies of the basket are being challenged, and core values concerning technique, virtuosity, and beauty are being energized by new artistic discourses regarding resources, data, space, and scale. The following are some brief observations on the current scene.

Found materials have been making their way into baskets for decades, but rising global concerns about sustainability have accelerated this trend in the basket-making world. This is paralleled by concerns over the dwindling of natural resources needed for traditional practice. As a result, many artists are working in this arena. For example, Bryant Holsenbeck's lively, random-woven goldfinches and crows are assembled with materials obtained through urban foraging, the current term for what used to be called trash picking, gleaning, dumpster diving, scavenging, salvaging, or curb crawling (see p. 150). Holsenbeck self-identifies as an environmentalist, and taking the position that we Americans are "blind to our waste," she employs found materials to transform them into something new in both small and large-scale formats (figure 1).[2] For Jerry Bleem, the container remains powerful and his forms, sometimes resembling organic forms like logs, arteries, or body parts, contrast with his assemblies of mass-produced, foraged materials sutured together with staples. In his absorption with the interior and exterior of these body-like vessels, Bleem transforms the ordinary through obsessive surface treatment (see p. 146).

Ann Weber, inspired by her teacher and ceramist Viola Frey and the cardboard furniture of Frank Gehry, uses interwoven cardboard strips to build sizeable sculptural forms in the round and in relief (figure 2). Weber typically covers the finished work with shellac or paint, using armatures within for strength, and when possible, scales up her ideas for public installations with bronze and Fiberglas casts.[3] Like Holsenbeck, Bleem, and Weber, Aaron Kramer finds it both inspiring and cost-effective to work with found materials, as with his *Half and Half* (see p. 155), composed of recycled street-sweeper bristles and reclaimed,

Fig. 1. Bryant Holsenbeck (b. 1949), *Bottle Fall*, 2015. Installation at Bucks County Community College, Newtown, Pennsylvania, composed of 20,000 bottles collected and cut by college and community members. *Courtesy of the artist*.

Fig. 2. Ann Weber (b. 1950), *Personages, Watch Over Me*, 2013. Found cardboard, staples, polyurethane: 90"–105". Photograph by M. Lee Fatherree. *Courtesy of the Dolby Chadwick Gallery, San Francisco.*

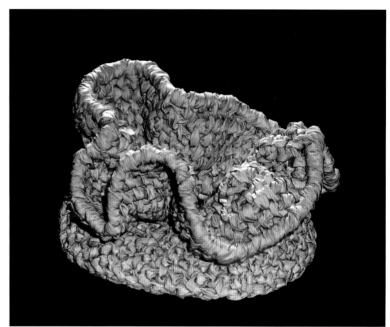

Fig. 3. Lara Knutson (b. 1974), *Soft Glass*, 2010. Reflective glass fabric, steel wire: 10.7" × 18". *Courtesy of the Corning Museum of Glass, New York.*

re-sawn hardwoods. Kramer applies his kinetic interests to foraged goods with surprising and joyful results, as with his *Spin Basket*, which employs a tin toy top, a bowling pin, washers, and wire. Who says baskets are supposed to be static?[4]

Many basket makers today use non-traditional materials in a variety of ways, and as a result, inventive ideas have emerged from within and beyond the basket world. Lara Knutson has made fresh inroads with Scotchlite reflective material. This 3M product, used to make workers and bicyclists visible at night, has been adapted into fabric lengths that she weaves on wire armatures to make vessel-like forms that give off an eerie glow (figure 3).[5] Glass may seem incompatible with basketmaking, but Charissa Brock combines bamboo with glass to create forms that sometimes resemble fossilized skeletons. A different approach is used by Kait Rhoads, who combines wire with hollow murine glass beads and mohair for added tactility (figure 4).[6] Exploring color rather than light, Jennifer Maestre manipulates colored pencils into bead-like elements, forming them into startling and spiky sculptural creations using a peyote stitch.

Fig. 4. Kait Rhoads (b. 1968), *Fluffy Cloud*, 2008. Blown glass, clear murine woven with copper wire, blue mohair on a steel stand: 17" × 13" × 10". *Courtesy of the artist.*

Fig. 5. Benjamin Aranda (b. 1973), Chris Lasch (b. 1972), Terrol Dew Johnson (b. 1973), *Endless Knot*, 2006. Wood, veneer, styrene, and sinew:15" × 36" × 18". *Courtesy of Aranda/Lasch & Terrol Drew Johnson.*

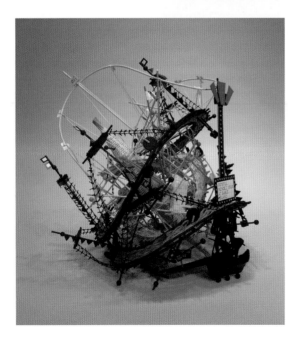

Fig. 6. Nathalie Miebach (b. 1972), *Fateful Rendevous at Sable Island*, 2014. Reed, wood, and data: 18" × 19" × 18". *Courtesy of the artist.*

Today most basket makers are deeply engaged in the analog realm. However, three artists are exploring the potential for digitally enhanced creativity in their field. Professional designers Benjamin Aranda and Chris Lasch made an intriguing start with Tohono O'odham basket weaver Terrol Dew Johnson. After seeing Johnson's vessels at the Museum of the American Indian in New York in 2004, the designers realized that his weavings were related to their own digital algorithmic experiments and proposed a collaborative project. Over the course of several months, Aranda/Lasch digitized some of Johnson's patterns, and Johnson then created baskets based on the algorithms provided by the designers. The resulting series featured the strong wave-like curve found in Johnson's original work, but transformed via their algorithmic application into something entirely new (figure 5).[7] Amit Zoran at the MIT Lab has also been investigating the use of digital frameworks for basket making. Still in an experimental phase, Zoran has been developing 3-D printed shapes that offer dynamic interactions for weavers.[8] These two experiments exemplify an exciting new agency among artists working in the fields of craft, design, and architecture, analog and algorithm-based processes, repetitive manual and automated practices. The collaborations and interdisciplinary nature of this work may bring about baskets as yet unimagined.

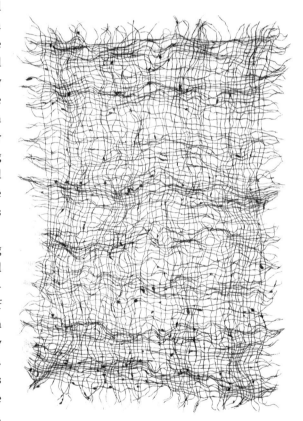

Data gathering and its interpretation by artists also has yielded promising if unorthodox results. A startling universe of complex forms has been created by basket maker Nathalie Miebach, who collects vast amounts of numerically-based information on weather formations in her region.[9] She gathers much of the data herself, complementing it with information obtained online. This data is translated into sculptural forms using plaiting techniques, common, brightly colored paper, and other found materials, as well as musical scores (figure 6). Her playful, colorful works vary in size and are studded with assorted elements and hand-written notations, creating unconventional forms that astonish the eye. Indeed, no two are alike; each one is a 3-D representation of specific data. Like the ancient Incans who developed *quipus* (or *khipus*, "talking knots") to record administrative data, Miebach has created a purposeful visual system to convey news of our fragile ecosystems.

Fig. 7. Kiyomi Iwata (b. 1941), *Southern Crossing Five*, 2014. Kibiso, dye: 87" × 60". © Tom Grotta, 2016. *Courtesy of browngrotta arts.*

These new data-driven expressions contrast with quieter experiments in space and light in which woven elements prompt discussions about what is seen and unseen, light and shadow, fragility and strength, gravity versus weightlessness. Such topics are the subject of sculptures by Nancy Koenigsberg, who works with layered arrangements of woven wire to convey lightness and breath within a network of line and shadow (see p. 155). Similarly, Japanese-born artist Kyomi Iwata uses kibiso, a silk factory byproduct that she mounts in loosely woven wall sculptures based upon drawn compositions (figure 7). Describing her process, Iwata says: "I am totally open, and because I'm open, I can float. For me, that's an exciting process in itself."[10]

Fig. 8. Martin Puryear (b. 1941),
*Brunhilde*, 1998–2000. Cedar
and rattan: 96" × 112.5" × 74".
© Martin Puryear. *Courtesy of
the Matthew Marks Gallery.*

Interstices of light and air in structural elements express the emotions; material densities express their compression, suppression, and release. Sculptor Martin Puryear investigates these concepts using wire, rattan, and wood. The artist employs pre-industrial skills in his practice as a way of meditating on craft, time, and labor, and his enigmatic forms include techniques and materials inspired by the world of basket making. His *Seer* (1984), a carved wooden handle or head set upon an open, bell-shaped framework of twisted wire simultaneously conveys transparency and enclosure, while the enormous, inverted basket entitled *Brunhilde* is filled with breath, as if waiting to exhale (figure 8).

The ties that bind the human psyche are probed in a tender, if troubling, manner by Robert Gober. Resurrecting the quotidian baskets of his suburban childhood, Gober wove a 1950s style laundry basket aggressively pierced with a large pipe, or culvert, one of the artist's preferred elements used to divert or wash away the indeterminate anguish of youthful memory. More recently, Gober created an oversized, intentionally clumsy, craft shop exercise with birch bark that on closer inspection reveals warp made of mangled fingers (figure 9). His painstakingly rendered works,

which include sinks, culverts, playpens, and doors, have been called by Roberta Smith a "sometimes subtle, sometimes furious protest against what might be called delusions of normalcy; the sexual, racial and religious prejudices these delusions engender are examined at their point of origin, the childhood home."[11]

The growing interest in large-scale work, land art, and installation art among basket makers began more than sixty years ago, with Ruth Asawa's sensuous biomorphic wire sculptures. Since then artists have been investigating a combination of approaches to create architecturally-scaled environmental installations, and the trend is growing. Random-weaving artists make use of brush, hay, branches, and twigs to transform interior spaces as well as landscapes, and Patrick Dougherty is one such artist whose gathered sculptures re-animate age-old harvest scenes. Dougherty's work, along with the dense hay constructs of Michael Shaughnessy and the wooded constructions of Barbara Andrus, embrace the gallery and the landscape as a stage for large-scale sculpture that draws strength from the natural materials of our environment (figure 10). These artists share a kinship with British artist Andy Goldsworthy,

Fig. 9. Robert Gober (b. 1954),
*Untitled*, 2015. Plaster, beeswax,
human hair, epoxy putty, cast
gypsum polymer, cast pewter, oil,
enamel paint: 41" × 43" × 7".
© Robert Gober. *Courtesy of
the Matthew Marks Gallery.*

who since the 1970s created environments using earth, wood, and stone. By virtue of scale and locale, such work appeals to new, often younger audiences primed for immersive installations and public venues.

Fig. 10. Michael Shaughnessy (b. 1958), *Confluence and Swirl*, 2011. Hay, twine: 20' × 34' × 22". Lehman College Art Gallery, New York City, New York. *Courtesy of the artist.*

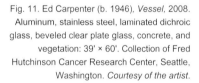

Fig. 11. Ed Carpenter (b. 1946), *Vessel,* 2008. Aluminum, stainless steel, laminated dichroic glass, beveled clear plate glass, concrete, and vegetation: 39' × 60'. Collection of Fred Hutchinson Cancer Research Center, Seattle, Washington. *Courtesy of the artist.*

Dichroic glass and steel may not be the first materials that come to mind when baskets are being discussed, but Ed Carpenter, who specializes in large scale installations, created one called *Vessel* as a "sanctuary" for people to enter and sit in (figure 11). His sculpture, located at Seattle's Fred Hutchinson Cancer Research Center, is a latticework of intersecting lines that form a basket, with three lateral rings to provide additional structure. His homage to the basketball hoop can be easily discerned once one recognizes that the Center was named for basketball great Fred Hutchinson. Carpenter's design includes honeysuckle vines to thread their way up the latticework and enhance the woven effect.[12] To be nestled inside a form of this size is to be quietly ensconced and gently held in a space that also offers light, breeze, and the sound of nature.

In another use of unconventional materials for basket making, Jason Hackenwerth reaches for the sky with his buoyant behemoths made of hundreds and sometimes thousands of colorful latex balloons (figure 12). Hackenwerth's sculptures have been featured at the Los Angeles Natural History Museum, the Guggenheim Museum, and Art Basel Miami Beach. Requiring the work of a team, sometimes crowd-sourced, his sculptures are tied together into basket-like forms like cornucopia and often resemble sea or microscopic creatures. Hackenwerth describes his ephemeral creations as "a journey into the unexpected, if only ever briefly, where viewers may feel transported to a quiet place where everything is possible and nothing more is needed."[13]

Fig. 12. Jason Hackenwerth (b. 1970), *Nucleotide*, 2011. Latex balloons: 28' × 23' × 26'. Long Beach Convention Center, Long Beach California. *Photograph courtesy of the artist.*

Fig. 13. Janet Echelman (b. 1966), *1.26 Durham*, 2015. Spectra fiber, high-tenacity polyester fiber, and interactive colored lighting: 240' × 90' × 46'. Photography by Melissa Henry. *Courtesy of Studio Echelman.*

Larger is the work of Janet Echelman, whose monumental, aerial forms got their start in the late 1990s with fishing nets when she was a Fulbright scholar in Mahaballipuram, India. Nowadays, her sculptures rise several stories in height and can be experienced in locations around the globe (figure 13). Brightly lit and held aloft by cables, her soft, undulating forms sway in the wind and look as much like sea anemones as large openwork bowls. Echelman achieves a subtle balance between structure and space, allowing the forces of nature—whether wind, water, or light—to allow movement within the whole.[14] Echelman employs computer-generated designs and a cadre of fabricators, thereby removing her hand from the process, but with more than a million knots in each project this is truly the work of many hands. In her desire for even greater public participation, the artist has offered viewers control over light projections with mobile devices, and engaged dancers whose movements are digitally connected to the nets. By prioritizing social interaction and community engagement, Echelman holds passersby in a joyful embrace.

When thinking big, it is worth remembering that the first forms of freestanding human shelter were made with naturally available materials and assembled with basket-making techniques. Today's ongoing debates regarding sustainability, climate change, and modern materials, with an assist from Buckminster Fuller's geodesic dome, demonstrate that baskets continue to be a major source of inspiration in construction, its global popularity perhaps best proved by the Bird's Nest (National) Stadium designed by Ai Wei Wei for the 2008 Summer Olympics and Paralympics in Beijing (figure 14).[15]

Fig.14. Ai Weiwei (b. 1957), Pierre de Meuron (b. 1950), Jacques Herzog (b. 1950), and Li Xinggang (b. 1969), Beijing National Stadium, 2003–2008. Photograph by Warren R. M. Stuart, Creative Commons.

Fig. 15. Foster + Partners, Swiss Re Headquarters in London, 1997–2004. Photograph by Aurelien Guichard, Creative Commons.

Since the introduction of strong, lightweight materials like carbon fiber revolutionized designs for airplanes, cars, boats, and even furniture, contemporary artists and architects have pushed beyond old boundaries, joining the tensile strength of carbon fiber with the binding structure afforded by basketry techniques. In 2008, the architectural firm Foster + Partners created a bullet-shaped building for Swiss Re headquarters in London (figure 15). Drawing carbon fiber from an oculus-shaped "start" at the top of the building, the strands spiral out and downward, enveloping a structure that is both light and strong. The power of the woven object is even more striking in the designs of Peter Testa, whose proposed *Carbon Tower* is inextricably bound to the notion that a basket offers the tensile strength to hold a building together (figure 16).[16]

Does Carpenter's *Vessel* qualify as a basket? Or Hackenwerth's and Echelman's airborne sculptures? The Swiss Re building? What about *Big Bambú: You Can't, You Don't and You Won't Stop*, the installation by Doug and Mike Starn on the rooftop of Metropolitan Museum in 2010 that was part sculpture, part architecture, and ongoing performance (figures 17 and 18)?[17] What about the bamboo scaffolding found throughout Asia and a mainstay of construction projects to this day? Is it necessary that these makers, designers, architects, and their works fit into some category, or can they compel us to think more broadly about the field? Basket artists and artists inspired by baskets are re-interpreting construction as well as the interstitial play of light and air that appears between woven elements. Investigating line and space, they explore the tension between interior and exterior, space and time, strength and fragility, self and other. In so doing, they unlock the potential of the basket to bind, free and interrogate the space between.

Fig. 16. Testa & Weiser, *Carbon Tower* (prototype, exterior rendering), 2013. Canadian Centre for Architecture, Montréal. Gift of Peter Testa and Devyn Weiser. © Peter Testa and Devyn Weiser.

Fig. 17. Doug Starn (b. 1961) and Mike Starn (b. 1961), *Big Bambú: You Can't, You Don't, and You Won't Stop*, April 27–October 31, 2010. Bamboo and nylon rope. The Iris and B. Gerald Cantor Roof Garden, Metropolitan Museum of Art. Photograph by Eileen Travell. *Courtesy of the artists.*

Fig. 18. *Big Bambú: You Can't, You Don't, and You Won't Stop* (detail). *Courtesy of the artists.*

ROOTED, REVIVED, REINVENTED:

Basketry in America

*ROOTED, REVIVED, REINVENTED: BASKETRY IN AMERICA* chronicles American basketry from its origins in Native American, immigrant, and slave communities to its presence within the contemporary fine art world. Historical baskets were rooted in local landscapes and shaped by cultural traditions. The rise of the Industrial Revolution and mass production at the end of the nineteenth century led basket makers to create works for new audiences and markets, including tourists, collectors, and fine art museums. Today the story continues. Some contemporary artists seek to maintain and revive traditions practiced for centuries. Others combine age-old techniques with nontraditional materials to generate cultural commentary. Still others challenge viewers' expectations by experimenting with form, materials, and scale. Baskets convey meaning through the artists' selection of materials, the techniques they use, and the colors, designs, patterns, and textures they employ.

*Rooted, Revived, Reinvented* is divided into five sections. "Cultural Origins" presents baskets created with traditional materials and techniques for utilitarian and ritual uses as well as the tourist trade. "The New Basketry" showcases artists who elevated basketry to a fine art by exploring the sculptural and expressive potential of traditional craft media. The remaining sections highlight three dominant strains in the contemporary basketry movement. "Living Traditions" encompasses works that are predicated on historical models but also express the artists' innovative contributions to them. In "Basket as Vessel," artists use the relationship between inside and outside inherent in the vessel form to explore conceptual concerns and generate social commentary. Finally, artists included in "Beyond the Basket" incorporate traditional and nontraditional techniques and materials to question cultural assumptions and address the nature of art itself.

## Part I: Cultural Origins

Although many cultural traditions influence American basketry, its roots are in Native America, Europe, and Africa. While individual groups developed their own forms and iconography, the craft has never been static. Basketry has been practiced and passed down within families and communities, and their makers consistently have responded to the availability of materials as well as regional trade and cultural exchange.

In addition to serving a myriad of utilitarian functions, basket making also played a major role in stimulating identity among many cultural groups. For example, The Akimel O'odham (Pima), like most Native cultures, created functional work such as the *kiaha* (burden basket) as well as ceremonial baskets used during rites like the *Víkita* (Harvest Dance). Irish, Scottish, French, and German settlers in the American northeast and Appalachia cemented their European roots in the New World through the continued production of willow and oak baskets, while African Americans from the South Carolina Lowcountry employed basketry as a means to survive and maintain connections to their cultural history.

Rowena Bradley (Eastern Band Cherokee, 1922-2003), *Flowing Waters Lidded Basket*, early 1990s. River cane: 11" × 8" × 8". *Courtesy of Lambert G. Wilson Collection.*

Eva Queen Wolfe (Eastern Band Cherokee, 1922-2004), *Lidded Double-weave Basket*, 1995. River cane: 9" × 6.5" × 6.5". *Courtesy of Lambert G. Wilson Collection.*

Ojibwe, formerly called Chippewa, *Basket with Lid*, 1900-1940. Birch bark, sweet grass, and porcupine quills: 2.5" × 2.75". *Courtesy of the Kansas City Museum and Union Station Kansas City, Kansas City, Missouri.*

Gullah, *Lunch basket*, circa 1970. Sea grass, pine straw, palmetto: 15" × 12" × 12.15". *Courtesy of the Mathers Museum of World Cultures, Indiana University.*

Marvin S. Peter (Inupiak, 1911-1962), *Baleen Basket with Walrus-head Carving*, circa 1961. Baleen, ivory: 3.5" × 4" × 4". *Courtesy of Lois Russell.*

Paiute, *Water Bottle*, 19th century. Wood, mud, horsehair: 21.25" × 13.25". *Courtesy of the University of Missouri Museum of Anthropology.*

Akimel O'odhamn, formerly called Pima, *Basket*, 1890–1910. Willow and devil's claw: 1.75" × 9.25". *Courtesy of the Kansas City Museum and Union Station Kansas City, Kansas City, Missouri.*

Akimel O'odham, formerly called Pima, *Basket*, 1880–1900. Willow and devil's claw: 2.25" × 14.5". *Courtesy of the Kansas City Museum and Union Station Kansas City, Kansas City, Missouri.*

After George Wharton James, *How to Make Indian and Other Baskets,* 1904. *Wristlets or Cuff Protectors*, early 20th century. Plant fiber: 6.25" × 6.5" × 2.5". *Courtesy of Jo Stealey.*

Quinault, *Basket*, 1903. Spruce root:
1.6" × 2.8". *Courtesy of the University
of Missouri Museum of Anthropology.*

Tlingit, *Berry Basket*, circa 1900.
Spruce root, bear grass: 6" × 8" × 8".
*Courtesy of Lois Russell.*

Tlingit, *Rattle-Top Basket*, circa
1875. Spruce root, bear grass:
3.5" × 5" × 5". *Courtesy of
Lois Russell.*

Central California (possibly Yokuts), *Coil Feather Basket*, circa 1890. Sumac, devil's claw, wool, quail feathers: 6" × 8" × 8". *Courtesy of Lois Russell.*

Modoc, *Quiver*, circa 1900. Tule stems: 17.5" x 4" x 3". *Courtesy of the University of Missouri Museum of Anthropology.*

Alvine Werner (Seven Villages of
the Amana Colonies), *Apple-
Picker Basket*, before 1931.
Cultured willow: 17" × 14" × 14".
*Courtesy of Joanna E. Schanz.*

Shaker, *White Oak Basket*, circa 1860. White oak:
12.5" × 14.25" × 12". *Courtesy of the South Union
Shaker Village, Auburn, Kentucky.*

## Part II: The New Basketry

New basketry emerged on the scene in the 1960s during an explosion of interest in all craft media. Artists were influenced by a confluence of factors, including the back-to-the-landers' creation of handmade products, the feminist movement's celebration of traditional crafts as art, and experimentation with architecturally scaled textiles. In light of all of these factors, artist and curator Mary Butcher concluded that basketry became "one of the most vital movements to emerge in the United States in the middle of the twentieth century."

Ed Rossbach, who coined the term "New Basketry," also helped forge this art movement. As a faculty member at the University of California, Berkeley, he integrated basketry into the Art and Design Curriculum and facilitated its introduction into contemporary art. His study of global weaving and textile traditions, both historical and contemporary, reflected his philosophy that baskets were as sculptural and architectural as the cast bronzes that adorn art museums and the skyscrapers that populate metropolitan cityscapes. Through his generous spirit, he inspired students and colleagues, including Joanne Segal Brandford, Lillian Elliott, Pat Hickman, Gyöngy Laky and others, who made California a hotbed of innovation that spread across the entire United States.

Joanne Segal Brandford (1933-1994), *Shoulder*, circa 1986. Bamboo, paint: 8" × 15" × 9". *Courtesy of Jo Stealey.*

Dorothy Gill Barnes (b. 1927), *Plaited Mulberry-Bark Basket*,
1985. Mulberry bark: 16.5" × 6.75" × 4.75". *Courtesy of the Ohio
Designer Craftsmen Permanent Collection.*

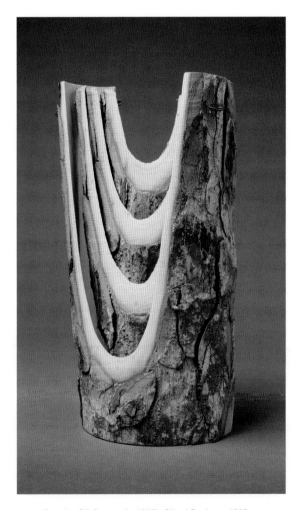

Dorothy Gill Barnes (b. 1927), *Sliced Buckeye*, 1998.
Buckeye wood, wire: 12" × 7" × 5". *Courtesy of the artist.*

Pat Hickman (b. 1941) and Lillian Elliott (1930-1994),
*Alien*, 1986. Gut, fiber, mixed media: 16.5" × 41" × 22".
*Courtesy of Gravers Lane Gallery, Philadelphia.*

Pat Hickman (b. 1941), *Fold*, 2001. Fiber: 20" × 13.5" ×
3.5". *Courtesy of the artist.*

Ferne Jacobs (b. 1942), *Heart Dance*, circa 1995. Waxed
linen: 10" × 14" × 10". *Courtesy of Martin Wice.*

Gyöngy Laky (b. 1944), *Traverser*, 2016.
Branches, commercial wood, screws, acrylic
paint: 24" × 24" × 24". *Courtesy of the artist.*

Kari Lønning (b. 1950),
*Square on Green*, 2011.
Reed: 4.75" × 6.75" × 6.75".
*Courtesy of Polly Allen.*

John McQueen (b. 1943), *Out of True*, 2014. Sticks, wood, waxed linen: 61" × 16" × 12". *Courtesy of the Duane Reed Gallery.*

Norma Minkowitz (b. 1937), *Final Resting Place*, 1987. Fiber, shellac, paint: 9" × 12" × 12". *Courtesy of the artist.*

Leon Niehues (b. 1951), *Emery Cloth Bird*, 2015. 3M emery
cloth, white oak, brass and stainless steel machine screws:
20" × 12" × 15". *Courtesy of the artist.*

Jane Sauer (b. 1937), *At Last*, 1999.
Waxed linen: 22" × 11" × 8". *Courtesy
of the David and Jacqueline Charak
Collection.*

Karyl Sisson (b. 1948), *Mixing Bowls*, 2003.
Vintage cloth tape measures, polymer: 1.75" × 2"
and 2.5" × 3.25" and 3.1" × 4.1". *Courtesy of the
Barn Gallery at Stonover Farm.*

Ed Rossbach (1914-2002), *Mickey Mouse Coil Basket*, 1975.
Synthetic raffia, sea grass: 6" × 9" × 9". *Courtesy of Jim Harris.*

Kay Sekimachi (b. 1926), *Basket with Sphere*, 2003.
Synthetic raffia: 6.5" × 14" × 14". *Courtesy of the artist.*

## Part III: Living Traditions

Basket makers from the Appalachians to the Sierra Nevadas continue the rich cultural histories of their craft while investing them with their personal styles. Some artists come from multi-generational families of basket makers. Others participate in and contribute to traditions through experimentation, apprenticeships, and professional workshops. While the baskets echo their historical antecedents and remain functional, they have become aestheticized objects in private and public collections.

This section showcases artists from the twentieth and twenty-first centuries whose baskets perpetuate and transform the historical traditions in which they work. Responding to the growth of the art market, the loss of conventional materials to environmental devastation, and socioeconomic issues facing their communities, these artists maintain basketry as living traditions.

JoAnn Kelly Catsos (b. 1956), *Charm*, 1997.
Pounded black ash, cherry: 2" × 1.5" x 1.5".
*Courtesy of the artist.*

Joe Feddersen (Confederated Tribes of the Colville Reservation, b. 1953), *Urban Indian Series: Cell Tower*, 2009. Waxed linen, cotton bias tape, cotton thread: 5.5" × 3" × 3". *Courtesy of Laura DeSimone and Bill Roulette;* and *Urban Indian Series: Freeway with HOV*, 2002. Waxed linen, cotton bias tape, cotton thread: 6" × 4" × 4". *Loaned anonymously.*

Pat Courtney Gold (Wasco Tribe, b. 1939), *Yuppie Indian Couple*, 2003. Acrylic yarn, Hungarian hemp: 9" × 7 "x 7". *Courtesy of the artist.*

Katherine Lewis (b. 1957), *Rope Coil*, 2016.
Willow: 7" × 16" x 16". *Courtesy of the artist.*

JoAnn Kelly Catsos (b. 1956), *Cherry Jubilee*, 2004. Black ash
splint, maple, stain: 7" × 9.5" x 9.5". *Courtesy of the National
Basketry Organization.*

José Formoso Reyes (1902-1980), *Nantucket Friendship Purse with Carved Seagull*, 1961. Oak, reed cane, ivory: 9" x 7" x 6.75". *Courtesy of the Nantucket Lightship Basket Museum.*

Leona Waddell (b. 1928), *White Oak Egg Basket*, 2004. White oak, brass pins: 10" × 13" × 8.5". *Courtesy of Scott Gilbert and Beth Hester.*

Cynthia W. Taylor (b. 1950), *Egg Basket with Side Handles (# 2004-1)*, 2004. Hand-split white oak: 5.5" × 9.5" × 8.5". *Courtesy of the artist.*

Stephen Zeh (b. 1952), *Pack Basket*, 2016. Brown ash, copper, silver, shearling, English bridle leather: 18" × 16" × 12". *Courtesy of the artist.*

Aaron Yakim (b. 1949), *Oval "Jesse-Style" Melon Basket*, 1996. Hand-split white oak: 8" × 9.5" × 11". *Courtesy of Scott Gilbert and Beth Hester*.

Jennifer Heller Zurick (b. 1955), *Entwined #1*, 2013. Willow bark, honeysuckle: 10" × 6" × 6". *Courtesy of the artist*.

Jennifer Heller Zurick (b. 1955), *#683-09*, 2009. Willow bark: 8.5" × 7" × 7". *Courtesy of Lila and Richard Bellando*.

Stephen Zeh (b. 1952), *Swing-Handle Apple Basket*, circa 1990. Brown ash: 17" × 14" x 14". *Courtesy of C. Edward and Mary Ellen Wall.*

## Part IV: Baskets as Vessels

The energy generated by the New Basketry fueled artists' exploration into baskets as sculpture. Artists experimented with old and new production methods and embraced a range of materials, from prunings to metals, from thread to filament, from paper to photographs. Their investigations, also motivated by modernism's emphasis on the medium as the primary carrier of meaning, produced a visual language that enabled artists to interrogate American history and culture.

While the works in this section retain their basket-ness, they are not utilitarian. Rather, the relationship between inside and outside inherent in the vessel form allows artists to reference the home, the human body, and the psyche, as well as to explore conceptual issues such as containment, freedom, and functionality itself. Through the selection of specific materials and techniques, artists create aestheticized objects intended for extended contemplation.

Darryl Arawjo (b. 1953) and Karen Arawjo (b. 1953), *Light Vessel CCCXXII*, 2004. Hand-split hickory, maple, monofilament: 8" x 8" × 8". *Courtesy of the artists.*

David Bacharach (b. 1949), *Blue II*, 2011.
Copper: 15" × 12" × 12.5". *Courtesy of the artist.*

Pamela Becker (b. 1943), *Tan with
Black Border*, 2011. Linen, rayon
thread, reed, twine: 8.75" × 15.75" ×
15.75". *Courtesy of the artist.*

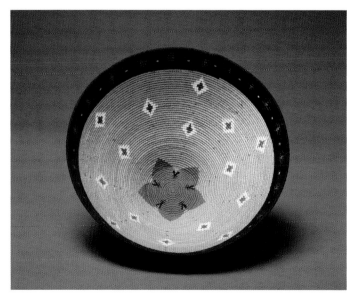

Clay Burnette (b. 1951), *Just Around the Curves*, 2008. Dyed and painted longleaf pine needles, waxed linen thread: 10" × 13" × 17". *Courtesy of the artist.*

Mary Giles (b. 1944), *Sunrise Sentinel*, 2007. Waxed linen, copper, iron: 26" × 6.25" x 6.25". *Courtesy of the artist.*

Jill Nordfors Clark (b. 1939), *April Snow*, 2010. Hog casings, twigs, gesso, silk thread: 30.5" × 19" × 5". *Courtesy of the artist.*

Lindsey Ketterer (b. 1974), *Calendula*, 2015. Window screen, washers, wire: 29" × 13" × 6".
*Courtesy of the artist.*

Steph Gorin (b. 1968), *#bringbackourgirls*, 2015. Steel, paper, vinyl: 48" × 30" × 30". *Courtesy of the artist.*

Shan Goshorn (Eastern Band Cherokee, b. 1957), *Preparing for the Fall*, 2012. Watercolor paper, archival inks, acrylic paint, gold foil: 12.5" × 12.5" × 15.25". *Courtesy of the Shan Goshorn Family*.

Carole Hetzel (b. 1942), *Brendan Basket #309*, 2012. Stainless steel cable, walnut-stained reed: 14.5" × 25" × 25". *Courtesy of the artist*.

Shan Goshorn (Eastern Band Cherokee, b. 1957), *They Were Called Kings* (set of 3), 2013. Watercolor paper, archival inks, acrylic paint: 13.5" × 8.5" × 7". *Courtesy of the Shan Goshorn Family*.

Marilyn Moore (b. 1945), *Balance*, 2014. Copper wire, coated copper wire: 3.5" × 9" × 6". *Courtesy of the artist.*

Deborah Muhl (b. 1957), *Untitled #983*, 1998. Sea grass, sinew, gourd, beads: 9" × 16" × 12". *Courtesy of Lois Russell.*

Bird Ross (b. 1957), *Cinch*, 2016. Vintage
fabric, found fabric, thread: 6" × 9" × 9".
*Courtesy of the artist.*

Lois Russell (b. 1951), *Magic Bus*, 2012.
Waxed linen: 9.25" × 11.5" × 10.5".
*Courtesy of Betsy Rowland.*

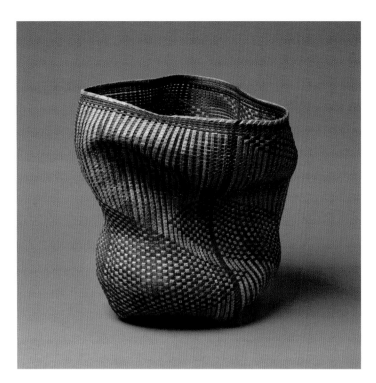

Polly Adams Sutton (b. 1950), *Merrill*, 2007. Western red cedar bark, dyed ash, magnet wire: 11.5" × 10" × 9". *Courtesy of the artist*.

JoAnne Russo (b. 1956), *Porcupine*, 1999.
Black ash, pine needles, porcupine quills:
7.75" × 5.5" × 5.5". *Courtesy of Polly Allen*.

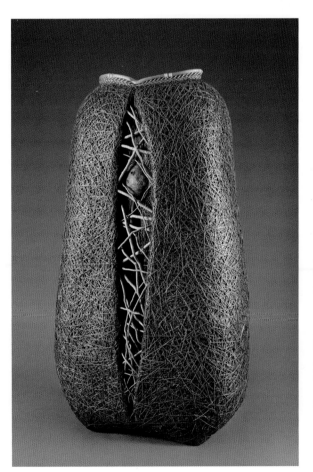

Dawn Nichols Walden (Ojibwe, b. 1949), *Random Order Series: Ties That Bind*, circa
2010. Cedar root, cedar bark, bear grass: 44" × 25" × 15". *Courtesy of Lois Russell*.

## Part V: Beyond the Basket

Current artists bridge the gap between the craft origins of basket making and the medium's new place within sculpture, textile, and installation art. By incorporating traditional and nontraditional techniques and materials and by exploring scale and dynamic form, these artists address a wide variety of ideas and issues, including the visualization of scientific data, cultural appropriation, and environmental politics. In addition, they address the nature of art itself; how form and materials can be the subject of art as well as its meaning; and how art navigates between and among utility, commodity, and the aestheticized object in the fine art world. Their work confirms basketry's status as a significant force in contemporary art.

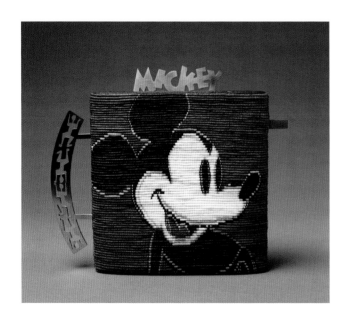

Kate Anderson (b. 1953), *Mickey Mouse Teapot/Warhol-Haring*, 2004. Waxed linen thread, stainless steel: 8.5" × 10.25" × 2". *Courtesy of the artist.*

Kate Anderson (b. 1953), *Lichtenstein
Teapot/Girl with Ribbon*, 2005. Waxed linen,
stainless steel: 8.5" × 9.25" × 1.75". *Courtesy
of David & Jacqueline Charak Collection.*

Lanny Bergner (b. 1952), *Celestial Vessel #7*, 2013. Stainless steel mesh, silicone, leather cord: 60" × 16" × 16". *Courtesy of Snyderman-Works Galleries.*

Nancy Moore Bess (b. 1943), *Kaki Shibu*, 2004. Waxed cotton, waxed linen, persimmon tannin, gessoed foam, dyed cane: 8.5" × 7" × 5.5" and 5" × 5.25" × 4". *Courtesy of browngrotta arts.*

Jerry Bleem (b. 1954), *Burden*, 2011.
Found paper, printed paper, acetate,
staples: 18.75" × 18.25" × 10.25".
*Courtesy of the artist*.

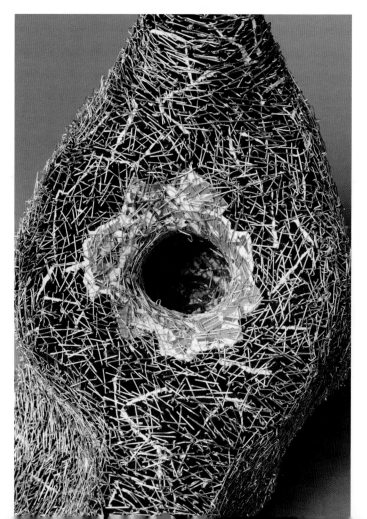

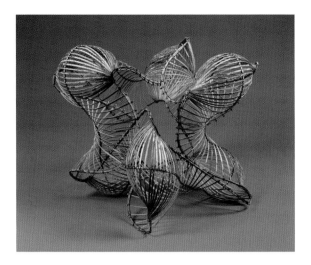

Charissa Brock (b. 1971), *Adagio*, 2012. Tiger bamboo, waxed linen thread: 33" × 31" × 24". *Courtesy of the artist*.

Ann B. Coddington (b. 1963), *Fingerprints*, 2013. Waxed linen, waxed cotton, wool, copper, paper cord, willow, reed, caning, artificial sinew, muslin: dimensions variable. *Courtesy of the artist*.

Ann B. Coddington (b. 1963), *Mother/Memory*, 2015.
Mixed fibers, found objects: dimensions variable.
*Courtesy of the artist.*

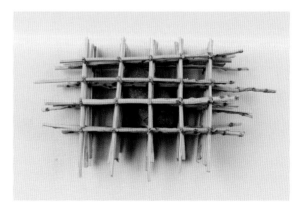

Leah Danberg (b. 1934), *Cock-a-Doodle-Do*, 2013. Waxed linen, acrylic, foam: 16" × 5.5" × 12". *Courtesy of the artist.*

Aron Fischer (b. 1980), *Work*, 2014. Ebonized white oak, walnut, leather, synthetic reed, Egyptian paste, steel: 24" × 48" × 4". *Courtesy of the artist.*

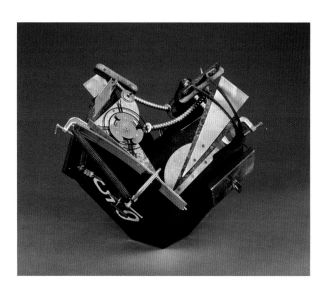

John G. Garrett (b. 1950), *The Builder's Basket*, 1999. Oxidized steel, aluminum, metal findings, c-clamps, springs, yardstick, vintage skate components, louvers, cigarette boxes, house numbers, drawer pull, circuit board, metal mesh, electrical conduit, tin, copper tubing, fan covers, washers, nuts, latches, rivets: 17.75" × 20" × 21". *Courtesy of the artist.*

Carol Eckert (b. 1945), *According to Isidore*, 2015. Linen, wire: 20" × 88" × 5". *Courtesy of the artist.*

Bryant Holsenbeck (b. 1949), *Crows*, 2014. Wire, plastic bags, broken records, string, fabric, found objects: 9" × 16" × 9" and 8" × 17" × 12". *Courtesy of the artist.*

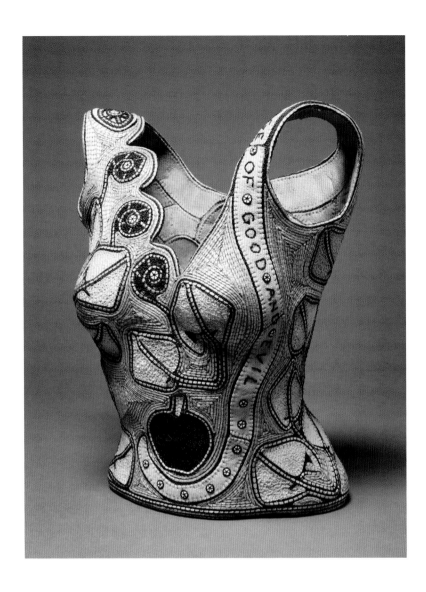

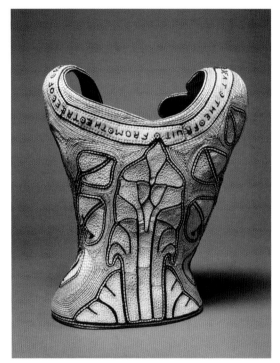

Jan Hopkins (b. 1955), *Forbidden*, 2010.
Grapefruit and cantaloupe peel, yellow cedar
bark, ostrich shell beads, waxed linen: 18" ×
15" × 9". *Courtesy of David and Jacqueline
Charak Collection.*

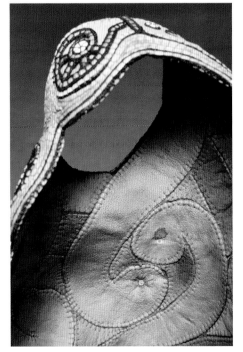

Lissa Hunter (b. 1945), *Pastime: Gardening*, 2005. Paper cord, waxed linen thread, paper, paint, bamboo, fiberboard, drywall compound, found clay pots: 24" × 18" × 3". *Courtesy of the artist.*

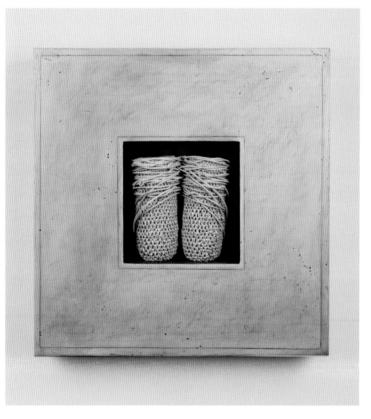

Lissa Hunter (b. 1945), *Duet*, 2008. Raffia, paper cord, rattan, paper, paint, fiberboard, drywall compound: 20" × 20" × 3.75". *Courtesy of the artist.*

Christine Joy (b. 1952), *Wave*,
2013. Willow: 20" × 16" × 10".
*Courtesy of the artist.*

Susan Kavicky (b. 1953), *Sitting*, 2010. Brown ash, fiberboard, oak: 16" × 18.5" × 13".
*Courtesy of Mary Anne Fray.*

Nancy Koenigsberg (b. 1927), *Caught*, 2006. Annealed steel wire, steel rods: 20" × 35" × 25". *Courtesy of the artist.*

Aaron Kramer (b. 1963), *Half and Half*, 2008. Reclaimed street-sweeper bristles, re-sawn hardwoods, washers, wire: 24" × 8" × 8". *Courtesy of the artist.*

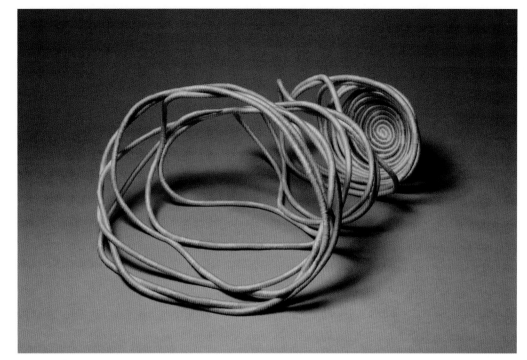

Amy Masters (b. 1984),
*Yellow*, 2013. Cord, yarn:
dimensions variable.
*Courtesy of the artist.*

Dorothy McGuiness (b. 1961),
*Satellite*, 2012. Watercolor
paper, acrylic paint, waxed
linen thread: 12" × 15" × 12".
*Courtesy of the artist.*

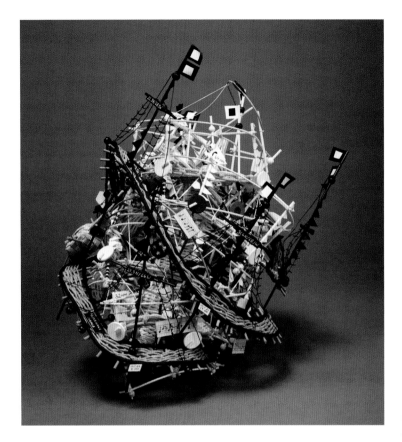

Nathalie Miebach (b. 1972), *The Halloween Grace*, 2015. Fiber rush, paper, wood, weather data: 18" × 18" × 18". *Courtesy of the artist.*

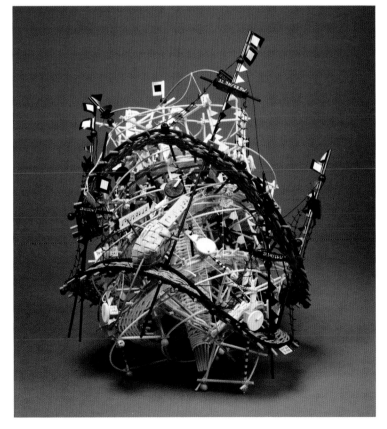

Leon Niehues (b. 1951),
*Bentwood Sphere*, 2015. White
oak, brass and stainless steel
machine screws, natural
walnut-hull dye: 22" × 17" ×
20". *Courtesy of the artist.*

Lois Russell (b. 1951), *5'2"*, 2013. Waxed
linen: 60" x 24" x 1". *Courtesy of the artist.*

Amanda Salm (b. 1961), *Showered with Laughter*, 2008. Horse hair,
natural dyes, metal hanger: 21.5" × 11.5" × 10.5". *Courtesy of the artist.*

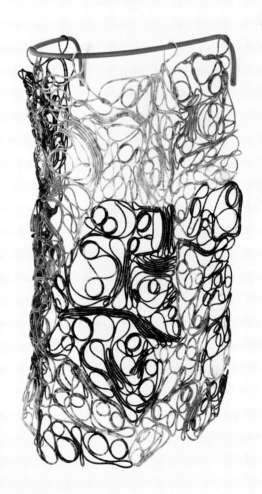

Biba Schutz (b. 1946), *Charlotte
Russe,* 2010. Bronze, copper, steel:
13" × 10" × 10". *Courtesy of the artist.*

Lisa Telford (Haida, b. 1957),
*Summer Night's Do*, 2007. Pounded
red cedar bark, cotton cord, vintage
mother-of-pearl buttons, feathers:
26" × 11". *Courtesy of Martin Wice.*

Lisa Telford (Haida, b. 1957), *Evening Out*, 2007. Red and yellow cedar bark: 5.5" × 3.12" × 8". *Courtesy of Martin Wice.*

Peggy Wiedeman (b. 1946), *Exploring Too*, 2006. Pine needles, Irish waxed linen: 8" × 11" × 9". *Courtesy of the artist.*

# Acknowledgments

*Rooted, Revived, Reinvented: Basketry in America* is the result of a remarkable partnership between the National Basketry Organization (NBO) and the University of Missouri Museum of Art and Archaeology, with special assistance from MU's Departments of Art, Art Education, and Art History and Archaeology.

Special thanks to the National Basketry Organization, its board, and its members for their unflinching support. The project began when Josephine Stealey, then chair of the exhibitions committee, and Lois Russell, then president, casually considered a traveling show that would highlight American basketry.

The project's transformation from idea to reality would not have been possible without the generous support of the University of Missouri's Museum of Art and Archaeology. Its director, Alec Barker, provided advice, guidance, and wisdom at every stage of the process. We also extend our gratitude to Jeffrey Wilcox, registrar and curator of collections; Barbara Smith, chief preparator, and her assistant, Matt Smith; and Cathy Callaway, educator. At the University of Missouri's Museum of Anthropology, Candace Sall, associate curator, and Audrey Gayou, collections manager, allowed us access to their collection and loaned us some wonderful works for the exhibition. Lisa Higgins, director of the Missouri Folk Arts Program, also provided assistance along the way.

We are thankful for the thoughtful contributions from each of the authors included in this volume: Carol Eckert, Jeannine Falino, Sybil E. Gohari, Jason Baird Jackson, Jon Kay, Patricia Malarcher, Margaret Fairgrieve Milanick, and Perry Allen Price. Our gratitude extends to Elissa Auther, Maria Elena Buszek, and Elizabeth Hutchinson as well, who provided advice early in the process.

We are indebted to all the collectors who loaned work for the show, including Polly Allen, Lila and Richard Bellando, David and Jacqueline Charak, Laura DeSimone and Bill Roulette, Mary Ann Fray, Beth Hester and Scott Gilbert, the Shan Goshorn Family, Jim Harris, Betsy Rowland, Lois Russell, Jo Stealey, and Lambert G. Wilson. The generous loans from brown grotta arts, Gravers Lane, Nantucket Lightship Museum, the National Basketry Organization, Ohio Designer Craftsmen, Duane Reed Gallery, Snyderman-Works Gallery, and University of Missouri Museum of Anthropology, have greatly enhanced the depth and breadth of the exhibition. This show would not exist without their willingness to share.

Our heartfelt gratitude extends to the many institutions and organizations that provided financial support: The Windgate Foundation; Center for Craft, Creativity and Design; the National Basketry Organization; and the University of Missouri. Individual "angels" contributed donations in support as well: Polly Allen, Lisa Crane, Emily Dvorin, Mary Anne Fray, Elizabeth Rowland, and additional anonymous donors. We thank, too, the museums and galleries that agreed to host the exhibition: Museum of Art and Archaeology, University of Missouri (Columbia, Missouri); 108 Contemporary (Tulsa, Oklahoma); Lauren Rogers Museum of Art (Laurel, Mississippi); Whatcom Museum (Bellingham, Washington); Houston Center for Contemporary Craft (Houston, Texas); South Dakota Art Museum (Brookings, South Dakota); Fuller Craft Museum (Brockton, Massachusetts); the Ruth Funk Center for Textile Arts at Florida Institute of Technology (Melbourne, Florida); and others.

As the project developed beyond our wildest expectations, we have been honored to work with a stellar team of graduate students—many of whom have long since graduated. Our admiration extends to Rachel Navarro, assistant curator; Patti Shanks, research and communications; Aron Fischer, administrative assistant; Danielle Langdon and Morgan Manning, graphic design; and Stefanie Gerber Darr and Tamryn McDermott, traveling exhibition coordinators.

To say this project has been a collaborative effort is an understatement; it could only have been realized with the vision and tenacity of everyone involved, including the graduate students who enrolled in our Museum Studies courses at MU. The exhibition served as the subject of three courses that included students from the departments of anthropology, art, art education, art history and archaeology, classics, and history (among others). The first group developed the exhibition's focus and structure, the second focused on the armature of the iCatalog, and the third centered on object-centered education in museum and online environments. Their research, writing, and innovative ideas have enriched every aspect of this exhibition, and their voices can be heard in this book as well as in the exhibition text, iCatalog, and museum education materials. These students include Mike Anthony, Kyle Bader, Jennifer Bennett, Leah Bowring, Shirley Boudreaux, Lorinda Bradley, Carina Carbone, Beth Collins, Jenna Covington, Aron Fischer, Julian Foley, Marni Gable, Kaitlyn Garbarino, Billy George, Laura Greeley, Kaitlin Grimes, Gretta Hempelmann, Devyn Hunter, Linda Ingalls, Kalina Irving, Nikos Karabetsos, Kenneth Kircher, Joshua Maier, Kelsey Frady Malone, Morgan Manning, Jeffrey Markworth, Katherine Mascari, Tamryn McDermott, Caleb McMurray, Margaret Milanick, Rachel Navarro, Zachary Nutt, Anthony Pierucci, Rebecca Pursley, Brittany Rancour, Mary Sandbothe, Ekaterina Shevchenko, and Gretchen Stricker.

We have been fortunate that so many of our colleagues at the University of Missouri have embraced the project and contributed their time and expertise. A very special thanks to our photographers, Joe Johnson and Sam Surgener, whose expert eyes and technical acumen resulted in outstanding images for the catalog and promotional materials. Special thanks to Chis Morrey, Zach Nutt, and Nikos Karabetsos. Their design and execution of the feedback station and touch panels have been a wonderful addition to the exhibition. Jean Brueggenjohann led an undergraduate design team that branded the exhibition and designed its prospectus: Zoe Ballam, Jacob Brcic, Danielle Fiesta, Catie Hoemann, Whitney Lockhart, Kristen Karpowicz,

Emmy Russell, Lili Sielert, and Danielle Yuede. Finally, Kathy Unrath and her art education graduate students developed museum education materials to accompany the show: Mike Anthony, Shirley Boudreaux, Abi Creech, Kristin Gantz, Lauren Holland, Michelle Livek, Kari Lomax, Amy Ruopp, Jon Sheltmire, Amy Tuchschmidt, and Danielle Vogel. Nancy Alexander, Curator of Visual Resources in the Department of Art History and Archaeology, provided much-needed insight into the world of digital images and databases.

All kinds of logistical support has been provided by the remarkable administrative team in the Art Department, namely Ferrie Craighead, Marcia Rackley, and Brenda Warren. Gaia Guirl-Stearley's editing of the manuscript and prepress formatting helped make this volume what it is today.

# Notes

## Chapter 1: Introduction: The Story of Contemporary American Basketry

1. On the role of girls and women in factory labor in Indiana, see Peggy Seigel, "Industrial Girls in an Early Twentieth-Century Boomtown: Traditions and Change in Fort Wayne, Indiana, 1900–1920," *Indiana Magazine of History* 99, no. 3: 231–253.

2. On the changing role of handmade baskets during the Industrial Revolution and Great Depression, please see Jon Kay's essay in this volume.

3. Gertrude Ashley and Mildred Ashley, *Raffia Basketry as a Fine Art* (Deerfield: Published by the Authors, 1915), 1–3.

4. On the role of perforated cardboard in the decorative arts, see Kenneth Ames, *Death in the Dining Room and Other Tales of Victorian Culture* (Philadelphia: Temple University Press, 1992).

5. On the Arts and Crafts movement, see Wendy Kaplan, *"The Art that is Life": The Arts and Crafts Movement in America, 1875–1920* (Boston: Museum of Fine Arts, 1987) and Eileen Boris, *Art and Labor: Ruskin, Morris, and the Craftsman Ideal in America* (Philadelphia: Temple University Press, 1989). There have been a number of regional studies, including: Marilee Boyd Meyer, ed., *Inspiring Reform: Boston's Arts and Crafts Movement* (Wellesley, MA: Davis Museum and Cultural Center, 1997); Lawrence Kreisman and Glenn Mason, *The Arts and Crafts Movement in the Pacific Northwest* (Portland, OR: Timber Press, 2007); and Judith A. Barter, *Apostles of Beauty: Arts and Crafts from Britain to Chicago* (Chicago: Art Institute of Chicago, 2009).

6. Madeline Yale Wynne, "Makers of Baskets," *Good Housekeeping* 33, no. 5: 370. *Good Housekeeping* was founded in Holyoke, Massachusetts, in 1885 "to produce and perpetuate perfection—or as near unto perfection as may be attained in the household." http://www.goodhousekeeping.com/institute/about-the-institute/a17940/good–housekeeping–institute–timeline/.

7. Wynne, "Makers of Baskets," 371–373.

8. T. J. Jackson Lears, *No Place of Grace: Antimodernism and the Transformation of American Culture, 1880–1920* (Chicago: University of Chicago Press, 1994).

9. Molly Lee, "Tourism and Taste in Alaska: Collecting Native Art in Alaska at the Turn of the Twentieth Century," in *Unpacking Culture: Art and Commodity in Colonial and Postcolonial Worlds*, ed. Ruth B. Phillips and Christopher B. Steiner (Berkeley: University of California Press, 1999), 273.

10. Otis T. Mason, "Aboriginal American Basketry: Studies in a Textile Art Without Machinery," *Annual Report of the U.S. National Museum* (Washington, DC: Smithsonian Institution, 1902): 187–188.

11. Rubie Watson, "Opening the Museum: The Peabody Museum of Archaeology and Ethnography," Occasional Papers, Vol. 1, Peabody Museum of Archaeology and Ethnography, Harvard University (Cambridge, MA: President and Fellows of Harvard College, 2001), 5.

12. George Wharton James, *How to Make Indian and Other Baskets* (New York: Frank M. Covert, 1903), 11. Wharton's sentiments were repeated by countless others. In her introduction, for example,

Wynne proclaimed: "In singleness of intent [the Indian woman of three centuries ago] wove her basket for use, and she made it strong because of her pride in her work. She made it beautiful because this basket, the product of her mind and hands, was the only permanent expression of her sense of the esthetic. With an antique basket before one it seems almost an impertinence to think of or to speak of basket making in our own day." Wynne, "Makers of Baskets," 369.

13. Eileen Boris, *Art and Labor: Ruskin, Morris, and the Craftsman Ideal in America* (Philadelphia: Temple University Press, 1989), 82.

14. William S. Marten, *Inexpensive Basketry* (Peoria, IL: Manual Arts Press, 1912).

15. Herbert J. Hall and Mertice M. C. Buck, *The Work of Our Hands: A Study of Occupations for Invalids* (New York: Muffat, Yard, and Company, 1915), 13.

16. William Rush Dunton, Jr., *Occupation Therapy: A Manual for Nurses* (New York: W. B. Saunders Company, 1915), 9.

17. Jennifer Laws, "Crackpots and Basket-Cases: A History of Therapeutic Work and Occupation," *History of Human Sciences* 24, no. 2: 70.

18. On Estelle Reed's Native Industries curriculum, please see Elizabeth Hutchinson, *The Indian Craze: Primitivism, Modernism, and Transculturation in American Art, 1890–1915* (Durham: Duke University Press, 2009), particularly Chapter 2, "The White Man's Indian Art," and Estelle Reed, *Course of Study for Indian Schools of the United States* (Washington, DC: Government Printing Office, 1901), 56–57.

19. For period histories, see Henry Wilder Foote, "The Penn School on St. Helena Island," *The Southern Workman* 31, no. 5: 263–270, and Rosa B. Cooley, *School Acres: An Adventure in Rural Education* (New Haven: Yale University Press, 1930).

20. *Annual Report of the Penn Normal, Industrial, and Agricultural School of St. Helena Island, 1905–1906* (Philadelphia: The John C. Winston Co., 1906), 17. According to folklorist Elsie Clews Parsons, Penn School helped revive the basketry industry and diversified it. Parsons, *Folk Lore of the Sea Islands, South Carolina* (Cambridge, MA: American Folk Lore Society, 1923), 208.

21. Quoted in Dale Rosengarten, *Row Upon Row: Sea Grass Baskets of the South Carolina Lowcountry*, reprint edition (Columbia, SC: University of South Carolina, 1994), 28. Interestingly, the basket making program at the Penn School maintained the historic division of labor among eighteenth and nineteenth century African American basket makers.

22. Ruth B. Phillips and Christopher B. Steiner, "Art, Authenticity, and the Baggage of Cultural Encounter" in *Unpacking Culture*, 4–6.

23. Hutchinson, *The Indian Craze*.

24. Leah Dilworth, *Imagining Indians in the Southwest: Persistent Visions of a Primitive Past* (Washington, DC: Smithsonian Institution Press, 1996), 82.

25. See also Jonathan Batkin, "Tourism Is Overrated: Pueblo Pottery and the Early Curio Trade, 1880–1910," in *Unpacking Culture*, 282–297, 367–369; Ruth B. Phillips, *Trading Identities: The*

*Souvenir in Native North American Art from the Northeast, 1700–1900* (Seattle: University of Washington Press, 1999); and Hutchinson, *The Indian Craze.*

26. "An Indian Cozy Corner," *Pearson's* (October 1902), np.

27. "The Basketry of the Northwest," *Papoose* (July 1903): 3, 6–7.

28. Phillips and Steiner, "Art, Authenticity, and the Baggage of Cultural Encounter," 4.

29. Susan C. Power, *Art of the Cherokee: Prehistory to the Present* (Athens, GA: University of Georgia Press, 2007). See Chapter 4 in particular, "New Markets and Revitalization." Any number of Native artists could be cited here, including Elizabeth Hickox (Karuk). See Marvin Cohodas, "Elizabeth Hickox and Karuk Basketry: A Study in Debates on Innovation and Paradigms of Authenticity," in *Unpacking Culture,* 143–161.

30. "The Washoe Baskets," *Papoose* (March 1903), 15–16. On the Cohns' marketing of Keyser, see Marvin Cohodas, "Louisa Keyser and the Cohns: Mythmaking and Basket Making in the American West" in *The Early Years of Native American Art History*, ed. Janet Catherine Berlo (Seattle: University of Washington Press, 1992), 88–133.

31. Jo Ann Nevers, "Dat So La Lee (Dabuda or Louisa Keyser, Washoe, 1835–1925)," *Infinity of Nations: Art and History in the Collection of the National Museum of the American Indian*, accessed July 29, 2016, http://nmai.si.edu/exhibitions/infinityofnations/california–greatbasin/118261.html#about.

32. For a study of how tourist baskets became part of native traditions in the American south, see Jason Baird Jackson's essay in this volume. For an examination of how a variation on a regional tradition became international by an artist's embrace of commercial trends and contemporary fashion, see Margaret Fairgrieve Milanick's contribution to the catalog.

33. Kate Carter, "Making History: Cherokee Indian Fair," 2009, Craft Revival: Shaping Western North Carolina Past and Present, A Project of Hunter Library Digital Initiatives at Western Carolina University, accessed May 19, 2017, http://www.wcu.edu/library/DigitalCollections/CraftRevival/about/index.html.

34. For a discussion of how Lowcountry "show baskets" became part of the fine art world, see Sybil E. Gohari's essay in this volume.

35. George Wharton James, *Indian Basketry*, 2nd ed. (New York: Henry Malkan, 1902), 175.

36. Arthur Wesley Dow, *Composition: A Series of Exercises in Art Structure for the Use of Students and Teachers*, 7th ed. (New York: Doubleday, Page, and Company, 1913), 4.

37. JoAnn Mancini, *Pre-Modernism: Art-World Change and American Culture from the Civil War to the Armory Show* (Princeton, NJ: Princeton University Press, 2005).

38. Katherine Caldwell with the assistance of Faye Harper, *From Mountain Hands: The Story of Allanstand Craft Shop's First 100 Years* (Asheville: Southern Highland Craft Guild, 1996).

39. Neil Harris, *Cultural Excursions: Marketing Appetites and Cultural Tastes in Modern America* (Chicago: University of Chicago Press, 1990).

40. Arthur Wesley Dow, "Ipswich As It Should Be," *Ipswich Chronicle,* May 9, 1891. Quoted in Frederick C. Moffatt, "Arthur Wesley Dow and the Ipswich School of Art," *New England Quarterly* 49, no. 3.

41. Van Wyck Brooks, "On Creating a Usable Past," *Dial,* April 11, 1918, 337–341.

42. Hutchinson, *The Indian Craze*, 3–4. See also W. Jackson Rushing, *Native American Art and the New York Avant-Garde: A History of Cultural Primitivism* (Austin: University of Texas Press, 1995) and Philip J. Deloria, *Playing Indian* (New Haven: Yale University Press, 1998).

43. Quoted in Robert Fay Schrader, *The Indian Arts and Crafts Board: An Aspect of New Deal Indian Policy* (Albuquerque: University of New Mexico Press, 1983), 13.

44. On American cultural nationalism, see Wanda Corn, *The Great American Thing: Modern Art and National Identity, 1915–1935* (Berkeley: University of California Press, 1999) and Benjamin Filene, *Romancing the Folk: Public Memory and American Roots Music* (Chapel Hill: University of North Carolina Press, 2000). On the politics of folk art, see Eugene W. Metcalf, Jr., "The Politics of the Past in American Folk Art History," in *Folk Art and Art Worlds*, eds. John Michael Vlach and Simon J. Bonner (Logan, UT: Utah State University Press, 1992), 27–50.

45. For an overview of the *Index of American Design*, see Virginia Tuttle Clayton, "Picturing a Usable Past" in *Drawing on America's Past: Folk Art, Modernism, and the Index of American Design,* ed. Virginia Tuttle Clayton et al. (Washington, DC: National Gallery of Art, 2002): 1–43.

46. Cahill argued against the inclusion of Native American arts because other agencies were pursuing that documentary work, and the lack of African American material can be partly explained by the lack of Southern state participation in the project. Nevertheless, culture brokers worked to locate America's heritage in the customs they believed constituted the nation's proper artistic and racial genealogy. See Ericka Doss, "American Folk Art's Distinctive Character: *The Index of American Design* and New Deal Notions of Cultural Nationalism," in Clayton et al., *Drawing on America's Past*, 60–73; Thomas L. Riedel, "Tradition Reconfigured: Juan A. Sanchez, Patrocino Barela, and New Deal Saint Making" in *Transforming Images: New Mexican Santos In-Between World*, eds. Claire Farago and Donna Pierce (State College, PA: Penn State University Press, 2006).

47. Elizabeth Stillinger, "From Attics, Sheds, and Secondhand Shops: Collecting Folk Art in America" in *Drawing on America's Past*, 54.

48. Glenn Adamson, "Serious Business: The Designer-Craftsman in Postwar California" in *California Design, 1930–1965: Living in a Modern Way,* ed. Wendy Kaplan (Boston: MIT Press, 2011), 203–231.

49. Elissa Auther, *String, Felt, Thread: The Hierarchy of Art and Craft in American Art* (Minneapolis: University of Minnesota Press, 2010), 10.

50. According to Walter Gropius, "There is no difference between the artist and the craftsman, the artist is merely a craftsman lifted to a higher plane." Quoted in Irene Waller, *Textile Sculptures* (Parkwest, FL: Taplinger, 1977), 7. For a more thorough discussion of the rise of the American studio craft movement, see Perry Allan Price in this volume.

51. Janet Koplos and Bruce Metcalf, *Makers: A History of American Studio Craft* (Asheville: Center for Craft, Creativity & Design, 2010).

52. Laurel Reuter, "The Walls Come Down: The Crafting of Art in America," in *Baskets: Redefining Volume and Meaning*, ed. Pat Hickman (Honolulu: University of Hawaii Press, 1993).

53. Waller, *Textile Sculptures*, 6.

54. Maria Elena Buszek, *Extra/Ordinary Craft and Contemporary Art* (Durham, NC: Duke University Press, 2011), 4.

55. Ed Rossbach, *The New Basketry* (New York: Van Nostrand Reinhold, 1976).

56. Auther, *String, Felt, Thread*, xxi.

57. Mildred Constantine and Jack Lenor Larsen, *Beyond Craft: The Art Fabric* (New York: Van Nostrand Reinhold, 1973), 31.

58. For a closer look at basketry's emergence as an art movement in the 1970s, 80s, and 90s, see Patricia Malarcher in this volume.

59. Rossbach graduated from Cranbrook in weaving and ceramics using the G.I. Bill according to Koplos and Metcalf, *Makers,* 265–267.

60. The West Coast became a fertile climate for artists. The University of California at Berkeley and Los Angeles, Pond Farm Workshops, the California School of Arts and Crafts, and many non-academic centers dotted the state. Waller, *Textile Sculptures*, 10.

61. Rossbach, *The New Basketry*, 86.

62. Dona Meilach and Dee Menagh, *Basketry Today with Materials from Nature* (New York: Crown Publishers, 1979).

63. Nicholas Bell, *A Measure of the Earth: The Cole-Ware Collection of American Baskets* (Chapel Hill, NC: University of North Carolina Press, 2013), 28.

64. Judy Chicago, *Through the Flower: My Struggle as a Woman Artist* (New York: Doubleday, 1975).

65. Mirra Bank, *Anonymous was a Woman: A Celebration in Words and Images and the Women Who Made It* (New York: St. Martin's Press, 1979).

66. Rose Silvka, "The American Craftsman," *Craft Horizons* 24 (May–June, 1964): 32. The back-to-the-land movement of the 1960s and 1970s was a modern iteration of Utopian ideals of the late nineteenth and early twentieth centuries.

67. While this survey of contemporary basketry focuses primarily on American artists and individual objects, essays by Carol Eckert and Jeannine Falino in this volume expand the discussion by looking at artists outside the United States; basketry's participation in installation and site-specific work; and basketry's entry into the arenas of architecture and design.

68. Bell, *A Measure of the Earth*, 28.

69. Ibid, 22–23.

70. Ibid, 22–23.

71. Rachel Nash Law and Cynthia W. Taylor, *Appalachian White Oak Basketmaking: Handing Down the Basket* (Knoxville: University of Tennessee Press, 1991).

72. Beth Hester, "Bearing White Oak Tradition" (unpublished manuscript, 2016).

73. From an interview with John McGuire in Bell, *A Measure of the Earth,* 30.

74. Ibid, 30.

75. Lucy Lippard, *Mixed Blessings: New Art in a Multicultural America* (New York: Pantheon, 1990).

76. Auther, *String, Felt, Thread,* 5–6.

77. Christine Joy, *Home,* accessed August 16, 2016, http://www.christinejoywillow.com/index.html.

78. Cited in Koplos and Metcalf, *Makers,* 266.

79. Ann B. Coddington, accessed May 12, 2017, http://ux1.eiu.edu/~abcoddington/portfolio/.

80. Susi Gablik, *The Reenchantment of Art* (New York: Thames & Hudson, 1995).

## Chapter 2: Native American Basketry from the Multicultural South: Craft, Labor, and Heritage

1. For more about the Native American peoples of the Southern United States, see Raymond D. Fogelson, ed., *Handbook of North American Indians*, Vol. 14. (Washington, DC: Government Printing Office, 2004).

2. For more about the similarities between the American Southeast and Amazonia, see John M. Goggin, "Plaited Basketry in the New World," *Southwestern Journal of Anthropology* 5, no. 2: 165–168. For an in-depth study of an Amazonian basketry tradition, see David M. Guss, *To Weave and Sing: Art, Symbol, and Narrative in the South American Rain Forest* (Berkeley: University of California Press, 1990). For an illustration of Asian bamboo basketry and its formal similarities to the cane basketry of the Southeast, see Louise Allison Cort and Nakamura Kenji, *A Basketmaker in Rural Japan* (Washington, DC: Smithsonian Institution, 1994). There is no major study of contemporary Chinese work baskets in English. For an account of Chinese basketry that emphasizes elite forms over the work baskets that share the most with the cane baskets of the Native South, see Simon Kwan, *Chinese Basketry* (Hong Kong: Muwen Tang Fine Arts Publications, 2010).

3. When discussing technical issues in the native basketry of the South, I rely upon the technical analysis developed by J. M. Adovasio, *Basketry Technology: A Guide to Identification and Analysis* (Walnut Creek, CA: Left Coast Press, 2010). My focus here is on basketry practices that are rooted within contemporary native communities and vernacular practices that are experienced locally and transmitted informally. I also recommend Sandy Heslop, ed., *Basketry: Making Human Nature* (Norwich: University of East Anglia, 2011); Betty J. Duggan, "Baskets of the Southeast" in *By Native Hands: Woven Treasures from the Lauren Rogers Museum of Art*, ed. Stephen Cook (Laurel, MS: Lauren Rogers Museum of Art, 2005), 26–72; Marshall Gettys, ed., *Basketry of the Southeastern Indians* (Idabel, OK: Museum of the Red River, 1984); J. Marshall Gettys, "Southeast" in *Woven Worlds: Basketry from the Clark Field Collection*, ed. Lydia L. Wyckoff (Tulsa: Philbrook Museum of Art, 2001), 173–191; and Jason Baird Jackson, "Southeastern

Indian Basketry in the Gilcrease Museum Collection," *American Indian Art* 25, no. 4: 46–55. Key sources for the river cane basketry of the region include Dayna Bowker Lee and H. F. Gregory, eds., *The Work of Tribal Hands: Southeastern Indian Split Cane Basketry* (Natchitoches, LA: Northwestern State University Press, 2006) and Dayna Bowker Lee and H. F. Gregory, eds., *Proceedings of the Southeastern Indian Basketry Gathering* (Natchitoches, LA: Northwestern State University, 2002).

4. For more on Eastern Cherokee basketry, see Sarah H. Hill, *Weaving New Worlds: Southeastern Cherokee Women and Their Basketry* (Chapel Hill: University of North Carolina Press, 1997). For the full range of Cherokee crafts in both North Carolina and Oklahoma, see Susan C. Power, *Art of the Cherokee: From Prehistory to the Present* (Athens, GA: University of Georgia Press, 2007). For more on Mississippi Choctaw basketry, see Bill Brescia and Carolyn Reeves, *By the Work of Our Hands: Choctaw Material Culture* (Philadelphia, MS: Choctaw Heritage Press, 1982). Brescia and Reeves' volume is especially important because it documents oak-splint basketry among the Mississippi Choctaw as well as the better-known river cane basketry of this community.

5. A rich resource dealing with the European American tradition of oak-splint basketry in Appalachia is Rachel Nash Law and Cynthia W. Taylor, *Appalachian White Oak Basketmaking: Handing Down the Basket* (Knoxville: University of Tennessee Press, 1991). Lucreaty Clark (1904–1986), a maker of white oak baskets in northern Florida, is among the best-documented African American makers of such baskets. See "Lucreaty Clark, White Oak Basket Maker: Photos and History," *Florida Memory,* accessed November 14, 2015, https://www.floridamemory.com/onlineclassroom/lucreaty/photos/.

6. For more on Florida Seminole basketry, both plaited work baskets and coiled market crafts, see David M. Blackard, *Patchwork and Palmettos: Seminole/Miccosukee Folk Art since 1820* (Fort Lauderdale: Fort Lauderdale Historical Society, 1990); Kathleen Deagan, "An Early Seminole Cane Basket," *Florida Anthropologist* 30, no. 1: 28–33; Kathleen Deagan, ed., *Florida Basketry, Continuity and Change: An Exhibit Featuring Both Traditional and Contemporary Florida Basketry Forms* (White Springs, FL: Florida Folklife Program, 1981); and Patsy West "Glade Cross Mission: An Influence on Florida Seminole Arts and Crafts," *American Indian Art* 9, no. 4: 58–67. For more on coiled basketry of the Sea Islands, see Dale Rosengarten, Theodore Rosengarten, Enid Schildkrout, and Judith Ann Carney, *Grass Roots: African Origins of an American Art* (New York: University of Washington Press, 2008).

7. See also Stephanie Anna May, "Alabama-Coushatta Pine Needle Basketry: A Meaningful Practice" (master's thesis, University of Texas, Austin, 1993), and Koasati Language Committee, *Ko·was·saa·ti Nas·ma·thaa·li A·saa·la / Coushatta Animal Baskets* (Kinder, LA: Koasati Language Committee, n.d.).

8. Shawna Cain, "Buckbrush: A Cherokee Source for Basketry," *Cherokee Phoenix,* December 3, 2009, accessed November 17, 2015, http://www.cherokeephoenix.org/Article/index/3462.

9. My use of the concept of heritage is shaped by recent work in folklore studies and emphasizes self-consciousness of cultural form, its links to identity, and a sense that active effort is required to perpetuate something that is seen as valuable.

10. Sammy Fretwell, "River Cane Could Stand Tall Again," *The State* (Columbia, SC), August 21, 2011, 35, accessed November 15, 2015, http://infoweb.newsbank.com/resources/doc/nb/news/13943C9C15564BA8?p=AWNB; "Canebrake Restoration," accessed November 15, 1015, http://www.rivercane.msstate.edu/research/restoration/; and Sean Gantt, "Rivercane Restoration: Linking Cultural, Biological, and Economic Values," accessed November 15, 2015, https://www.youtube.com/watch?v=4cXaHHUN43I. The environmental concerns of basket makers from a number of Southern communities are conveyed in Lee and Gregory, *The Work of Tribal Hands*, especially in Section II: "Partnerships and Environmental Issues."

11. "Cultural Classes," Cherokee Heritage Center, accessed November 17, 2015, http://www.cherokeeheritage.org/cultural-outreach/cultural-classes/. See also Will Chavez, "Cherokee Basket Maker Shares Her Talent," *Cherokee Phoenix,* September 30, 2004, accessed November 17, 2015, http://www.cherokeephoenix.org/Article/index/679; Anonymous, "World's Largest Cherokee Basket Nears Completion," *Cherokee Phoenix,* April 18, 2012, accessed November 17, 2015, http://www.cherokeephoenix.org/Article/index/6178; Will Chavez, "Program Teaches Basket Making from Start to Finish," *Cherokee Phoenix,* September 5, 2014, accessed November 17, 2015, http://www.cherokeephoenix.org/Article/index/8494; Roger Graham, "Cherokee National Treasure Shares Basket Weaving Expertise," *Cherokee Phoenix,* February 4, 2015, accessed November 17, 2015, http://www.cherokeephoenix.org/Article/index/9051; and "TCCO to Host Meeting, Basket Weaving Class Oct. 6," *Cherokee Phoenix,* October 5, 2015, accessed November 17, 2015, http://www.cherokeephoenix.org/Article/index/9686.

12. Cherokee National Cultural Arts Department and Cherokee Heritage Center, "The Lost Arts Program—1988" (program, circa 2010), accessed November 17, 2015, http://www.cherokeeheritage.org/wp-content/uploads/2013/08/ProgramWeb.pdf.

13. Oklahoma Native American Basketweavers Association, accessed November 17, 2015, http://onaba.org/; Cherokee Heritage Center, accessed November 17, 2015, http://www.cherokeeheritage.org/; and Five Civilized Tribes Museum, accessed May 17, 2017, http://www.fivetribes.org/.

## Chapter 3: Coiled Baskets of the South Carolina Lowcountry: Who Knew the Art World Would Embrace Baskets as Works of Art?

1. Throughout this paper, reference to coiled basketry utilizes the following distinction made by historian Dale Rosengarten: "The bulrush 'work' basket, once essential to rice production and traditionally made by men, almost disappeared. Sweetgrass 'show' baskets, on the other hand, based on household forms and made primarily by women, began to be produced for a new

market, leading to the artistic efflorescence taking place today." Dale Rosengarten, "Missions and Markets: Sea Island Basketry and the Sweetgrass Revolution," in *Grass Roots*, ed. Dale Rosengarten, Theodore Rosengarten, Enid Schildkrout, and Judith Ann Carney, 128.

2. James E. Newton writes, "Slave art was an art of anonymity—an art which rose from slavery in the form of skilled handicrafts—an art descended from the remoteness of African imagery and later channeled as a functional aesthetic" in "Slave Artisans and Craftsmen: The Roots of Afro-American Art," in *The Other Slaves, Mechanics, Artisans and Craftsmen*, ed. James E. Newton and Ronald L. Lewis (Boston: G.K. Hall & Co., 1978), 233.

3. Many of the plant fibers, palm, and grasses used in this production grew in Africa during this time. William S. Pollitzer, *The Gullah People and Their African Heritage* (Athens, GA: University of Georgia Press, 1999), 182.

4. Specifically, the fanner basket was used to hold and throw the rice into the air so that the wind could blow away the debris. Pollitzer, *The Gullah People and Their African Heritage*, 182.

5. Rosengarten, *Row Upon Row,* 9.

6. Ibid.

7. Baskets were so essential to rice production that plantation owners demanded higher prices for slaves skilled in coiled basketry production. The *Charleston Gazette and Advertiser* announced in an advertisement on February 15, 1791, "A good jobbin carpenter and an excellent basket maker." The implication here is that basket making is a valuable skill, and once an individual could no longer work in the fields, he could still continue to produce baskets. See Pollitzer, *The Gullah People and Their African Heritage*, 182.

8. This shift coincides with the automation of rice production and eventually its outsourcing to other countries. Rosengarten further acknowledges this aspect of the changing history: "African American sea grass basketry has evolved over 300 years from an agricultural and household craft practiced primarily in the slave quarters of Lowcountry plantations to a modern art form produced for sale." Rosengarten, *Row Upon Row,* 18.

9. Rosengarten, "Missions and Markets," 128.

10. Gerald Davis explains, "New residential developments, shopping centers, recreational centers, and the like are all using areas of land that once bountifully supplied basketry materials." Gerald Davis, "Afro-American Coil Basketry in Charleston County, South Carolina: Affective Characteristics of an Artistic Craft in a Social Context," in *Afro-American Folk Arts and Crafts*, ed. William Ferris (Boston: G.K. Hall & Co., 1983), 244.

11. Rosengarten, *Row Upon Row,* 33.

12. Judge Dennis Auld, too, purchased many baskets for his friend "Doc" Lachichotte, who, in turn, sold them in his hammock shop located on the beach resort of Pawley's Island and specializing in local craftwork. Not only did Lachichotte sell the baskets, but he also produced a brochure that described the baskets as "reminiscent" objects that "will be relegated to the lost arts,"

thereby attempting to imbue the baskets with an air of a bygone product, soon to be unavailable. Rosengarten, *Row Upon Row,* 38.

13. Davis, "Afro-American Coil Basketry," 244.

14. South Carolina Information Highway (SCIWAY), "Where to Find Sweetgrass Baskets Today," accessed July 15, 2016, http://www.sciway.net/facts/sweetgrass-baskets.html.

15. Patricia Jones-Jackson, *When Roots Die: Endangered Traditions of the Sea Islands* (Athens, GA: University of Georgia Press, 1987), 18. As an aside, additional contemporary reception reveals focus on a number of factors: "Mary Jackson brings the best of two worlds to her art—a rich cultural heritage and a contemporary artistic vision that merge in the creation of her uniquely beautiful sweetgrass baskets." Roberta Kefalos, "Sweetgrass Baskets by Mary Jackson" (pamphlet, Gibbs Museum of Art, n.d.), 1.

16. See, for example, Lucy Lippard, *Mixed Blessings: New Art in a Multicultural America* (New York: The New Press, 2000).

17. "Mary Jackson, Fiber Artist," MacArthur Fellows Program, published January 27, 2008, accessed October 1, 2015, https://www.macfound.org/fellows/800/.

18. Quoted in Sokolitz, "Sweetgrass Baskets by Mary Jackson."

19. See interview with Joyce Lovelace, "Root and Branch," *American Craft,* published March 16, 2015, accessed October 1, 2015, http://craftcouncil.org/magazine/article/root-and-branch.

20. Quoted in Sokolitz, "Sweetgrass Baskets by Mary Jackson."

21. "Meet the 2008 MacArthur Fellows," MacArthur Foundation, accessed October 1, 2015, https://www.macfound.org/fellows/class/2008/.

22. "Mary Jackson, Fiber Artist," MacArthur Fellows Program.

23. Susan Sully, "Dream Weaver: Artist, Teacher, and Activist Mary Jackson Has Helped Revitalize South Carolina's Sweetgrass Basketmaking Tradition," *Southern Accents* (September/October 2002): 102–106.

24. Interview with Lovelace, "Root and Branch."

25. Ibid.

26. Marguerite S. Middleton and Mary A. Jackson. "Sweetgrass Baskets of Mount Pleasant, South Carolina" (Mt. Pleasant, SC: 2002), cover.

27. For example, one of Jackson's sweetgrass baskets is described in literature produced by the Renwick Gallery with the following: "The unbound basket handle bursts forth, while the intricate weaving of palmetto, bulrush and sweetgrass creates exquisite light and dark patterns. By exaggerating the size and curve of the basket handle . . . Jackson . . . creates an intensely elegant form." "The Renwick Invitational: Five Women in Craft," Smithsonian American Art Museum, revised January 15, 2011, accessed March 18, 2005, http://www.tfaoi.com/aa/laa.

28. Kenneth Trapp. "Mary Jackson, Biography," Smithsonian American Art Museum, accessed March 18, 2005, http://www.americanart.si.edu/search/artist_bio.

29. Bo Peterson, "S.C. May Designate Sweetgrass Basket as Official 'State Handcraft,'" *Post and Courier* (Charleston, SC), February 4, 2005, accessed March 18, 2005.

30. See "South Carolina," accessed July 25, 2016, http://www.netstate.com/states/symb/crafts/sc_sweet_grass_basket.htm.

31. Angela Rucker, "Festival Helps Promote a S. C. Artistic Tradition," *Post and Courier* (Charleston, SC), June 30, 1995, accessed March 18, 2005.

32. Linda L. Meggett, "Basket Weavers Caught in a Bind," *Post and Courier* (Charleston, SC), February 22, 1999, accessed March 18, 2005.

## Chapter 4: The Oak-Rod Baskets of Brown County, Indiana

1. For a detailed description of this creative process, see: Rosemary O. Joyce, *A Bearer of Tradition: Dwight Stump, Basketmaker* (Athens: University of Georgia Press, 1989). Joyce discusses the oak-rod baskets made by an Ohio tradition bearer. A comprehensive survey of basket makers is found in: Rachel Nash Law and Cynthia W. Taylor, *Appalachian White Oak Basketmaking: Handing Down the Basket* (Knoxville: University of Tennessee Press, 1991).

2. Henry Hovis's father, John Hovis (1784–1858), was born in York County, Pennsylvania. The 1850 census lists his occupation as a "basket maker." For more about the Hovis family, see: Kenneth J. Reeve and Helen H. Reeve, "Henry Hovis," in *Family Studies of Brown County, Indiana #113* (1998).

3. Ping was a vernacular photographer who provided photographic services for his neighbors in southern Brown County. W. Douglas Hartley, *Otto Ping: Photographer of Brown County, Indiana 1900–1940* (Indianapolis: Indiana Historical Society, 1994).

4. For more about Hubbard and his "Abe Martin" cartoons, see: Davis S. Hawes, *The Best of Kin Hubbard: Abe Martin's Sayings and Wisecracks, Abe's Neighbors, His Almanack, Comic Drawings* (Bloomington: Indiana University Press, 1995). While based mostly on the cartoonist's childhood memories from Ohio, his work stoked urban interest in what many saw as the peculiar people in Brown County.

5. For more about the Brown County art colony, see: Lyn Letsinger-Miller, *The Artists of Brown County* (Bloomington: Indiana University Press, 1994).

6. John Kay, "Oak-Rod Baskets in Brown County: Historic Photographs of a Craft Tradition" in *International Oaks* 25, no. 1 (2014): 85–92; and Kay, "A Picture of an Old Country Store: The Construction of Folklore in Everyday Life" in *Museum Anthropology Review* 4, no. 2 (2010), accessed April 5, 2017, https://scholarworks.iu.edu/journals/index.php/mar/article/view/914/1032.

7. "Ludlow Seeks Means of Preserving Simplicity of Brown County Natives," *Indianapolis Star*, January 13, 1941, 16.

8. For more about Hohenberger and his photography, see: Dillon Bustin, *If You Don't Outdie Me: The Legacy of Brown County* (Bloomington: Indiana University Press, 1982) and Cecil K. Byrd, *Frank M. Hohenberger's Indiana Photographs* (Bloomington: Indiana University Press, 1993). Hohenberger's undated diary is included in the Hohenberger Collection at the Lilly Library at Indiana University in Bloomington, Indiana.

9. The Bohall Brothers included Joseph "Josey" Bohall (1872–1960), George Bohall (1873–1959), John Bohall (1878–1936), Charlie Bohall (1880–1949), and Levi Bohall (1885–1957). Their sister Anna (Bohall) Shipley (1873–1958) also made a few baskets.

10. Claudia Pomatto, unpublished transcript of interview with Howard Bruce Hovis, Bloomington, IN, December 2, 1973.

11. Frank Michael Hohenberger, "Joe Bohall, Down in the Hills of Brown," in *Indianapolis Star,* November 2, 1924.

12. Kay, "A Picture of an Old Country Store."

13. Victor Green, "3 Brown County Brothers Uphold Family Basket-Weaving Tradition," in *Indianapolis Star,* May 15, 1927.

14. Henry Wood, "Willow Weaver: A Once Flourishing Southern Indiana Business Now Is Practiced by Only a Handful of Hoosiers," in *Indianapolis Sunday Star Magazine,* May 15, 1949, 20.

15. Green, "3 Brown County Brothers," 1927.

16. Green, "3 Brown County Brothers," 1927.

17. Hohenberger, "Joe Bohall," 1924.

18. For a discussion of Cannon County's exporting of baskets, listen to: John Kay, "Episode 34: Cannon County Baskets a Tennessee Tradition," *The Artisan Ancestors Podcast* (2013), accessed April 5, 2017, http://www.artisanancestors.com/2013/02/18/episode-34-cannon-county-baskets-a-tennessee-tradition/.

19. Anonymous, *Handicrafts in Indiana* (Bloomington, IN: Indiana University Extension Division, Public Welfare Service and Indiana Federation of Art Clubs, 1940), 6. Oak-rod basket making was almost exclusively a male craft in Brown County because of the strength required to pull rods. However, as noted above, Anna Shipley, James Bohall's daughter, made a few baskets, which helped support the widow's family.

20. Kay, "Oak-Rod Baskets in Brown County," 89.

21. Pomatto, Unpublished transcript of interview with Howard Bruce Hovis.

22. I am thankful to folklorist and basket scholar Beth Hester for identifying these fancy baskets as being made in western Kentucky.

23. Warren Roberts, "Basketry in Brown County, Indiana" (unpublished manuscript, n.d.), Warren Roberts Collection, Bloomington, IN: Indiana University Archive.

24. Frank Michael Hohenberger, *Nashville Observer*, April 1955.

25. According to an unpublished transcript of an interview with Margaret Morgan in 1973, John

Bohall taught oak-rod basket making to his friend Edward Morgan (1875–1961) while on a fishing trip in the late 1890s. Edward would eventually learn to weave a variety of useful forms, such as harvest baskets, picnic baskets, sewing baskets with lids, round laundry baskets, and clothes hampers. When Edward's eldest son, Reuben Morgan (1900–1981), was twelve-years-old, he began helping his father make and weave oak-rods. During the Depression, just as William Bohall had done, Reuben and his father traveled the countryside selling and bartering their baskets. After years of not making baskets, Reuben began weaving again when he retired. Reuben Morgan, interview with Margaret Morgan, October 31, 1973, Indiana University Archive, Bloomington, IN (unpublished). See also: Gary Stanton, "The Tradition of Oak-Rod Baskets in Southern Indiana" (unpublished manuscript, 1975), 3–4.

26. Cynthia Anne Clark, interview with Howard Bruce Hovis, March 25, 1973, Indiana University Archive, Bloomington, IN.

27. Riving is the process of splitting a piece of wood along the grain often using a fro, a special kind of hand ax, which is hit with a mallet. As the wedge-shaped blade rips into the wood, the short handle can be used to twist the blade to make the wood split down the grain of the wood.

28. Randing is the basic weaving pattern in rod basketry.

29. Clark, 1973. In the 1970s, oak-rod baskets were not the only kind still being made in southern Indiana. Pearl Higdon of Shelby County and John Adams of Harrison County both wove baskets from flat, white oak splits. Higdon plaited exquisite Appalachian-style baskets, a craft she and her family brought to Indiana from Grayson County, Kentucky, in the 1920s. Adams produced round workbaskets from flat strips of oak, a craft he learned in his youth and one he revived for fun in his retirement years. Like many older folk artists, their making of art was not purely utilitarian nor solely an expression of cultural heritage, but more a form of material life review—a practice by which they could both recall their personal history and share their work with others. Both Higdon and Adams demonstrated their craft at state parks and local heritage events.

30. Clark, 1973.

31. Stanton, "The Tradition of Oak-Rod Baskets."

## Chapter 5: Fashioning Nantucket Mink: From Nantucket Lightship Basket to Friendship Purse

I wish to, first and foremost, thank Kristin Schwain for two dynamic courses she taught in collaboration with Dr. Josephine Stealey on American basketry. The seed for this paper started to germinate in the first course and grew into a full paper in the second course, fed by the fruitful environment of inquiry Schwain facilitates in her courses. I wish to thank Stealey for opening my senses and mind to a field of artistic expression I was not familiar with. It has been a fun journey of discovery. I also wish to thank both Maryann Wasik, Executive Director and Mary Bergman, Director of the Nantucket Lightship

Basket Museum, for agreeing to loan a Reyes friendship purse to the exhibition and for helpful sources, and to Marie Henke, Photo Archives Specialist, Nantucket Historical Association, for help with images.

1. Michael Jehle, organizer. "A Report on the NHA Symposium: Nantucket and the Native American Legacy of New England," accessed March 2017, www.nha.org/library/hn/HN-winter96-symposium.htm.

2. As the whale population dwindled in the Atlantic, the whaling industry undertook the increased expense and risk of voyaging to the Pacific to hunt for whales. Ric Burns, *Into the Deep: America, Whaling, and the World*, accessed April 5, 2017, http://www.pbs.org/wgbh/americanexperience/films/whaling/.

3. By 1750 a brick oven furnace, called a trywork, was invented to render whale blubber into oil aboard ship during long voyages. Coopers were important crewmembers who built barrels for the oil during voyages.

4. José Formoso Reyes, interview by Henry Coffin Carlisle, 1958, Nantucket Historical Association. "Personal History and Craft of Lightship Baskets," accessed March 2017, http://www.nantuckethistoricalassociation.net/images/DBText/audiofiles/CT-38a&b_JoseReyes_1958_01.mp3.

5. Katherine and Edgar Seeler, *Nantucket Lightship Baskets* (Nantucket, MA: Deermouse Press, 1972), 44, 56, 60.

6. Susan Fernald, "Nantucket Lightship Handbags and Baskets," *Historic Nantucket* 16 (1969): 23–24.

7. Martha Lawrence, *Lightship Baskets of Nantucket* (Atglen, PA: Schiffer Publishing, Ltd.), 23.

8. The first hotel on Nantucket, Ocean House Hotel, opened in 1847, and the second, the Atlantic Hotel, in 1848. By 1855, regular ferry service to Nantucket was established from Hyannis.

9. Seeler, *Nantucket Lightship Baskets*, 76.

10. Fernald, "Nantucket Lightship Handbags and Baskets," 24. Fernald writes that the crew of the South Shoal Lightship reportedly had a lathe aboard, among other necessary tools for making lightship baskets.

11. Clinton Mitchell "Mitchy" Ray, a third-generation lightship basket maker, descended from Captain Charles B. Ray, who as a lightship captain made baskets that include the following poem on the bottom of each: "I was made on Nantucket, I'm strong and I'm stout. Don't lose me or burn me, and I'll never wear out." It emphasized that strength and durability were sought-after qualities in an era when things were made by hand.

12. Ex-whalers from Nantucket may have served also on other lightships marking dangerous shoals in the Cape Cod, Martha's Vineyard, and Nantucket area, such as the *Cross Rip*, *Great Round Shoals*, *Handkerchief*, or *Pollack Rip Shoals*.

13. The area of the Old and New South Shoals is one hundred square miles extending thirty-five miles south of Nantucket Island, and is made up of shallow waters over shifting sandbars. Swept by vicious cross currents and winds, large waves and dense fogs are common occurrences.

14. In the early days of the South Shoal lightship service, crews served eight months total per year aboard ship in two four-month tours of duty with two months' leave between each tour. The lightship's only connection with land was a tender that brought provisions, mail, and fresh crews. In modern times, tours of duty were a more humane thirty days. The South Shoal lightship, the last lightship in the United States service, was decommissioned in 1985 and replaced by a navigational buoy.

15. Crewmen's wages were set at twenty cents per day. Willard Flint, "A History of U.S. Lightships," accessed November 2015, www.uscg.mil/history/articles/lightships.pdf.

16. Flint, "A History of U.S. Lightships," 11.

17. In an interview with Dorr Kahn in 1975, José Formoso Reyes said when he first came to Nantucket Island in 1945, no one was interested in Nantucket lightship baskets. Nantucket Historical Society, accessed March 2016, https://www.nantucketlightshipbasketmuseum.org/research-collections/biographies/jose-formoso-reyes-1902-1980.

18. The culturally diverse Philippines were ceded to the United States by Spain in 1898, after the Spanish-American War.

19. Ellen Melinkoff, *What We Wore: An Offbeat Social History of Women's Clothing, 1950 to 1980* (New York: William Morrow, 1984), 21.

20. Myles A. Garcia, "The Filipino Who Made a Prized, World-Famous Basket," Last modified April 17, 2015, http://globalnation.inquirer.net/120811/the-filipino-who-made-a-prized-world-famous-basket.

21. In a 1975 interview, Reyes admitted that he thought he invented the covered basket but over time realized much earlier makers had made covers for lightship baskets. The lids were flat, not domed, were not hinged, and although they had wooden pieces in the center, they were much smaller and not embellished. "José Formoso Reyes (1902–1980)," Nantucket Lightship Basket Museum, accessed April 5, 2017, https://www.nantucketlightshipbasketmuseum.org/research-collections/biographies/jose-formoso-reyes-1902-1980.

22. Dror Kahn interview with José Formoso Reyes in 1975.

23. Henry Coffin Carlisle. "Personal History and Craft of Lightship Baskets," interview with José Formoso Reyes, Nantucket Historical Society, 1958, http://www.nantuckethistoricalassociation.net/images/DBText/audiofiles/CT-38a&b_JoseReyes_1958_01.mp3.

24. To accomplish their goal, they had to place their order months in advance because of Reyes' backlog. Lawrence, *Lightship Baskets,* 67.

25. Roger B. May, "Costly Cane-Craft Is Nantucket's Bag—And Sinatra Has 3," *Wall Street Journal*, September 17, 1975.

26. *Haute couture* translates to "high-quality sewing."

27. William R. Leach, "Transformations in a Culture of Consumption: Women and Department Stores, 1890–1925" in *The Journal of American History* 71, no. 2 (1984): 327.

28. Paul F. Whitten, *The Friendship Baskets and Their Maker, José Formoso Reyes*, 1960. Reprinted September 2002 by The Nantucket Lightship Basket Makers and Merchants Association.

29. Valerie Steele, *Fifty Years of Fashion: New Look to Now* (New Haven, CT: Yale University Press, 1997), 34.

30. Melinkoff, *What We Wore,* 48.

31. Joan Ockman, "Mirror Images: Technology, Consumption and the Representation of Gender in American Architecture Since World War II" in *American Architectural History*, ed. Keith L. Eggener (New York: Routledge, 2004), 347.

32. Anne Fogarty, *Wife-Dressing* (New York: Julian Messner, 1959), 10.

33. Whitten, *The Friendship Baskets and Their Maker*

34. "Nantucket Lightship Baskets: A Historic Perspective," Nantucket Lightship Basket Museum, accessed December 2015, https://www.nantucketlightshipbasketmuseum.org/research-collections/history-of-baskets.

35. Whitten, *The Friendship Baskets and Their Maker.*

36. Seeler, *Nantucket Lightship Baskets*, 2.

## Chapter 6: Beyond Summer Camp and Merit Badges: The Studio Craft Movement, Education, and the American Basket

1. Ed Rossbach, *The Nature of Basketry* (West Chester, PA: Schiffer Publishing Ltd., 1986), 13.

2. Rossbach, *The Nature of Basketry*, 10.

3. The origin of the idiom "underwater basket weaving" is best left to the linguists, but it is certainly conceivable that the soaking of basket materials in water in preparation for weaving contributed to its development and use.

4. Gertrude and Mildred Ashley, *Raffia Basketry as a Fine Art* (Deerfield: Published by the Authors, 1915).

5. Ed Rossbach, *The New Basketry* (New York: Van Nostrand Reinhold, 1976), 26.

6. George Wharton James, *Indian Basketry* (New York: Dover, 1972), 227.

7. Koplos and Metcalf, *Makers*, 110–111. Koplos and Metcalf provide a summary of Keyser's relationship to the Cohns and the numerous fabrications they employed to profit from her baskets.

8. Ellen Taubman and David Revere McFadden, *Changing Hands: Art Without Reservation 3, Contemporary Native North American Art from the Northeast and Southeast* (New York: Museum of Arts and Design, 2012), 171.

9. Otto Salomon, *The theory of educational sloyd: the only authorised ed. of the lectures of Otto Salomon/ rev. and ed. for English and American students by an inspector of schools; together with a résumé of the history of manual training, and a portrait and biography of Herr Salomon* (Boston: Silver, Burdett, 1907), 1.

10. Calvin Woodward, *Manual Training in Education* (New York: Charles Scribner's Sons, 1892), 231–232

11. Ibid.

12. Nicholas R. Bell, *A Measure of the Earth: The Cole-Ware Collection of American Baskets* (Washington, DC: Smithsonian American Art Museum, 2013), 28–35.

13. Robin Dreyer, "The Joy of Hands at Work: Penland School and the Evolution of Craft Education," in *The Nature of Craft and the Penland Experience,* ed. Jean W. McLaughlin (New York: Lark Books, 2004), 10–15.

14. Ibid., 17.

15. Keith W. Olson, "The G. I. Bill and Higher Education: Success and Surprise," *American Quarterly* 25 (December 1973): 596–610.

16. In a letter to the editor published in the November/December 1961 issue of *Craft Horizons*, MacKenzie compares the works of Voulkos and his contemporaries as covered in Rose Slivka's "The New Ceramic Presence" in the July/August issue of the same publication to the "big pile in our neighbor's cow pasture."

17. Rose Slivka, *Peter Voulkos: A Dialogue with Clay* (New York: New York Graphic Society, 1978), 9.

18. David Lewis, *Warren MacKenzie: An American Potter* (New York: Kodansha International, 1991), 44–45.

19. Vincent Katz, "Black Mountain College: Experiment in Art," in *Black Mountain College: Experiment in Art*, ed. Vincent Katz (Cambridge, MA: MIT Press, 2013), 20–25.

20. Gerald W. R. Ward, ed., *Craft Transformed: Program in Artisanry* (Brockton, MA: Fuller Museum of Art, 2003), 13–17, 24–25.

21. Gary Smith, *Daniel Rhodes: The California Years* (Sanata Cruz, CA: The Art Museum of Santa Cruz County, 1986), 3, 24.

22. Kathleen Maclay, "UC Berkeley Textile Expert Ed Rossbach Dies At 88," press release, October 16, 2002.

23. Koplos and Metcalf, *Makers,* 266.

24. Koplos and Metcalf describe the 1960s as a time when "almost any talented MFA recipient could get a teaching job" in *Makers: A History of American Studio Craft*, 309.

25. Koplos and Metcalf, *Makers*, 266–267.

26. Published in 1976, Ed Rossbach's *The New Basketry* is seen as a watershed moment for the recognition and later explosion of a different category of basketry, frequently called New Basketry in reference to the book's title.

27. Rossbach, *The New Basketry*, 35, 62, and 66.

28. Jack Lenor Larsen, *The Tactile Vessel: New Basket Forms* (Erie, PA: Erie Art Museum, 1989), 15.

29. Examples include *The Modern Basket: A Definition at the Pittsburgh Center for the Arts* in 1987 or the traveling *The New American Basket* in 1984 at Brainerd Art Gallery, State University College, Potsdam, New York.

30. Ulysses G. Dietz, *Great Pots: Contemporary Ceramics from Function to Fantasy* (Madison, WI: Guild Publishing), 25–33.

31. Rossbach, *The New Basketry*, 86.

32. Auther, *String, Felt, Thread*, 136–140.

33. On ceramics, see Garth Clark, "Diaspora: Two Years that Have Changed Ceramics Forever," last modified November 4, 2015, https://cfileonline.org/commentary-diaspora-two-years-that-have-changed-ceramics-forever-contemporary-ceramic-art-cfile/. On fiber, see Porter, Jenelle. *Fiber Sculpture: 1960–Present.*

**Chapter 7: New Basketry Beginnings: 1970–1990**

1. Mildred Constantine and Jack Lenor Larsen, *Beyond Craft: The Art Fabric* (New York: Van Nostrand Reinhold, 1973), 221.

2. Ed Rossbach, *The New Basketry* (New York: Van Nostrand Reinhold, 1976), 9.

3. Ed Rossbach, *Baskets as Textile Art* (New York: Van Nostrand Reinhold, 1973).

4. Harriet Nathan, *Charles Edmund Rossbach: Artist, Mentor, Professor, Writer* (Berkeley: University of California, 1987), 91.

5. Joan Sterrenburg, e-mail message to author, August 10, 2015. Patricia Malarcher, telephone conversation with author, August 12, 2015.

6. Lillian Elliott, "Baskets: Direct and Natural," *Arts and Activities* (January 1983): 21.

7. In a conversation with Patricia Malarcher, Pat Hickman recalled that Ed Rossbach and his students frequented the Caning Shop in Albany, California (now in Berkeley), for discarded chair caning material and basketry supplies.

8. Lillian Elliott, *Lillian Elliott: Artist, Instructor, and Innovator in Fiber Arts*, interview by Harriet Nathan, 1989.

9. Joanne Segal Brandford, "Breathing Baskets" (lecture, University of Hawaii, Honolulu, March 31, 1993).

10. Anne Wilson, curator, *Ethnic Costume* (exhibition, Downtown Center of the DeYoung Museum, San Francisco, California, 1977).

11. Sterrenburg, correspondence.

12. Suellen Glashausser and Carol Westfall, *Plaiting: Step by Step* (New York: Watson-Guptill, 1976).

13. Arline Fisch and Carol Shaw-Sutton, e-mail correspondence with Patricia Malarcher, July 23, 2015 and September 16, 2015, respectively.

14. Shaw-Sutton, correspondence.

15. *Sculpture Textile: 12th International Biennial of Tapestry* (Lausanne, Switzerland: Centre International de la Tapisserie Ancienne et Moderne and Musée cantonal des Beaux-Arts, 1985), 108.

16. Ferne Jacobs, telephone conversation with Patricia Malarcher, July 13, 2013.

17. Rossbach, *The New Basketry*.

18. Ibid., 84, 62.

19. John Garrett, e-mail correspondence with Patricia Malarcher, n.d.

20. Rob Pulleyn, ed., *The Basketmaker's Art: Contemporary Baskets and Their Makers* (Asheville, NC: Lark Books, 1986), 62–67.

21. *Basketry: Tradition in New Form* (exhibition, Institute of Contemporary Art, Boston, January 12–February 28, 1982; at the Cooper-Hewitt Museum, New York, June 19–August 29, 1982; and at the Greenville County Museum of Art, Greenville, South Carolina, September 18, 1982–January 3, 1983). A nineteen-page illustrated catalog was published.

22. Mildred Constantine and Jack Lenor Larsen, *The Art Fabric: Mainstream* (New York: Van Nostrand Reinhold, 1981).

23. Patricia Malarcher, "What Makes a Basket a Basket?" *Fiberarts* 11 (January–February 1984): 38.

24. John McQueen, telephone conversation with Patricia Malarcher, July 28, 2015.

25. Nathan, *Charles Edmund Rossbach*, 112.

26. McQueen, telephone conversation.

27. Nathan, *Charles Edmund Rossbach,* 66.

28. McQueen telephone conversation with Malarcher.

29. Carol and Dan Hart, *Natural Basketry* (New York: Watson-Guptill, 1976).

30. Kari Lonning, telephone conversation with Patricia Malarcher, July 24, 2015.

31. Virginia I. Harvey, *The Techniques of Basketry* (New York: Van Nostrand Reinhold, 1974).

32. Hideyuki Oka, *How to Wrap 5 Eggs: Traditional Japanese Packaging* (Boston: Weatherhill, 1975).

33. Nancy Moore Bess, e-mail correspondence with Patricia Malarcher, July 22, 2015.

34. Hisako Sekijima, e-mail correspondence with Patricia Malarcher, July 28, 2015.

35. *The Tactile Vessel: New Basket Forms*. Catalog for exhibition curated by Jack Lenor Larsen. Erie Art Museum, 1989, 56–57.

36. Patricia Malarcher, "A Basketmaker's Year Down Under," *Fiberarts* 8 (July–August 1981): 47–49.

37. "Douglas Fuchs' *Floating Forest*: 30th Anniversary Exhibition," Ararat Rural City Council Events Calendar, Ararat, VIC, Australia. This exhibition took place February 17–April 1, 2012 at the Ararat Regional Art Gallery in partnership with the Powerhouse Museum, Sydney, which had acquired key components of the work. See also http://debbieherd.blogspot.com/2012/02/douglas-fuchs-floating-forest-30th.html.

38. "The New Basket: A Vessel for the Future" (exhibition, Brainerd Art Gallery, SUNY Potsdam, June 16–July 15, 1984, later at the Rochester Institute of Technology, Rochester, NY; New York State Museum, Albany; and the Southern Highland Handicraft Guild, Asheville, NC).

39. Dona Z. Meilach, *A Modern Approach to Basketry with Fiber and Grasses Using Coiling, Twining, Weaving, Macramé, Crocheting* (New York: Crown Publishing, 1974).

40. Jane Sauer, telephone conversation with Patricia Malarcher, July 30, 2015.

41. Nancy N. Rice, Review of Jane Sauer show, B. Z. Wagman Gallery, St. Louis, Missouri, *New Art Examiner* (September 1986): 60.

42. Robert Maloney, "New York in Review," *Arts* 63 (January 1989): 101.

43. Pat Hickman, *Baskets: Redefining Volume and Meaning* (Honolulu: The University of Hawaii Art Gallery, 1993), 11.

## Chapter 8: Diverse Structures, Dissolving Boundaries

1. Bruce W. Pepich, *Collection Focus in Fiber: John McQueen* (Racine, Wisconsin: Racine Art Museum, 2010), 9.

2. Janet Koplos, "Why Basketry Matters." Keynote address for the biennial conference of the National Basketry Organization, Macalester College, St. Paul, Minnesota, July 14, 2015.

3. Judy Metro, ed., *An Eye for Art* (Washington, DC: National Gallery of Art, 2013), 172.

4. Natasja Sheriff, "Everything is Nothing: The Art of Sopheap Pich," *Hyperallergic*, June 11, 2013, accessed April 13, 2017, https://hyperallergic.com/73086/everything-is-nothing-the-artwork-of-sopheap-pich/.

5. Turner Contemporary, a visual arts venue in Margate, Kent, United Kingdom.

6. Lauren A. Wright, ed., *Maria Nepomuceno, Tempo para Respirar* (*Breathing Time*) (Kent, England: Turner Contemporary, 2012), 5.

7. Joyce Lovelace, "Composing Chaos," *American Craft*, December/January, 2014.

8. Barbara Shapiro, "Political Voices of Three Left Coast Artists: Gyongy Laky, Linda Gass, Linda MacDonald" (Textile Society of America Symposium Proceedings, Washington, DC, September 19–22, 2012), http://digitalcommons.unl.edu/tsaconf/743.

9. David M. Roth, "Gyöngy Laky @ b.sakata garo." *Squarecylinder.com*, September 8, 2012, accessed April 13, 2017, http://www.squarecylinder.com/2012/09/gyongy-laky-b-sakata-garo/.

10. Andreas Pohancenik, "Organic* Lettering and Signage in Landscape and Environmental Design" (master's dissertation, Central Saint Martens College of Art and Design, 2004).

11. Maxwell Tielman, "Studio Tour & Interview: Doug Johnston," *Design Sponge*, March 13, 2013, accessed April 13, 2017, http://www.designsponge.com/2013/03/studio-tour-interview-doug-johnston.html.

12. Lowery Stokes Sims, "Stephen Burks: A Hybrid Making on Earth," in *Stephen Burks: Man Made*, ed. Naomi Beckwith (New York: The Studio Museum in Harlem, 2011), 6.

13. University of East Anglia. "Basket Weaving May Have Taught Humans to Count," *ScienceDaily*, accessed February 18, 2016, www.sciencedaily.com/releases/2009/06/090604222534.htm.

14. Chris Drury, "Working Outside the System," *Elephant*, July 15, 2015, accessed April 13, 2017, http://www.elephantmag.com/chris-drury-working-outside-the-system/.

15. Also known as TICKON, founded in Langeland, Denmark, in 1993 by Alfio Bonanno.

16. John K. Grande, *Art Nature Dialogues* (New York: State University of New York, 2004), 235.

17. Nina Azzarello, "Nicolay Polissky Wraps Abandoned Soviet Shop in Undulating Wooden Jacket," *Design Boom*, September 3, 2015, accessed April 13, 2017, http://www.designboom.com/art/ nikolay-polissky-selpo-ugra-national-park-zvizzhi-village-russia-09-03-2015/.

18. Noah Sneider, "Myth and Reality: Nikolay Polissky's Timeless Land Art," *Calvert Journal,* July 16, 2013, accessed April 13, 2017, calvertjournal.com/articles/show/1219/myth-reality-nikolay-polissky-timeless-land-art.

19. Eugenia Flynn and Tiriki Onus, "The Tjanpi Desert Weavers Show Us That Traditional Craft is Art," *The Conversation*, August 12, 2014, accessed April 23, 2017, http://theconversation.com/ tjanti-desert-weavers-show-us-that-traditional-craft-is-art-30243.

20. Janelle Carrigan, "Australian Policies at the Venice Biennale," *New York Times*, May 6, 2015.

## Chapter 9: The Space Between

The author wishes to thank Marisa Bartolucci for her insightful comments on an early draft of this essay.

1. For a timely look at the field in general and this sentiment in particular, see Emily Zilber, "The Object in Flux," *Crafted: Objects in Flux* (Boston: Museum of Fine Arts, Boston, 2015), 9–15. This essay's opening line owes a debt to the title of Zilber's catalogue.

2. Holsenbeck's full quote can be found at http://www.bryantholsenbeck.com/, accessed January 7, 2016.

3. Peter Selz, "Ann Weber, Dolby Chadwick Gallery, San Francisco," *Sculpture* 32, no. 4 (May 2013): 73–74.

4. To see Kramer's *Spin Basket in Action*, see Aaron Kramer, "Spin Basket," YouTube video, 0:20, uploaded November 5, 2007, accessed May 17, 2017, https://www.youtube.com/watch?v =HvjdqdQo2mo.

5. Nicholas R. Bell, *40 under 40: Craft Futures* (New Haven, CT: Yale University Press), 146–147. Author's conversation with the artist occurred on January 9, 2016.

6. Rhoads, who is primarily considered a glass artist, was included in *Game Changers: Fiber Art Masters and Innovators*, Fuller Craft Museum, July 5–November 23, 2014. I am indebted to Pat Warner for bringing this exhibition to my attention.

7. Paola Antonelli and Michele Millar Fisher, "If Not Museums, Then Where? Adding Ancient Algorithms and New Biological Futures to MoMA's Collection," *MoMA Inside/Out*, July 6, 2015, accessed January 9, 2016, http://www.moma.org/explore/inside_out/2015/07/08/if-not-museums-then-where-adding-ancient-algorithms-and-new-biological-futures-to-momas-collection. I am grateful to Marisa Bartolucci for bringing this collaboration to my attention.

8. Amit Zoran, "Hybrid Basketry: Interweaving Digital Practice within Contemporary Craft," *Leonardo* 46, no. 4 (2013): 324–331. For an overview of his projects, see Amit Zoran Homepage, accessed

May 17, 2017, www.amitz.com, particularly Hybrid Basketry (2013) and Hybrid Bricolage (2016).

9. According to Miebach's artist statement, "My aim . . . is to reveal patterns in the data to musicians who might identify that which I have failed to see." Artist statement, Nathalie Miebach: Sculpture, accessed May 17, 2017, www.nathaliemiebach.com/statement.html. For an excellent video on the artist's intent, see Miebach's 2011 TED Talk: Nathalie Miebach, "Nathalie Miebach: Art Made of Storms," TED Video, 4:19, filmed July 2011, accessed March 17, 2017, http://www.ted.com/talks/nathalie_miebach.

10. Joyce Lovelace, "Always Unfolding." American Craft. November 17, 2015, accessed April 13, 2017, https://craftcouncil.org/magazine/article/always-unfolding.

11. Roberta Smith, "Against Delusion: Robert Gober's Nuts-and-Bolts Americana," New York Times, August 23, 2007.

12. Suzanne Beal, "Basket of Light," American Craft 69, no. 1 (February/March 2009): 36.

13. Jason Hackenwerth, "Mandarin Oriental Lobby Balloons with New Art Installation" (video), accessed January 5, 2015, http://hk.localiiz.com/video-mandarin-oriental-lobby-balloons-with-new-art-installation/#.Vow1rFJZg2a>.

14. Echelman uses triple-braided, ultra-high-molecular-weight polyethylene (a lightweight fiber fifteen times stronger than steel) that gives shape and support to the bottom, hanging net panels spun from polytetrafluoroethylene (ensuring color quality and ultraviolet resistance). Olivia Schwob, "Net Effects," Harvard Magazine, May–June 2015, accessed January 1, 2016, http://harvardmagazine.com/2015/05/net-effects. For a video of the mockup and later installation, see http://www.echelman.com/project/impatient-optimist/.

15. Darvas, György, Symmetry: Cultural-historical and ontological aspects of science-arts relations; the natural and man-made world in an interdisciplinary approach, trans. David Robert Evans (Berlin: Springer Science & Business Media, 2007), 236–237.

16. Matilda McQuaid, et al., Extreme Textiles, Designing for High Performance (New York: Princeton Architectural Press, 2005), 109–110.

17. For information on Big Bambú, see http://www.dmstarn.com/big_bambu_met.html. As stated in a press release from Metropolitan Museum of Art on April 27, 2010, "The work will embody a contradictory nature: It is always complete, yet it is always unfinished. Working on the sculpture while the exhibition is open to the public, the artists and teams of rock climbers (six to twenty of whom will be present during different phases of the project) will provide visitors with a rare opportunity to experience their work as it unfolds. It is a temporary structure in a sense, but it is a sculpture—not a static sculpture, it's an organism that we are just a part of—helping it to move along."

# Bibliography

Adamson, Glenn. *The Invention of Craft.* New York: Bloomsbury, 2013.

———. "Serious Business: The Designer-Craftsman in Postwar California." In *California Design, 1930–1965: Living in a Modern Way,* edited by Wendy Kaplan, 203–232. Boston: MIT Press, 2011.

Adovasio, J. M. *Basketry Technology: A Guide to Identification and Analysis.* Walnut Creek, CA: Left Coast Press, 2010.

Ames, Kenneth. *Death in the Dining Room and Other Tales of Victorian Culture.* Philadelphia: Temple University Press, 1992.

*Annual Report of the Penn Normal, Industrial, and Agricultural School of St. Helena Island, 1905–1906.* Philadelphia: The John C. Winston Co., 1906.

Antonelli, Paola, and Michele Millar Fisher. "'If Not Museums, Then Where?' Adding Ancient Algorithms and New Biological Futures to MoMA's Collection," *Inside/Out* (blog), Museum of Modern Art, July 8, 2015, http://www.moma.org/explore/inside_out/2015/07/08/if-not-museums-then-where-adding-ancient-algorithms-and-new-biological-futures-to-momas-collection.

Antonsen, Lasse. *Pat Hickman*: *Traces of Time*. Dartmouth, MA: University of Massachusetts, 2012.

Ashley, Gertrude and Mildred. *Raffia Basketry as a Fine Art.* Deerfield: Published by the Authors, 1915.

Auther, Elissa. *String, Felt, Thread*: *The Hierarchy of Art and Craft in American Art*. Minneapolis, MN: University of Minnesota Press, 2010.

Azzarello, Nina. "Nicolay Polissky Wraps Abandoned Soviet Shop in Undulating Wooden Jacket," *Design Boom,* September 3, 2015. http://www.designboom.com/art/nikolay-polissky-selpo-ugra-national-park-zvizzhi-village-russia-09-03-2015/.

Bank, Mirra. *Anonymous Was a Woman: A Celebration in Words and Images and the Women Who Made It.* New York: St. Martin's Press, 1979.

Barnes, Marianne. *New and Different Materials for Weaving and Coiling.* Atglen, PA: Schiffer, 2012.

Barter, Judith A. *Apostles of Beauty: Arts and Crafts from Britain to Chicago.* Chicago: Art Institute of Chicago, 2009.

*Basketry: Tradition in New Form.* Exhibition at the Institute of Contemporary Art, Boston, January 12–February 28, 1982; at the Cooper-Hewitt Museum, New York, June 19–August 29, 1982; and at the Greenville County Museum of Art, Greenville, South Carolina, September 18, 1982–January 3, 1983.

Batkin, Jonathan. "Tourism Is Overrated: Pueblo Pottery and the Early Curio Trade, 1880–1910." In *Unpacking Culture: Art and Commodity in Postcolonial Worlds,* edited by Ruth B. Phillips and Christopher B. Steiner, 282–300. Berkeley: University of California Press, 1999.

Beal, Suzanne. "Baskets of Light." *American Craft* 69, no. 1 (February/March 2009): 36–37.

Beckwith, Naomi, Thelma Golden, Lowery Stokes Sims, and Keith Recker. *Stephen Burks: Man Made.* New York: Studio Museum in Harlem, 2011.

Bell, Nicholas R. *40 under 40: Craft Futures.* New Haven, CT: Yale University Press, 2012.

———. *A Measure of the Earth*: *The Cole-Ware Collection of American Baskets*. Chapel Hill, NC: University of North Carolina Press, 2013.

Blackard, David M. *Patchwork and Palmettos: Seminole/Miccosukee Folk Art Since 1820*. Fort Lauderdale: Fort Lauderdale Historical Society, 1990.

Bohall, William, interview by Claudia Pomatto, December 2, 1973. Unpublished transcript. Box 4, M/C 73/41, Indiana University Folklore Institute Material Culture Papers, University Archives, Indiana University, Bloomington.

Boris, Eileen. *Art and Labor: Ruskin, Morris, and the Craftsman Ideal in America*. Philadelphia: Temple University Press, 1989.

Brandford, Joanne Segal. "Breathing Baskets." Transcript of a lecture presented at the University of Hawaii, Honolulu, March 31, 1993.

Brescia, Bill, and Carolyn Reeves. *By the Work of Our Hands: Choctaw Material Culture*. Philadelphia, MS: Choctaw Heritage Press, 1982.

Brooks, Van Wyck. "On Creating a Usable Past." *Dial* (April 11, 1918): 337–341.

Bryan-Wilson, Julia. "Eleven Propositions in Response to the Question 'What Is Contemporary about Craft?'" *Journal of Modern Craft* 6, no. 1 (2013): 7–10.

Bustin, Dillon. *If You Don't Outdie Me: The Legacy of Brown County*. Bloomington, IN: Indiana University Press, 1982.

Buszek, Maria Elena. *Extra/Ordinary: Craft and Contemporary Art*. Durham, NC: Duke University Press, 2011.

Butcher, Mary. *Contemporary International Basketmaking*. London: Merrell Holberton, 1999.

Byrd, Cecil K. *Frank M. Hohenberger's Indiana Photographs*. Bloomington, IN: Indiana University Press, 1993.

Cain, Shawna. "Buckbrush: A Cherokee Source for Basketry." *Cherokee Phoenix,* December 3, 2009. Accessed November 17, 2015. http://www.cherokeephoenix.org/Article/index/3462.

Caldwell, Katherine. *From Mountain Hands: The Story of Allanstand Craft Shop's First 100 Years*. Asheville: Southern Highland Craft Guild, 1996.

Carrigan, Janelle. "Australian Policies at the Venice Biennale." *New York Times,* May 6, 2015.

Carter, Kate. "Making History: Cherokee Indian Fair." *Craft Revival: Shaping Western North Carolina Past and Present*. A Project of Hunter Library Digital Initiatives at Western Carolina University. Accessed April 13, 2017. http://www.wcu.edu/library/DigitalCollections/CraftRevival/about/index.html.

Cashdan, Marina. "Interview: Maria Nepomuceno." *Blouinartinfo International,* June 18, 2010. Accessed April 13, 2017. http://www.blouinartinfo.com/news/story/276944/interview-maria-nepomuceno.

Chavez, Will. "Cherokee Basket Maker Shares Her Talent." *Cherokee Phoenix,* September 30, 2004. Accessed November 17, 2015. http://www.cherokeephoenix.org/Article/index/679.

———. "Program Teaches Basket Making from Start to Finish." *Cherokee Phoenix,* September 5, 2014. Accessed November 17, 2015.

Chicago, Judy. *Through the Flower: My Struggle as a Woman Artist*. New York: Doubleday, 1975.

Clark, Garth. "Diaspora: Two Years that Have Changed Ceramics Forever." Cfile.daily, November 4, 2015, https://cfileonline.org/commentary-diaspora-two-years-that-have-changed-ceramics-forever-contemporary-ceramic-art-cfile/.

Clayton, Virginia Tuttle, ed. *Drawing on America's Past: Folk Art, Modernism, and the Index of American Design.* Washington, DC: National Gallery of Art, 2002.

Clayton, Virginia Tuttle. "Picturing a Usable Past." In *Drawing on America's Past: Folk Art, Modernism, and the Index of American Design,* edited by Virginia Tuttle Clayton, 1-43. Washington, DC: National Gallery of Art, 2002.

Coakley, Joyce V. *Sweetgrass Baskets and the Gullah Tradition.* Charleston, SC: Arcadia, 2005.

Cohodas, Marvin. "Elizabeth Hickox and Karuk Basketry: A Study in Debates on Innovation and Paradigms of Authenticity." In *Unpacking Culture: Art and Commodity in Colonial and Postcolonial Worlds,* edited by Ruth B. Phillips and Christopher B. Steiner, 143–161. Berkeley: University of California Press, 1999.

Cohodas, Marvin. "Louisa Keyser and the Cohns: Mythmaking and Basket Making in the American West." In *The Early Years of Native American Art History,* edited by Janet Berlo. Seattle: University of Washington Press, 1992.

Constantine, Mildred, and Jack Lenor Larsen. *The Art Fabric*: *Mainstream.* New York: Van Nostrand Reinhold, 1982.

———. *Beyond Craft*: *The Art Fabric.* New York: Van Nostrand Reinhold, 1973.

Cooley, Rosa B. *School Acres: An Adventure in Rural Education.* New Haven: Yale University Press, 1930.

Corn, Wanda. *The Great American Thing: Modern Art and National Identity, 1915–1935.* Berkeley: University of California Press, 1999.

Cort, Louise Allison, and Nakamura Kenji. *A Basketmaker in Rural Japan.* Washington, DC: Smithsonian Institution, 1994.

Davis, Gerald. "Afro-American Coil Basketry in Charleston County, South Carolina: Affective Characteristics of an Artistic Craft in a Social Context." In *Afro-American Folk Arts and Crafts,* edited by William Ferris, 235-258. Boston: G.K. Hall & Co., 1983.

Deagan, Kathleen. "An Early Seminole Cane Basket." *Florida Anthropologist* 30 (1) (1977): 28–33.

Deagan, Kathleen, ed. *Florida Basketry, Continuity and Change: An Exhibit Featuring Both Traditional and Contemporary Florida Basketry Forms.* White Springs, FL: Florida Folklife Program, 1981.

Deloria, Philip J. *Playing Indian.* New Haven: Yale University Press, 1998.

Dietz, Ulysses G. *Great Pots: Contemporary Ceramics from Function to Fantasy.* Madison, WI: Guild Publishing, 2004.

Dilworth, Leah. *Imagining Indians in the Southwest: Persistent Visions of a Primitive Past.* Washington, DC: Smithsonian Institution Press, 1996.

Doss, Erika. "American Folk Art's Distinctive Character: *The Index of American Design* and New Deal Notions of Cultural Nationalism." In *Drawing on America's Past: Folk Art, Modernism, and the Index of American Design,* edited by Virginia Tuttle Clayton, 61–73. Washington, DC: National Gallery of Art, 2002.

Dow, Arthur Wesley. *Composition: A Series of Exercises in Art Structure for the Use of Students and Teachers.* 7th ed. New York: Doubleday, Page, and Company, 1913.

Drury, Chris. "Working Outside the System." *Elephant.* July 15, 2015, http://www.elephantmag.com/chris-drury-working-outside-the-system/.

Duggan, Betty J. "Baskets of the Southeast." In *By Native Hands: Woven Treasures from the Lauren Rogers Museum of Art,* edited by Stephen Cook, 26-73. Laurel, MS: Lauren Rogers Museum of Art, 2005.

Dunton, William Rush, Jr. *Occupation Therapy: A Manual for Nurses.* New York: W. B. Saunders Company, 1915.

Eckert, Carol, and Lena Vigna. *Collection Focus: Carol Eckert at RAM.* Racine, WI: Racine Art Museum, 2010.

Elderfield, John. *Martin Puryear.* New York: Museum of Modern Art, 2007.

Elliott, Lillian. "Baskets: Direct and Natural." *Arts and Activities* (January 1983): 21–23.

Elliott, Lillian, and Ed Rossbach. *Artist, Instructor, and Innovator in Fiber Arts: Oral History Transcript.* Reprint, Charleston, SC: Nabu Press, 2010.

Falino, Jeannine. *Crafting Modernism: Midcentury American Art and Design.* New York: Abrams, 2011.

Fariello, M. Anna, and Paula Owen. *Objects and Meaning: New Perspectives on Art and Craft.* Lanham, MD: Scarecrow Press, 2004.

Fernald, Susan. "Nantucket Lightship Handbags and Baskets." *Historic Nantucket* 16 (1969).

Filene, Benjamin. *Romancing the Folk: Public Memory and American Roots Music.* Chapel Hill: University of North Carolina Press, 2000.

Flint, Willard. *A History of U.S. Lightships.* Washington, DC: Coast Guard Historian's Office and the Internal Relations Branch, 1993. Accessed June 10, 2017. www.uscg.mil/history/articles/lightships.pdf.

Fogarty, Ann. *Wife-Dressing.* New York: Julian Messner, 1959.

Fogelson, Raymond D., ed. *Handbook of North American Indians.* Vol. 14. Washington, DC: Government Printing Office, 2004.

Foote, Henry Wilder. "The Penn School on St. Helena Island." *The Southern Workman* 31, no. 5 (1902): 263–270. https://hdl.handle.net/2027/hvd.32044042995100.

Fretwell, Sammy. "River Cane Could Stand Tall Again." *The State* (South Carolina), August 21, 2011. Accessed November 15, 2015. http://infoweb.newsbank.com/resources/doc/nb/news/13943C9C15564BA8?p=AWNB.

Gablik, Susi. *The Reenchantment of Art.* New York: Thames and Hudson, 1991.

*Game Changers: Fiber Art Masters and Innovators.* Fuller Craft Museum. July 5–November 23, 2014.

Gantt, Sean. "Rivercane Restoration: Linking Cultural, Biological, and Economic Values." YouTube video, 7:05. Posted May 6, 2011. https://www.youtube.com/watch?v=4cXaHHUN43I.

Garcia, Myles A. "The Filipino Who Made a Prized, World-Famous Basket." *Inquirer.net,* April 17, 2015. Accessed April 13, 2017. http://globalnation.inquirer.net/120811/the-filipino-who-made-a-prized-world-famous-basket.

Gettys, J. Marshall, ed. *Basketry of the Southeastern Indians*. Idabel, OK: Museum of the Red River, 1984.

Gettys, J. Marshall. "Southeast." In *Woven Worlds: Basketry from the Clark Field Collection,* edited by Lydia L. Wyckoff, 173-191. Tulsa: Philbrook Museum of Art, 2001.

Glashausser, Suellen, and Carol Westfall. *Plaiting: Step by Step*. New York: Watson-Guptill, 1976.

Goggin, John M. "Plaited Basketry in the New World." *Southwestern Journal of Anthropology* 5, no. 2 (Summer 1949): 165–168. http://www.jstor.org/stable/3628633.

Graham, Roger. "Cherokee National Treasure Shares Basket Weaving Expertise." *Cherokee Phoenix,* February 4, 2015. Accessed November 17, 2015. http://www.cherokeephoenix.org/Article/index/9051.

Grande, John K. *Art Nature Dialogs: Interviews with Environmental Artists*. New York: State University of New York, 2004.

Green, Victor. "3 Brown County Brothers Uphold Family Basket-Weaving Tradition." *Indianapolis Star,* May 15, 1927.

Greer, Betsy. *Craftivism*: *The Art of Craft and Activism*. Vancouver: Arsenal Pulp Press, 2014.

Guss, David M. *To Weave and Sing: Art, Symbol, and Narrative in the South American Rain Forest*. Berkeley: University of California Press, 1990.

Hackenwerth, Jason. "Video: Mandarin Oriental Lobby Balloons with New Art Installation." *Localiiz: The Site with Insight,* March 13, 2015. http://hk.localiiz.com/video-mandarin-oriental-lobby-balloons-with-new-art-installation/#.WTwU4RPytE4.

Hall, Herbert J., and Mertice M. C. Buck. *The Work of Our Hands: A Study of Occupations for Invalids*. New York: Muffat, Yard, and Company, 1915.

Halper, Vicki, and Ed Rossbach. *John McQueen*: *The Language of Containment*. Washington, DC: Smithsonian Institution, 1991.

*Handicrafts in Indiana*. Bloomington, IN: Indiana University Extension Division, 1940.

Harris, Neil. *Cultural Excursions: Marketing Appetites and Cultural Tastes in Modern America*. Chicago: University of Chicago Press, 1990.

Hart, Carol, and Dan Hart. *Natural Basketry*. New York: Watson-Guptill, 1976.

Harvey, Virginia I. *The Techniques of Basketry*. New York: Van Nostrand Reinhold, 1974.

Hawes, David S. *The Best of Kin Hubbard: Abe Martin's Sayings and Wisecracks, Abe's Neighbors, His Almanack, Comic Drawings*. Bloomington: Indiana University Press, 1995.

Held, Peter, and Heather Sealy Lineberry. *Rethinking Contemporary Craft*: *Crafting a Continuum*. Tempe, AR: Arizona State University Art Museum, 2013.

Hemmings, Jessica, ed. *The Textile Reader*. New York: Berg, 2012.

Heslop, Sandy, ed. *Basketry: Making Human Nature*. Norwich: University of East Anglia, 2011.

Hester, Beth. "Bearing the White Oak Tradition." Unpublished manuscript, 2016.

Hickman, Pat. *Baskets: Redefining Volume and Meaning*. Honolulu: University of Hawaii, 1993.

Hill, Sarah H. *Weaving New Worlds: Southeastern Cherokee Women and Their Basketry*. Chapel Hill: University of North Carolina Press, 1997.

Hohenberger, Frank Michael. *Down in the Hills O' Brown County*. Nashville, Indiana: Self-published, 1952.

———. "Joe Bohall, Down in the Hills of Brown." *Indianapolis Star,* November 2, 1924.

———. *Nashville Observer* (Indiana), April 1955.

Hovis, Howard Bruce, interview with Cynthia Anne Clark, March 25, 1973. Unpublished transcript. M/C 73/44, Box 4, Indiana University Folklore Institute Material Culture Papers, University Archives, Indiana University, Bloomington.

Hunter, Catherine K. "Part 2: Pat Hickman." *NBO Quarterly Review* (Spring 2012): 14–20.

Hutchinson, Elizabeth. *The Indian Craze: Primitivism, Modernism, and Transculturation in American Art, 1890–1915*. Durham, NC: Duke University Press, 2009.

Irwin, John Rice. *Baskets and Basket Makers in Southern Appalachia*. Exton, PA: Schiffer, 1982.

Jackson, Jason Baird. "Southeastern Indian Basketry in the Gilcrease Museum Collection." *American Indian Art* 25, no. 4 (Autumn 2000): 46–55.

James, George Wharton. *How to Make Indian and Other Baskets*. New York: Frank M. Covert, 1903.

———. *Indian Basketry*. 2nd ed. New York: Henry Malkan, 1902.

Jehle, Michael. "A Report on the NHA Symposium: Nantucket and the Native American Legacy of New England." *Historic Nantucket* 44, no. 3 (Winter 1996): 98–100. Accessed November 2015. www.nha.org/library/hn/HN-winter96-symposium.htm.

Jones-Jackson, Patricia. *When Roots Die, Endangered Traditions of the Sea Islands*. Athens, GA: University of Georgia Press, 1987.

Joyce, Rosemary O. *A Bearer of Tradition: Dwight Stump, Basket Maker*. Athens, GA: University of Georgia Press, 1989.

Kany, Daniel. "Every Decade or So PMA's Biennial Is Extra Special." *Portland Press Herald-Post,* April 17, 2011.

Kaplan, Wendy, ed. *"The Art That Is Life": The Arts and Crafts Movement in America, 1875–1920*. Boston: Museum of Fine Arts, 1987.

Kardon, Janet, ed. *Revivals! Diverse Traditions, 1920–1945: The History of Twentieth-Century American Craft*. New York: Abrams, 1994.

Katz, Vincent, ed. *Black Mountain College: Experiment in Art*. Cambridge, MA: MIT Press, 2013.

Kay, Jon. Episode 34. *Cannon County Baskets: A Tennessee Tradition*. Podcast audio. Artisan Ancestors: Researching Creative Lives and Handmade Things. MP3, 60:47. Accessed June 10, 2017. http://www.artisanancestors.com/2013/02/18/episode-34-cannon-county-baskets-a-tennessee-tradition/.

———. "Oak-Rod Baskets in Brown County: Historic Photographs of a Craft Tradition." *International Oaks* 25, no. 1 (2014): 85–92.

———. "A Picture of an Old Country Store: The Construction of Folklore in Everyday Life." *Museum Anthropology Review* [Online] 4, no. 2 (27 October 2010).

Kefalos, Roberta. "Sweetgrass Baskets by Mary Jackson." Pamphlet distributed at The Gibbs Museum of Art, n.d.

Kester, Bernard. *Basketry*: *Tradition in New Form*. Boston: Institute of Contemporary Art, 1981.

Kieffer, Susan Mowery. *500 Baskets*: *A Celebration of the Basketmaker's Art*. New York: Lark Books, 2006.

Kishkovsky, Sophia. "A Defunct Collective Finds Its Muse." *New York Times,* June 24, 2010.

Koasati Language Committee. *Ko·was·saa·ti Nas·ma·thaa·li A·saa·la / Coushatta Animal Baskets*. Kinder, LA: Koasati Language Committee, n.d.

Koplos, Janet. "Why Basketry Matters." Keynote address for the biennial conference of the National Basketry Organization, Macalester College, St. Paul, Minnesota, July 14, 2015.

Koplos, Janet, and Bruce Metcalf. *Makers: A History of American Studio Craft Makers*. Chapel Hill, NC: University of North Carolina Press, 2010.

Kramer, Aaron. *Spin Basket*. YouTube video, 0:20. Posted November 5, 2007. Accessed April 13, 2017. https://youtube/HvjdqdQo2mo.

Kreisman, Lawrence and Glenn Mason. *The Arts and Crafts Movement in the Pacific Northwest*. Portland, Oregon: Timber Press, 2007.

Kwan, Simon. *Chinese Basketry*. Hong Kong: Muwen Tang Fine Arts Publications, 2010.

Larsen, Jack Lenor. *The Tactile Vessel: New Basket Forms*. Erie, WI: Erie Art Museum, 1989.

Lasansky, Jeannette. "Pennsylvania-German Round-Rod Oak Baskets." *Antiques* 127, no. 4 (April 1984): 886–895.

———. *Willow, Oak & Rye: Basket Traditions in Pennsylvania*. University Park, PA: Keystone Books, 1979.

Law, Rachel Nash, and Cynthia W. Taylor. *Appalachian White Oak Basket Making*: *Handing Down the Basket*. Knoxville: University of Tennessee Press, 1991.

Lawrence, Martha. *Lightship Baskets of Nantucket*. Atglen, PA: Schiffer Publishing, Ltd., 2000.

Laws, Jennifer. "Crackpots and Basket-Cases: A History of Therapeutic Work and Occupation." *History of Human Sciences* 24, no. 2 (2011): 65–81.

Leach, William R. "Transformations in a Culture of Consumption: Women and Department Stores, 1890–1925." *The Journal of American History* 71, no. 2 (September 1984): 319–342. http://www.jstor.org/stable/1901758.

Lears, T. J. Jackson. *No Place of Grace: Antimodernism and the Transformation of American Culture, 1880–1920*. Chicago: University of Chicago Press, 1994.

Lee, Dayna Bowker, and H. F. Pete Gregory, eds. *Proceedings of the Southeastern Indian Basketry Gathering, May 16–17, 2002*. Natchitoches, LA: Northwestern State University, 2002.

———. *The Work of Tribal Hands: Southeastern Indian Cane Basketry*. Natchitoches, LA: Northwestern State University Press, 2006.

Lee, Molly. "Tourism and Taste in Alaska: Collecting Native Art in Alaska at the Turn of the Twentieth Century." In *Unpacking Culture: Art and Commodity in Colonial and Postcolonial Worlds,* edited by Ruth B. Phillips and Christopher B. Steiner, 267-281. Berkeley: University of California Press, 1999.

Leier, Ray, Jan Peters, and Kevin Wallace. *Baskets: Tradition and Beyond*. Madison, WI: Guild Publishing, 2000.

Letsinger-Miller, Lyn. *The Artists of Brown County*. Bloomington, IN: Indiana University Press, 1994.

Lewis, David. *Warren MacKenzie: An American Potter*. New York: Kodansha International, 1991.

Lippard, Lucy. *Mixed Blessings: New Art in a Multicultural America*. New York: Pantheon, 1990.

Lønning, Kari. *The Art of Basketry*. New York: Sterling, 2000.

Lovelace, Joyce. "Always Unfolding." *American Craft,* November 17, 2015. https://craftcouncil.org/magazine/article/always-unfolding.

———. "Composing Chaos." *American Craft,* November 19, 2013. https://craftcouncil.org/magazine/article/composing-chaos.

———. "Root and Branch." *American Craft,* March 16, 2015. http://craftcouncil.org/magazine/article/root-and-branch.

"Ludlow Seeks Means of Preserving Simplicity of Brown County Natives." *Indianapolis Star,* January 13, 1941.

Malarcher, Patricia. "A Basketmaker's Year Down Under." *Fiberarts* 8 (July–August 1981).

———. "What Makes a Basket a Basket?" *Fiberarts* 11 (January–February 1984).

Maloney, Robert. "New York in Review." *Arts* 63 (January 1989).

Mancini, JoAnn. *Pre-Modernism: Art-World Change and American Culture from the Civil War to the Armory Show*. Princeton, NJ: Princeton University Press, 2005.

Marten, William S. *Inexpensive Basketry*. Peoria, IL: Manual Arts Press, 1912.

"Mary Jackson, Fiber Artist." MacArthur Fellows Program. January 27, 2008. https://www.macfound.org/fellows/800/.

May, Roger B. "Costly Cane-Craft Is Nantucket's Bag—And Sinatra Has 3." *Wall Street Journal,* September 17, 1975.

May, Stephanie Anna. "Alabama-Coushatta Pine Needle Basketry: A Meaningful Practice." M.A. Thesis, University of Texas, Austin. 1993.

McLaughlin, Jean W., ed. *The Nature of Craft and the Penland Experience*. New York: Lark Books, 2004.

McQuaid, Matilda, ed. *Extreme Textiles: Designing for High Performance*. New York: Smithsonian, Cooper-Hewitt, National Design Museum, and Princeton Architectural Press, 2005.

McWhite, Wyona. *All Things Considered VI: Juried & Invitational Exhibition, July 30–December 11, 2011.* Brasstown, NC: National Basketry Organization, 2011.

Meggett, Linda L. "Basket Weavers Caught in a Bind." *Post and Courier* (Charleston, SC), August 9, 1998, EC Zone, B1.

Meilach, Dona. *Basketry Today with Materials from Nature.* New York: Crown, 1979.

———. *A Modern Approach to Basketry with Fiber and Grasses Using Coiling, Twining, Weaving, Macramé, Crocheting.* New York: Crown Publishing, 1974.

———. *Soft Sculpture and Other Soft Art Forms.* New York: Crown, 1974.

Melinkoff, Ellen. *What We Wore: An Offbeat Social History of Women's Clothing, 1950 to 1980.* New York: William Morrow, 1984.

Metcalf, Jr., Eugene W. "The Politics of the Past in American Folk Art History." In *Folk Art and Art Worlds,* edited by John Michael Vlach and Simon J. Bonner, 27–50. Logan, UT: Utah State University Press, 1992.

Metro, Judy, ed. *An Eye for Art.* Washington DC: National Gallery of Art, 2013.

Meyer, Marilee Boyd, ed. *Inspiring Reform: Boston's Arts and Crafts Movement.* Wellesley, MA: Davis Museum and Cultural Center, 1997.

Moffatt, Frederick C. "Arthur Wesley Dow and the Ipswich School of Art." *New England Quarterly* 49, no. 3 (September 1976): 339–355. http://www.jstor.org/stable/364678.

Monem, Nadine, ed. *Contemporary Textiles: The Fabric of Fine Art.* London: Black Dog Publishing, 2008.

Morgan, Reuben, interview by Margaret Morgan, October 31, 1973. Unpublished transcript. M/C 73/43, Box 4, Indiana University Folklore Institute Material Culture Papers, University Archives, Indiana University, Bloomington.

"Nantucket Lightship Baskets: A Historic Perspective." Nantucket Lightship Basket Museum. Accessed December 2015. https://www.nantucketlightshipbasketmuseum.org/research-collections/history-of-baskets.

Nathan, Harriet. *Charles Edmund Rossbach: Artist, Mentor, Professor, Writer.* Berkeley: University of California, 1987.

———. *Lillian Elliott: Artist, Instructor, and Innovator in Fiber Arts.* Berkeley: University of California, 1992.

Nevers, Jo Ann. "Dat So La Lee (Dabuda or Louisa Keyser, Washoe, 1835–1925)." *Infinity of Nations: Art and History in the Collection of the National Museum of the American Indian,* National Museum of the American Indian, Smithsonian Institutions. Accessed July 29, 2016. http://nmai.si.edu/exhibitions/infinityofnations/california–greatbasin/118261.html#about.

Newman, Thelma R. *The Container Book.* New York: Crown, 1977.

Newton, James E. "Slave Artisans and Craftsmen: The Roots of Afro-American Art." In *The Other Slaves, Mechanics, Artisans and Craftsmen,* edited by James E. Newton and Ronald L. Lewis, 233-421. Boston: G.K. Hall & Co., 1978.

Ockman, Joan. "Mirror Images: Technology, Consumption and the Representation of Gender in American Architecture Since World War II." In *American Architectural History*, edited by Keith Eggener, 342-351. New York: Routledge, 2004.

Oka, Hideyuki. *How to Wrap 5 Eggs: Traditional Japanese Packaging*. Boston: Weatherhill, 1975.

Oliver, Valerie, and Glenn Adamson. *Hand Made: The Performative Impulse in Art and Craft*. Houston, TX: Contemporary Arts Museum Houston, 2010.

Olson, Keith W. "The G. I. Bill and Higher Education: Success and Surprise." *American Quarterly* 25 (December 1973): 596–610.

Onus, Tiriki, and Eugenia Flynn, "The Tjanpi Desert Weavers Show Us That Traditional Craft Is Art." *The Conversation*. August 12, 2014. theconversation.com/tjanti-desert-weavers-show-us-that-traditional-craft-is-art-30243.

Openshaw, Jonathan. *Postdigital Artisans: Craftsmanship with a New Aesthetic in Fashion, Art, Design, and Architecture*. Amsterdam: Frame Publishers, 2015.

Parsons, Elsie Clews. *Folk Lore of the Sea Islands, South Carolina*. Cambridge, MA: American Folk Lore Society, 1923.

Pasquine, Ruth, ed. *Making a Difference: Fiber Sculpture by Jane Sauer*. Little Rock: Arkansas Arts Center, 2000.

Pepich, Bruce W. *Collection Focus in Fiber: John McQueen*. Racine, WI: Racine Art Museum, 2010.

Peters, Jan. *Baskets: Tradition and Beyond*. Cincinnati, OH: F&W Publications, 2001.

Peterson, Bo. "Sweetgrass Baskets May Become Official 'State Handicraft.'" *Post and Courier* (Charleston, SC), February 4, 2005.

Phillips, Ruth B. *Trading Identities: The Souvenir in Native North American Art from the Northeast, 1700–1900*. Seattle: University of Washington Press, 1999.

Phillips, Ruth B., and Christopher B. Steiner. "Art, Authenticity, and the Baggage of Cultural Encounter." In *Unpacking Culture: Art and Commodity in Colonial and Postcolonial Worlds*, edited by Ruth B. Phillips and Christopher B. Steiner, 3-19. Berkeley: University of California Press, 1999.

Pohancenik, Andreas. "Organic* Lettering and Signage in Landscape and Environmental Design." M.A. Dissertation, Central Saint Martens College of Art and Design, 2004.

Pollard, Ann, and Rebecca A.T. Stevens, eds. *Ed Rossbach: 40 Years of Exploration and Innovation in Fiber Art*. Asheville, NC: Lark Books, 1990.

Pollitzer, William S. *The Gullah People and Their African Heritage*. Athens, GA: University of Georgia Press, 1999.

Porter, Frank W., ed. *The Art of Native American Basketry: A Living Legacy*. New York: Greenwood Press, 1990.

Porter, Jenelle, ed. *Fiber: Sculpture 1960–Present*. New York: Delmonico Books, 2014.

Power, Susan C. *Art of the Cherokee: Prehistory to the Present*. Athens, GA: University of Georgia Press, 2007.

Pulleyn, Rob, ed. *The Basketmaker's Art*: *Contemporary Baskets and Their Makers*. Asheville, NC: Lark Books, 1986.

Reed, Estelle. *Course of Study for Indian Schools of the United States*. Washington: Government Printing Office, 1901.

Reeve, Kenneth J., and Helen H. Reeve. "Henry Hovis." *Family Studies of Brown County, Indiana (#113)*, 1998.

"The Renwick Invitational: Five Women in Craft." Smithsonian American Art Museum. Accessed March 18, 2005. http://www.tfaoi.com/aa/laa.

Reyes, José Formoso, interview by Henry Coffin Carlisle, 1958. CT-38a&b, Henry Coffin Carlisle Oral History Collection, Nantucket Historical Association, Nantucket, MA.

Reyes, José Formoso, interview by Dror Khan, 1975. Film, Nantucket Historical Association. Accessed April 13, 2017. https://www.nantucketlightshipbasketmuseum.org/research-collections/biographies/jose-formoso-reyes-1902-1980.

Rice, Nancy N. "Review of Jane Sauer show, B. Z. Wagman Gallery, St. Louis, Missouri." *New Art Examiner* (September 1986): 60.

Riedel, Thomas L. "Tradition Reconfigured: Juan A. Sanchez, Patrocino Barela, and New Deal Saint Making." In *Transforming Images: New Mexican Santos In-Between World*, edited by Claire Farago and Donna Pierce, 213-28. State College, PA: Penn State University Press, 2006.

Roberts, Warren. "Basketry in Brown County, Indiana." Warren Roberts Collection. Bloomington, IN: Indiana University Archive. Unpublished.

Rosengarten, Dale. *Row Upon Row: Sea Grass Baskets of the South Carolina Lowcountry*. Reprint edition. McKissick Museum: University of South Carolina, 1994.

Rosengarten, Dale, Theodore Rosengarten, Enid Schildkrout, and Judith Ann Carney. *Grass Roots: African Origins of an American Art*. New York: University of Washington Press, 2008.

Rossbach, Ed. *Baskets as Textile Art*. New York: Van Nostrand Reinhold, 1979.

———. *The Nature of Basketry*. Atglen, PA: Schiffer, 1986.

———. *New Basketry*. New York: Van Nostrand Reinhold, 1980.

Roth, David M. "Gyöngy Laky @ b.sakata garo." Squarecylinder.com, September 8, 2012, http://www.squarecylinder.com/2012/09/gyongy-laky-b-sakata-garo/.

Rucker, Angela. "Festival Helps Promote a S. C. Artistic Tradition." *Post and Courier* (Charleston, SC), June 30, 1995.

Rushing, W. Jackson. *Native American Art and the New York Avant-Garde: A History of Cultural Primitivism*. Austin: University of Texas Press, 1995.

Russell, Carol K. *Fiber Art Today*. Atglen, PA: Schiffer, 2011.

Salomon, Otto. *The theory of educational sloyd: the only authorised ed. of the lectures of Otto Salomon/ rev. and ed. for English and American students by an inspector of schools; together with a résumé of the history of manual training, and a portrait and biography of Herr Salomon*. Boston: Silver, Burdett, 1907.

Schrader, Robert Fay. *The Indian Arts and Crafts Board: An Aspect of New Deal Indian Policy*. Albuquerque: University of New Mexico Press, 1983.

Schwob, Olivia. "Net Effects." *Harvard Magazine* (May–June 2015). Accessed January 1, 2016. http://harvardmagazine.com/2015/05/net-effects.

*Sculpture Textile: 12th International Biennial of Tapestry*. Lausanne, Switzerland: Centre International de la Tapisserie Ancienne et Moderne and Musée cantonal des Beaux-Arts, 1985.

Seeler, Katherine and Edgar. *Nantucket Lightship Baskets*. Nantucket, MA: Deermouse Press, 1972.

Seidenfaden, Eva. *The Art of Basketmaking: The Périgord Technique and Tradition*. La Vendée, France: Pollina, 2006.

Seigel, Peggy. "Industrial Girls in an Early Twentieth-Century Boomtown: Traditions and Change in Fort Wayne, Indiana, 1900–1920." *Indiana Magazine of History* 99, no. 3 (September 2003): 231–253.

Selz, Peter. "Ann Weber, Dolby Chadwick Gallery, San Francisco." *Sculpture* 32, no. 4 (May 2013): 73–74.

Shapiro, Barbara. "Political Voices of Three Left Coast Artists: Gyöngy Laky, Linda Gass, Linda MacDonald." In *Textiles and Politics: Textile Society of America 13th Biennial Symposium Proceedings, Washington, DC, September 18–September 22, 2012*. University of Nebraska-Lincoln Digital Commons, http://digitalcommons.unl.edu/tsaconf/743/.

Shaw, Robert. *American Baskets: A Cultural History of a Traditional Domestic Art*. New York: C. Potter, 1999.

Sheriff, Natasja. "Everything Is Nothing: The Art of Sopheap Pich." *Hyperallergic,* June 11, 2013. https://hyperallergic.com/73086/everything-is-nothing-the-artwork-of-sopheap-pich/.

Sims, Lowery Stokes. "Stephen Burks: A Hybrid Making on Earth." In *Stephen Burks: Man Made*, edited by Naomi Beckwith. New York: The Studio Museum in Harlem, 2011.

Slivka, Rose. *Peter Voulkos: A Dialogue with Clay*. New York: New York Graphic Society, 1978.

Smith, Gary. *Daniel Rhodes: The California Years*. Santa Cruz, CA: The Art Museum of Santa Cruz County, 1986.

Smith, Roberta. "Against Delusion: Robert Gober's Nuts-and-Bolts Americana." *New York Times*, August 23, 2007.

Sneider, Noah. "Myth and Reality: Nikolay Polissky's Timeless Land Art." *Calvert Journal,* July 16, 2013, http://calvertjournal.com/articles/show/1219/myth-reality-nikolay-polissky-timeless-land-art.

Sokolitz, Roberta. "Sweetgrass Baskets by Mary Jackson." Mary A. Jackson, Inc. Charleston, SC: n.d.

Stanton, Gary. *The Tradition of Oak Rod Baskets in Southern Indiana*. Unpublished Manuscript, 1975.

Steele, Valerie. *Fifty Years of Fashion: New Look to Now*. New Haven, CT: Yale University Press, 1997.

Stillinger, Elizabeth. "From Attics, Sheds, and Secondhand Shops: Collecting Folk Art in America." In *Drawing on America's Past: Folk Art, Modernism, and the Index of American Design,* edited by Virginia Tuttle Clayton, 44-59. Washington, DC: National Gallery of Art, 2002.

Sudduth, Billie Ruth. *Baskets: A Book for Makers and Collectors*. Madison, WI: Hand Books Press, 1999.

Sully, Susan. "Dream Weaver: Artist, Teacher, and Activist Mary Jackson Has Helped Revitalize South Carolina's Sweetgrass Basketmaking Tradition." *Southern Accents* (September/October 2002): 102–106.

Taubman, Ellen Napiura, and David Revere McFadden. *Changing Hands*: *Art without Reservation.* New York: Museum of Arts and Design, 2012.

Teiwes, Helga. *Hopi Basket Weaving*. Tucson: University of Arizona Press, 1996.

Tielman, Maxwell. "Studio Tour & Interview: Doug Johnston," *Design Sponge,* March 13, 2013. http://www.designsponge.com/2013/03/studio-tour-interview-doug-johnston.html.

Trapp, Kenneth. "Mary Jackson, Biography." Smithsonian American Art Museum. Accessed March 18, 2005. http://www.americanart.si.edu/search/artist_bio.

Turnbaugh, Sarah Peabody, and William A. Turnbaugh. *Basket Tales of the Grandmothers*. Narragansett, RI: Thornbrook, 1999.

———. *Indian Baskets*. West Chester, PA: Schiffer, 1986.

University of East Anglia. "Basket Weaving May Have Taught Humans to Count." *ScienceDaily*. Accessed February 18, 2016. www.sciencedaily.com/releases/2009/06/090604222534.htm.

Waller, Irene. *Textile Sculpture*. New York: Taplinger, 1977.

Ward, Gerald W. R., ed. *Craft Transformed: Program in Artisanry*. Brockton, MA: Fuller Museum of Art, 2003.

West, Patsy. "Glade Cross Mission: An Influence on Florida Seminole Arts and Crafts." *American Indian Art Magazine* 9, no. 4 (Autumn 1984): 58–67.

Whitten, Paul F. *The Friendship Baskets and Their Maker, José Formoso Reyes*. 1960. Reprint. Nantucket, MA: The Nantucket Lightship Basket Makers and Merchants Association, 2002.

Wood, Henry. "Willow Weaver: A Once Flourishing Southern Indiana Business Now Is Practiced by Only a Handful of Hoosiers." *Indianapolis Sunday Star Magazine*, May 15, 1949, 20.

Woodward, Calvin. *Manual Training in Education*. New York: Charles Scribner's Sons, 1892.

Wright, Lauren A., ed. *Maria Nepomuceno, Tempo para Respirar* [*Breathing Time*]. Margate, England: Turner Contemporary, 2012.

Wynne, Madeline Yale. "Makers of Baskets." *Good Housekeeping* 33, no. 5 (November 1901): 369-373.

Zilber, Emily. *Crafted*: *Objects in Flux*. Boston: Museum of Fine Arts, Boston, 2015.

Zoran, Amit. "Hybrid Basketry: Interweaving Digital Practice within Contemporary Craft." *Leonardo* 46, no. 4 (2013): 324–331.

# Index

Africa, basketry origins, 8, 13, 16, 33, 40–41

Albers, Joseph and Anni, 72

Aleutian Islands, 76

Al-Hilali, Neda, 80

Allanstand Cottage Industries, 17–18

Amana Colonies, 19

American Craft Council, 22, 72

American Craftsman's Educational Council, 72

Anderson, Kate, 27, 143, 144

Andrus, Barbara, 102

Appropriation, 26, 27

Aranda, Benjamin, 100, 101

Arawjo, Darryl and Karen, 24, 25, 132

Architecture, 95, 104–105

Arrowmont School of Arts and Crafts, 21, 71

Art departments: effect of GI Bill on, 19–20, 71–72; introduction of craft media, 19–21, 71–74. *See also:* Charles "Ed" Rossbach; University of California at Berkeley

Art education: apprenticeships 24–25; Arthur Wesley Dow, 17–18; assimilation, 11–13; journals and periodicals, 22; workshops, 21–22, 25, 66, 71, 96, 124. *See also:* Art departments; Immersive Craft Schools; Manual Training Movement

Art world: audiences, 40; criticism, 16–17, 20, 45–44; development of, 19, 40, 46; display, 17–18; diversification of, 43; hierarchies, 20–21, 27, 28, 30, 33–34, 40, 44–46, 74–75, 76, 86; market, 15–16, 42, 73, 93

Arts and Crafts Movement, 10–12, 17, 24, 30, 68, 82

Artschwager, Richard, 76, 77

Asawa, Ruth, 21, 102

Austin, Joan, 79, 80

Auther, Elissa, 26, 74

Bacharach, David, 133

Back-to-the-Land Movement, 19, 22–24, 70

Barnes, Dorothy Gill, 116

Bauhaus (German Art School), 20, 72

Becker, Pamela, 133

Bell, Nicholas, 23–24, 70

Bergner, Lanny, 145

Bess, Nancy Moore, 84, 145

Bishop, Mary Beasom, 71

Black Mountain College, 72

Bleem, Jerry, 98, 146

Bohall Family, 48, 50–54, 178; Elizabeth, 50; John, 52, 178; Joseph "Josey," 51, 53, 178; Levi, 52; William, 51, 53, 54, 179

Boston University Program in Artisanry, 72–73

Bradley, Rowena, 32, 109

Brandford, Joanne Segal, 21, 26, 76–79, 115

Brock, Charissa, 99, 147

Brown, William J., 71

Burks, Stephen, 93

Burnette, Clay, 134

Butcher, Mary, 115

Cahill, Holger, 18–19

California College of Arts and Crafts/California College of Art, 78Carpenter, Ed, 103–105

Catsos, JoAnn Kelly, 24, 124, 126

Cherokee: buckbrush basketry, 36; Cherokee Fair, 16; Cherokee National Treasure program, 37–38, conservation efforts, 36–37; continuing education, 38; double-weave basketry, 32–33, 36; river-cane basketry, 32–33; tourism, 16, 36; white oak basketry, 33–34

Clark, Jill Nordfors, 134

Coddington, Ann B., 28, 147, 148

Cohn, Abe and Amy, 15, 68, 169

Craft: as counter-culture, 22–23; economic renewal, 36, 70–71, 93, 95, 96; hobbyists, 10, 67; markets and shows, 24, 33, 46; therapeutic value of, 12, 67, 73; wholesale distribution, 11–16, 22, 42–43, 53–54, 93. *See also:* Arts and Crafts Movement

Craft Associations, 72. *See also:* American Craft Council

Cranbrook Academy of Art, 71, 73, 80

Cultural Preservation, 25–26, 36–38, 46, 60–64

Danberg, Leah, 149

Data, as material, 92, 98, 100–101, 143, 157

Design, 20, 72, 76, 88, 90, 92–93, 101, 105, 115

Dougherty, Patrick, 102

Dow, Arthur Wesley, 17–18

Drury, Chris, 94–95

Echelman, Janet, 104–105, 188

Eckert, Carol, 150, 206

Ecology, 36–37, 46, 92, 96

Elliott, Lillian, 21, 22, 26, 78–79, 80, 115, 117

Environmental art, 29, 92, 93–95, 98, 101, 102, 104

Exhibitions: 12th International Biennial of Tapestry, 22–23, 79, 80; *Basketry: Tradition in New Form*, 82; *A Measure of the Earth: The Cole-Ware Collection of American Baskets*, 24, 70

Fashion, 25, 58, 62–64

Feddersen, Joe, 125

Fiber art: influence in New Basketry, 20–21, 73–74, 76, 78–83, 89, 93, 101

Fiberworks Center for Textile Arts, 21, 78

Fisch, Arline, 80

Fischer, Aron, 30, 149

Fred Harvey Company, 14–15

Fuchs, Douglas, 85

Garrett, John, 26, 82, 149

George, Lucy N., 37

Giles, Mary, 134

Glashausser, Suellen, 79

Gober, Robert, 86, 102

Gold, Pat Courtney, 25–26, 125

Goldsworthy, Andy, 102

Gorin, Stephanie, 136

Goshorn, Shan, 27–28, 137, 138

Greenberg, Clement, 20, 26

Gropius, Walter, 72, 170

Hackenwerth, Jason, 103–104, 105

Hall, Fiona, 96

Hammond, Harmony, 74

Handmade, value of, 10–13, 23, 30, 41, 46, 48–49, 53, 56, 60, 63, 68, 70, 115

Harvey, Virginia, 84

Haystack Mountain School of Crafts, 71

Hepper, Carol, 86

Heslop, Sandy, 93

Hess-Boson, Marie, 94

Hetzel, Carole, 137

Hickman, Pat, 21, 22, 79, 86, 89, 115, 117

Holsenbeck, Bryant, 28–29, 98, 150

Hopkins, Jan, 151

Hovis family, 48–51, 52, 54–56; Henry, 48, 54, 177; Henry W., 48, 50– 51; Bruce, 54–56; Jacob, 48–49; John, 48–49; Lewis, 48

Hunter, Lissa, 79, 152

Identity: local identity (Nantucket), 58, 62, 64; cultural identity, 8, 40–41, 108; national identity, 8, 18–19, 20, 32–33, 46; Native identity, 12–13, 25–26, 32–38; regional identity, 46, 48, 50–56

Immersive Craft Schools, 70–71. *See also:* Arrowmont School of Arts and Crafts; Haystack Mountain School of Crafts; Penland School of Crafts

*Index of American Design*, 19

"Indian Craze," 11, 14–17, 68

Indiana University in Bloomington, 79

Industrial Revolution, 8–10, 14, 41, 48, 59, 66, 108

Installation art, 28–29, 30, 85, 88–90, 95– 96, 98, 102–104, 105, 143, 171
Intercultural Contact, 8, 14–15, 24–25, 32–33, 58, 61, 79, 88
Itter, Diane, 79
Iwata, Kyomi, 101
Jackson, Mary, 40, 42–46, 85, 176
Jackson-Pierite, Rose, 34–35
Jacobs, Ferne, 80–81, 82, 117
James, George Wharton, 11, 16–17, 68, 111
Johnson, Terrol Dew, 100, 101
Johnston, Doug, 93
Joy, Christine, 27, 153
Kavicky, Susan, 154
Kester, Bernard, 82
Ketterer, Lindsey, 135
Keyser, Louisa, 15
Knutson, Lara, 99
Koenigsberg, Nancy, 101, 155
Koplos, Janet, 73, 89
Kramer, Aaron, 98–99, 155
Laky, Gyöngy, 21, 78, 92–93, 115, 118. *See also:* Fiberworks Center for Textile Arts
LaPlantz, Shereen, 22, 83
Larsen, Jack Lenor, 21, 74, 85
Lasch, Chris, 100, 101
Lewis, Katherine, 24, 25, 126
Lønning, Kari, 84, 118
MacKenzie, Warren, 72, 183
Maestre, Jennifer, 99
Manual Training Movement, 11–13, 68–71
Marketing and Distribution, 15, 16, 17–18, 22, 30, 40, 42, 53–54, 56, 68, 71, 169
Mass production: influence on basketry, 8–10, 15, 23, 29, 48–49, 59, 108
Masters, Amy, 156
McGuiness, Dorothy, 156

McQueen, John, 23, 28, 83, 84, 88–89, 119
Meilach, Dona, 21
Metcalf, Bruce, 73
Miebach, Nathalie, 92, 100, 101, 157, 188
Minkowitz, Norma, 26, 119
Modernism: and anti-modernism, 10–12, 50; art movement, 14, 19–20, 30, 44–45, 132; and authenticity, 10–11, 14, 18, 30; and folk art, 18–19; and "Primitivism," 11, 14–15, 18–19; and tradition, 14–19; and "usable past," 18
Montclair State University, 79
Moore, Marilyn, 139
Morgan, Lucy, 70–71
Morgan, Reuben, 54, 179
Muhl, Deborah, 139
Music, 37, 92, 93, 101
Nepomuceno, Maria, 90–91
New Basketry, 19–23, 73–74, 76, 82, 84, 85, 108, 115, 132, 183; African influences on, 8, 40, 42–46, 66, 90; Global influences on, 24–25, 28, 58–61, 64, 72, 76, 79, 84–85, 86, 90; Native American influences on, 8, 11, 14–17, 66, 67–68, 76, 79, 80, 81, 82, 83, 84, 89. *See also:* Art Departments, Charles "Ed" Rossbach
Niehues, Leon, 24, 25, 120, 158
Occupational Therapy, 12, 73
Peabody Museum of Archaeology and Ethnology at Harvard University, 11, 25, 79
Peleg, Rina, 82
Penland School of Crafts, 21, 70–71
Penn Normal, Industrial, and Educational School, 13
Pich, Sopheap, 90
Polissky, Nikolay, 95
Pujol, Elliott, 82
Puryear, Martin, 90, 102
Ray, Clinton Mitchell "Mitchy," 61, 180

Reed, Estelle, 12–13

Reyes, José Formoso, 61–64, 127, 181

Rhoads, Kait, 99, 100

Rochester Institute of Technology, 72

Ross, Bird, 140

Rossbach, Charles "Ed," 19–22, 23, 26, 27, 66, 67, 73–74, 76–78, 79, 80, 81, 82, 83, 115, 122, 171

Russell, Lois, 140, 159, 163

Russo, JoAnne, 24, 142

Salm, Amanda, 159

San Diego State University, 80

Sauer, Jane, 22, 85–86, 121

Schutz, Biba, 160

Sekijima, Hisako, 84–85

Sekimachi, Kay, 82, 123

Seventy, Sylvia, 78

Shaker, 19, 30, 114

Shaughnessy, Michael, 102, 103

Shaw-Sutton, Carol, 22, 80–81, 82

Sheehan, Diane, 79

Sisson, Karyl, 26, 121

Site-Specific work, 88, 93–95, 102–104

Slavery, 8, 13, 16, 33, 40–41, 46, 108, 174–175

South Carolina Lowcountry baskets: African origins, 13, 16; fine art world, 42–45; Highway 17, 16, 41–42, 46; marketing and sales, 13, 16, 41–42; Penn Normal, Industrial, and Educational School, 13; rice cultivation, 16, 40–41; "show" baskets, 16, 40- 41, 45–46, 174

Souvenirs, 8, 14–16, 48, 50–53, 59

Smith, Roberta, 102

Standardization, 8–10, 51, 59–60

Starn, Doug and Mike, 105–106

Stereotypes, challenges to, 25, 27, 68

Sterrenburg, Joanne, 76, 79

Sturtevant, William C., 32

Sutton, Polly Adams, 24, 141

Taylor, Cynthia, 24, 128, 173

Taylor, Julia, 33–34

Telford, Lisa, 25, 26, 160, 161

Tjanpi Desert Weavers, 96

Tourism, 14–16; 34–36, 48–51, 53–56, 59–60, 61, 108

Tradition: and modernity, 11–13, 14–19, 68, 73–74; expression of, 33–34, 43–46; family, 51; local, 48–50, 58, 64, 88; preservation of, 8, 18–19, 23–26, 43–46, 54–56, 108, 115; revival of, 23–25, 62, 64, 70, 85, 124; tribal, 32–38

Tremblay, Gail, 68, 69

Trentham, Gary, 79

Tyler University, 83

University of California at Berkeley, 21, 73, 76, 78, 79, 115

University of California at Davis, 78

University of California in Los Angeles, 82

University of Massachusetts Dartmouth's College of Visual and Performing Arts, 73

Voulkos, Peter, 19–20, 72, 183

Waddell, Leona, 24, 127

Walden, Dawn Nichols, 142

Weber, Ann, 98–99

Werner, Alvine, 114

Westfall, Carol, 79

Wiedeman, Peggy, 161

Wolfe, Eva Queen, 109

Women's Rights Movement (1960s): 19, 22, 26

Yakim, Aaron, 24, 129

Zeh, Stephen, 24, 128, 130–131

Zoran, Amit, 101

Zurick, Jennifer Heller, 129

# About the Contributors

**Carol Eckert**, artist, critic and curator. In addition to appearing in exhibitions nationally and internationally, Eckert's work is part of many public and private collections, including the Museum of Art and Design, New York; the Renwick Gallery of the Smithsonian American Art Museum, Washington, DC; and the Racine Art Museum in Wisconsin. Since 2012, she has authored a well-respected blog, *Contemporary Basketry: Concepts, Forms, Materials, Techniques, and Processes Related to Basketry.*

**Jeannine Falino**, independent curator and scholar. Falino has served as an adjunct curator and edited exhibition catalogs for the Museum of Arts and Design in New York since 2007, including *Crafting Modernism: Midcentury American Art and Design* (2011). Concurrently, she has curated exhibitions and edited catalogs at a variety of institutions, including the Museum of the City of New York and Fuller Craft Museum in Brockton, Massachusetts. Falino was the Carolyn and Peter Lynch Curator of Decorative Arts and Sculpture at the Museum of Fine Arts in Boston until 2003.

**Sybil E. Gohari**, PhD, art historian whose scholarship focuses on race and gender as well as the impact of the art market on the production, proliferation, and reception of art. Gohari's professional and scholarly experience as a teacher, author, and advisor spans some of the leading academic and artistic institutions in Washington, DC. The recipient of numerous academic awards and honors, she held the Black Entertainment Television (BET) Fellowship during the course of her doctorate. Gohari has been published in a number of academic publications, including *Woman's Art Journal.* She has also written book chapters and exhibition reviews and presented papers at various conferences and symposia.

**Jason Baird Jackson**, Associate Professor, Department of Folklore and Ethnomusicology at Indiana University, Bloomington. As the Director of Indiana University's Mathers Museum of World Cultures and editor of *Museum Anthropology Review*, an open-access, peer-reviewed journal, Jackson pursues projects on emerging issues of intellectual and cultural property as well as heritage policy. His long-term research on Oklahoma's Euchee/Yuchi people appears in his 2003 monograph, *Yuchi Ceremonial Life: Performance, Meaning, and Tradition in a Contemporary American Indian Community* (2003), and in a variety of journals and edited volumes, including his own, *Yuchi Indian Histories Before the Removal Era* (2012).

**Jon Kay**, Professor of Practice, Department of Folklore and Ethnomusicology at Indiana University, Bloomington. Kay directs Traditional Arts Indiana, a statewide traditional arts program, based at

IU's Mathers Museum of World Cultures. In that capacity, he conducts fieldwork; hosts the podcast *Artisan Ancestors*; produces documentaries about the state's traditional artists and art forms; and organizes exhibitions. He recently curated *Working Wood: Oak-Rod Baskets in Indiana* (2015) and the traveling exhibit *Indiana Folk Arts: 200 Years of Tradition and Innovation* (2016), and authored *Folk Art and Aging: Life-Story Objects and Their Makers* (2016).

**Patricia Malarcher**, writer and artist. Malarcher served as the editor of *International Surface Design Journal*, one of the foremost contemporary textile periodicals, from 1993 to 2011. She has written a series of catalog essays and book chapters on significant textile artists, including Eszter Bornemisza, Kiyomi Iwata, Helena Hernmarck, and Michael James. She has also authored essays on basketry and criticism, including "Basketry Interpretations" for the Museum for Textiles in Toronto, Ontario (1989) and "Approaches to Criticism: Fragments of an Evolution" in *Objects and Meaning: New Perspectives on Art and Craft* (2005).

**Margaret Fairgrieve Milanick**, PhD candidate in Art History and Archaeology, University of Missouri. After completing an MS thesis at Southern Connecticut State University entitled "Random Mutagenesis of Amino Acid Transporters," Milanick turned to the study of art history, earning an MA in eighteenth-century European Art before starting her doctorate in American Art. She has published on a broad array of subjects, including an eighteenth-century French snuffbox and the *Missouri: Heart of the Nation* collection of mid-twentieth-century regionalist paintings.

**Perry Allen Price**, Executive Director for the Houston Center for Contemporary Craft. Price has served as Director of Education of the American Craft Council and Curator of Exhibitions and Collections at the Fuller Craft Museum in Brockton, Massachusetts. He holds an MA in Museum Studies from the Cooperstown Graduate Program at the State University of New York at Oneonta and the New York State Historical Association. He lectures widely on American craft, juries national exhibitions, and contributes to the journal *American Craft*.

**Kristin Schwain**, Associate Professor of American Art, University of Missouri. After receiving a joint PhD in Art History and Humanities from Stanford University, Schwain joined the Department of Art History and Archaeology at the University of Missouri in 2001. In addition to her book *Signs of Grace: Religion and American Art in the Gilded Age* (2008), Schwain has contributed chapters to edited volumes and journals on artists of the African diaspora, including Jacob Lawrence, Henry Ossawa Tanner, and Rolando Estévez, as well as historiographical and methodological studies on the intersection of American art and religion. She has also curated exhibitions on American and Afro-Cuban artists for the University of Missouri's Museum of Art and Archaeology.

**Josephine Stealey**, PhD, artist, curator, and Professor of Art at the University of Missouri. Stealey is a nationally recognized artist in the contemporary basketry movement. Her work is exhibited widely and appears in many private and public collections, including the National Portrait Gallery and the Smithsonian American Art Museum. She is a contributing author for the *International Surface Design Journal*, *FiberArts* magazine, and the National Basketry Organization's *Quarterly Review*. She teaches workshops across the country; curates and juries exhibitions; and lectures on contemporary American basketry at national and international conferences. After leading the Fiber program for more than thirty years, Stealey became chair of the University of Missouri's Department of Art in 2015.